S0-BES-603

# SYDNOR KNOWS THE ANSWER

## A Memoir

To Denise -
expert in alumni
affairs -
with warmest personal regards.
Sydnor

By Sydnor Thompson, Jr.

©Copyright 2006 by Sydnor Thompson, Jr.
Second Edition 2007
All rights reserved

Cover Illustration by Gene Payne
Cover Design by Joseph F. Thompson

By the author of

*The Sydnor Family Saga* –
*The English Forebears and American Descendants of*
*Fortunatus Sydnor (ca 1640 – ca 1682), the Immigrant*

A portion of Chapter 1 of this book appeared in *The Lynch's Ferry*
magazine (Fall/Winter 2002/2003 issue) of Lynchburg, Virginia and
is reprinted here by permission.

Library of Congress Control Number: 2006936792

ISBN: 1-59948-056-5

Pure Heart Press/
Main Street Rag Publishing Company
4416 Shea Lane
Charlotte, NC 28227
www.MainStreetRag.com

To my mother
Helen Josephine Layne Thompson Grose,
who taught me the meaning of unconditional love and absolute trust.

# PREFACE

"Sydnor knows the answer!" were the words I heard from the lips of my eighth grade classmate, pronounced in a tone that was obviously not complimentary. I had raised my hand to volunteer the answer to a question the teacher had put to the class; and for the first time in my life, I suddenly became aware that volunteering an answer might be a questionable act in the eyes of one's schoolmates. Stunned by the reproach, I may not have volunteered another answer for at least a week.

Rarely is one given an opportunity to ruminate publicly upon the life he knew as a lad in what was once his hometown. In 2002 I had occasion to do just that. Upon the suggestion of Robert Garbee and through the good offices of Jane Davis, I was invited to speak at a public forum at Jones Memorial Library in Lynchburg, Virginia. Given carte blanche, I chose to speak on the subject of my formative years in that southern town. I was especially pleased when a number of my classmates agreed to attend the session (at my invitation) to help me reminisce.

After performing that exercise, I decided to expand upon my talk at a somewhat greater length. The first chapter of this book is the product of that undertaking. Once I started I found I couldn't stop, as the temptation to bring the story up to date proved irresistible. I confess that by its very nature, this work is an exercise in vanity. My excuse for persisting is the hope that these reminiscences may prove of special interest to those who have shared in the experiences and perhaps to others who can identify with them from similar events in their own lives. On that account I have included the names of many friends and acquaintances who have accompanied me in my journey.

I appreciate that the tale is not yet finished, but that is the nature of memoir. With great effort, I have drawn the line at December 31, 2004, although other notable events have occurred and continue to occur while publication is pending.

Karen Handerhan, who works in the word processing department at Parker Poe Adams & Bernstein, has been exceptionally faithful in typing out the manuscript on her own time, for which I am most appreciative. I am also grateful to my brother Joseph F. "Chick" Thompson and to my friend Lucia V. Halpern for having reviewed drafts of the manuscript and to Chick for the cover design and photographic layout. I am especially grateful to Annie Maier for her patient editing of this work, a process that has contributed significantly to its succinctness and clarity.

Sydnor Thompson, Jr.
October 10, 2006

# TABLE OF CONTENTS

# PART ONE
# THE LYNCHBURG YEARS

# CHAPTER 1
## THE LYNCHBURG I REMEMBER

It has always been something of a regret to me that I first saw the light of day in Baltimore, Maryland rather than in Lynchburg, Virginia. A week before I was to be born, Mother took a train from Lynchburg to Baltimore so that she could benefit from the care of Daddy's mother during her confinement. I was born on February 18, 1924, before she returned home. By such a narrow margin was I deprived of being a natural-born citizen of the Old Dominion.

When I was growing up there, Lynchburg was a city of about 40,000 souls, once the center of a thriving tobacco market that gave way in the late 1800s to a railroad center, boasting the lines of three railway companies. Like Rome, it was built on seven hills, and at one time or another, I lived on most of them. It was incorporated in the late 1700s and bears the name of its founder, John Lynch.

One of my earliest memories is that of Mother walking up the stairs with my new little sister Barbara Jane in her arms. It was early October 1927 and I was three and a half years old. Bobbie's birth was for me the highlight of my time on Memorial Avenue, where I lived with my mother and father and my male dolls Otticle and Bitticle in a second floor apartment.

Another particularly fond memory of those early years is of the time my father took me to the Isis Theatre to see a film starring Al Jolson. Despite my youth, I have never forgotten it. Jolson sang "Climb upon my knee, Sonny Boy," and I identified with his child, who was only slightly younger than I. When Sonny Boy died, I was virtually inconsolable.

### ENGLEWOOD AVENUE

Within a year or two of Bobbie's arrival, we bought a modest house at 1331 Englewood Avenue in Fort Hill between what was then the Fairground and Thornhill Wagon Company. The house was on a lot that fell off to the rear, just enough for one to be able to drop a cat from the back steps and thrill to watch it land on its feet. Sunflowers nodded their heads majestically at the side of the garage, which was far enough from the house for six year old boys to play doctor with six year old neighborhood girls without fear of being surprised by their elders. Our education in that regard was derived primarily from the friends with whom we smoked cigarettes made of corn silk behind the garage.

There was a small neighborhood grocery store on Fort Avenue across from the Fairground. When I was seven years old, a boy who was working on a soft drink truck ran from the grocery into the path of a moving streetcar whose tracks were laid directly in front of the store. I arrived in time to see the youngster's body still lying on the tracks. Though someone had shown enough sensitivity to cover him

1

with a cloth, my whole system underwent a shock that I have never forgotten.

In a more salutary vein, that same store supplied us with small cards which pictured various professional baseball players. Some enterprising marketer had convinced the bubble gum manufacturer to enclose the cards with the gum as a sales gimmick. There was usually a brisk trade in those cards in the neighborhood as well as on the school playground. In fact, it was not long before imaginative youngsters invented a game of chance ("for keeps" of course) in which the cards were flipped to the ground in much the same fashion as coins had been in a common gaming contest. One of the gamesters was selected to call out "odds" or "evens" before the cards fell to the ground and the winner took both cards home with him. I understand that adults who have saved baseball cards have been offered great sums for them today. I was not so farsighted. Another favorite pastime was shooting marbles, which occupied our leisure time at home and at school. It was not a game at which I excelled.

I made several good friends while living on Englewood Avenue. One of them was Fred Harrison, who lived next door. Fred and I struck up a friendship that lasted until he went to work for The Academy Theater some years later and refused to let me in on a ten cent ticket because he knew I was more than 12 years old. Until then, being small had had its compensations.

Billy Dooley, who was a year or so younger than I, lived up the street. It was Billy who introduced me to fighting. One day, he threw me to the ground without warning and pummeled me mercilessly. Billy was a tough little customer and it was several months before I was able to pass his house without fear of being mugged. Eventually I learned to fight back. My technique was to get my arms around my adversary's neck and choke him until he gave up – not exactly in accordance with the Marquis of Queensbury rules but effective. Anyhow Billy eventually relented. His brother Paul was later a member of my high school class. He was a saint compared to Billy.

Lois Lichtenstein lived next door. Lois' grandfather had established a clothing store on Main Street in the late 1800s and her father succeeded him there. My greatest malefaction on Englewood was setting the lot between our houses on fire. My playmate and I stood transfixed as the circle of fire widened beyond our ability to stamp it out. When the fire trucks arrived I was in my bedroom under the bed. No doubt that's why my mother concluded that I was responsible for it. Lois remained one of my dearest friends through high school, despite my having nearly set her house on fire.

Perhaps my best friend growing up was my brother Joe, named for our grandfather and nicknamed "Chick" by my father. Chick was born in 1931 and despite the discrepancy in our ages, or perhaps because of it, he soon became my faithful sidekick. Through the years we have grown even closer. In a sense it is a case of history's repeating itself because our father, also named Sydnor, and his brother Joseph were close as well.

Next to my friends, the best thing about life on Englewood Avenue was attending Fort Hill School. There I learned to play the triangle in kindergarten under the tutelage of Miss Kasey and Miss Graves, which proved to be the apex of my career as an instrumentalist. My favorite teacher at Fort Hill School was Miss Purvis in what was known as High 3 (the second semester of the third grade). Miss Purvis was pretty, but she was also very kind to me. She always sat on the side of the streetcar from which she could see me walking home so that we could wave to one another. I was quite stricken with her. Within a year or so after I left the third grade, she married - I still haven't quite forgiven her.

That crush was the first evidence of those incipient male hormones that would in time become quite active – sometimes enough so to get me in trouble. But that's another story and one I'm not likely to relate! Anyone who may have paid me the compliment of joining me in any such "peccadillo of a bygone time" (in the words of Edmund Fuller) need not be concerned that her tryst will come to light here. Those who are especially interested in such matters will have to read between the lines. I am reminded that a friend once wrote a novel and brought it to Harry Golden for criticism. Harry's verdict was "There isn't enough fucking in it." But then I never expected this to be a *New York Times* best seller.

While I was still under Miss Purvis' tutelage, I was chosen to represent my class in the annual school posture contest and was awarded the city-wide High 3 first prize - a blue ribbon. That was the closest I ever came to succeeding in any physical activity at school. I've no doubt, however, that it was the military bearing I learned at Miss Purvis' hands that enabled me to scale the ranks to private first class in the U.S. Army in World War II.

To the best of my recollection, it was also in High 3 that I was surprised to read the following item in *The Lynchburg News*: "NAME OMITTED. The name of Sydnor Thompson was inadvertently omitted from the list of Honor Roll students in High 3 at Fort Hill School." The item caught my eye because it appeared on the same page as my favorite Adventures of Uncle Wiggly, so I knew all of my friends had read it as well. This constituted me something of a local celebrity.

It was no small thing that my classmate Ann Holston lived across the street from the school. I liked Ann but didn't get up enough nerve to ask her if I could come over for a visit until high school when we were both selected to compete in the Virginia State High School Latin Tournament at Randolph-Macon Woman's College. The fact that Ann "got it for prettiest" in our high school graduating class attests to my good judgment in wanting to share her company. I wasn't exactly a Don Juan as far as the girls were concerned. In fact, I didn't manage my first kiss until I was sixteen years old and then only because the bottle stopped spinning in front of my victim at Kitty Davis' birthday party.

Another highlight of living on Englewood was the Craddock-Terry "Cutters" baseball team that played at the nearby Fairground. My first cousin Newton Shearer (Dr. Newton Shearer of Kingsport, Tennessee), who was several years my senior, often came all the way from his house on Rivermont Avenue to Fort Hill to go to a game with me. After Billy Dooley and I were reconciled, he and Paul gave Newt and me license to climb the fence in their backyard to avoid having to pay the fare for admission to the Fairground. In fact, in time there was quite a heavy traffic over his fence. The Cutters were presumably employees of the Craddock-Terry Shoe Company, though that principle may have been honored in the breach as the season became more competitive.

Lynchburg eventually drew a minor league professional team to the Fairground and Newt and I continued our patronage via the Dooleys' backyard. On one occasion, a foul ball hit me in the face and I awoke from the resultant concussion in the arms of a baseball player who was pouring water over my face from the water fountain. Fortunately that was the only treatment that proved necessary.

I learned about more than baseball at the fairground. One of my early childhood recollections is that of a shell-shocked veteran who often attended the games. I watched as his companion wiped dribble from his chin. For a boy, that veteran's plight was frightening testimony to the horror of World War I. It seems my childhood was punctuated with tragic occurrences. Or perhaps those are the memories that come most easily to mind.

## FAMILY BACKGROUND
### The Thompson Line

My paternal grandfather Joseph Frank Thompson moved his with wife and four daughters from Martinsburg, West Virginia to Baltimore, Maryland and thence to Lynchburg in about 1929, following my father who had accepted a post as traffic clerk in the freight offices of the Chesapeake and Ohio Railway there. My father, the eldest child, was a natural pathfinder for the family.

A staunch Democrat, Granddaddy lost his position as postmaster of Martinsburg upon the election of the Republican President Warren G. Harding. He and his older brother James Furlong Thompson had earlier operated a clothing store in Martinsburg under the name "J. F. Thompson and Brother" (they were both "J.F.s"). My grandfather was a representative of a family that had immigrated to West Virginia from Scotland in the early years of the nineteenth century. The immigrant Joseph Thompson took a

4

position as a weaver on a plantation in Berkeley County. Granddaddy, who was Joseph's great grandson, was one of thirteen siblings who were born and lived in Martinsburg for most of their lives. Granddaddy's father Samuel Jasper Thompson served in the Confederate Army and later worked as a conductor on the B&O railway.

After Granddaddy lost his job as postmaster, he began to travel for a men's clothing firm headquartered in Baltimore. When he moved to Lynchburg, he bought a brown shingle house on Wilson Avenue across the street from the rear of Fort Hill Methodist Church, which my siblings and I regularly attended. Probably because Granddaddy's income was contingent upon his success in making sales, my father was called upon to co-sign the note and mortgage on the Wilson Avenue house. Like my father, my grandfather was soft-spoken and gentle, though unlike my father, he rose early in the morning to prepare breakfast for the family. My grandmother had trained him well.

## The Sydnor Line

My father was named for his maternal grandfather Dr. Charles William Sydnor of Strasburg, Virginia, who was a surgeon in the Confederacy's Army of Northern Virginia. As my father's first born, I was named Charles William Sydnor Thompson, Jr. Early in life, I learned that Dr. Sydnor was a representative of a somewhat illustrious family that had immigrated to America from England in colonial times, a fact which eventually led me to devote many hours of my adult life to tracing our shared ancestry. The letters Dr. Sydnor wrote my great grandmother Mary Louisa "Mollie" Davis of Lovingston, Virginia during the war are now in the Southern Historical Collection at the University of North Carolina. One such letter, written just before they were to be married, began as follows:

Hospital A.V.D.
Feb. 5th 1865

My Dear Mollie:

Your letter was received this morning quite to my gratification and after reading & rereading it - I believe there are but two exceptions to be taken to its contents, the first of which is the cold and formal manner in which you began. Any one not acquainted with the existing facts could not come to any other conclusion than that you were addressing a strictly business and formal communication to some unknown individual whose person you had never seen and whose acquaintance you had no desire to cultivate. The second objection is found in the conclusion of the aforesaid document. If after this year's hard labor during which time I have striven most diligently both with pen & living to accomplish something of importance that would tend to my present and future welfare, you can find no more meaning and expressive terms with which to end your letters than the chilly, hackneyed, unmeaning word "your friend", then I fear my efforts have all been in vain. Whilst I and every one else must admit it to be an honor to be termed even a friend by you, yet I think the near approach of our wedding would justify language of a more affectionate character even from the most fastidious.

You are no doubt aware there exist two kinds of living creatures termed by physiologists cold and warm blooded animals. Now I belong to the last named class of creatures such as inhabit the woods, fields, cities, towns &c. And if you do not wish to curdle the blood in my veins, causing me to imagine myself a member of that society, the cold blooded race who have their abodes in the mighty deep as well as the smaller streams, never sign your name at the conclusion of a letter to me as "your friend."

As his letter exemplifies, Great Grandfather had a keen sense of humor. I could not help but note that he signed his letter "Yours truly, C.W. Sydnor," which I deem to be no more intimate than her "your friend." It seems that such formality was in keeping with the custom of the day – even between those who were betrothed.

My grandmother Bessie Sydnor Thompson ("Nanny") was one of my dearest friends and in later years became like a second mother to me under circumstances that I shall recount. It was she who first led me to understand that her father's family had an illustrious history. Nanny dropped out of Mary Baldwin College at age 21 to marry my grandfather, whom she met in Martinsburg, West Virginia, while visiting her sister Anna. Anna had married Dr. Clarence Stealey, pastor of Martinsburg's First Baptist Church. Their son Dr. Sydnor Stealey, an outstanding liberal Baptist theologian, became the first president of Southeastern Baptist Seminary in Wake Forest, North Carolina in 1955. I visited him in the president's home before the rugs had been unrolled. Dr. Stealey started the Seminary off on the right foot but unfortunately it has since fallen into the hands of the reactionary Southern Baptist Convention. He is no doubt spinning in his grave.

Nanny's first three children were boys. The first, named Frank, Jr., died at three years of age. My father was the second child. When the youngest, named Walter Lee for her sister's husband, died within a year of his birth, Nanny "took to her bed." One day Daddy, the sole surviving son, came to her bedside and asked why she didn't get up. She explained to him that she had been struck down by the untimely deaths of his two brothers. Then, as Nanny never tired of relating, my two-year old father exclaimed "But you still have me!" She got out of bed and in time was healed of her depression.

Nanny was an inveterate fan of President Franklin D. Roosevelt and together we listened to his radio fireside chats. She also taught me to play bridge, which she considered necessary to a proper upbringing. Crossword puzzles were her passion, however, and she bought them by the gross in magazines. I seem to have inherited that interest, as has my brother Chick.

Daddy had dropped out of Washington and Lee Law School in 1922 as a result of Granddaddy's having lost his postmaster position. This was especially unfortunate in view of the fact that Daddy had been elected president of the intermediate law class. In time, leaving law school proved to be a defining event in his life. In any event, that's how Daddy happened to move to Lynchburg to work for the

Chesapeake & Ohio Railway. He soon met Mother who was a native of Lynchburg and they were married within a year.

## The Layne and Hill Lines

Mother's parents were Arthur Layne and Martha Jane "Mattie" Hill Layne. Both of them were from Amherst County, Virginia, which adjoins Lynchburg. Arthur traveled for a Lynchburg pharmaceutical firm. Mattie was one of seven siblings in the family of Confederate veteran Joseph Henry Hill and his wife Serena Louise Landrum, a school teacher. A letter Mattie wrote in 1894 from Lynchburg to her youngest sister Delia, who had married Walter L. Bailey and moved to his farm near Waugh, Virginia, read in part as follows:

My dear Delia

I shall attempt to address you a short letter in this eve and it is certainly my desire to write you something cheerful and edifying, but when I reflect that you are parted from us and we cannot possibly in the future be together as in the past it gives me oh such wretched feelings; truly in accordance with this dreadful day for it is indeed one of the worst it has ever been my privilege to experience; so very different from yesterday – though it may seem quite the reverse to you, one who is just entering a life of bright hopes and anticipations. I have only to call to recollection what my own were on a like occasion – the natural thoughts and feelings of all who bow at Cupid's shrine. May the Dispenser of all vicissitudes grant your every wish, and the disappointments of life be like angel's visits.

Evidence of Mattie's mother Serena's strong religious bent appears in a letter which she wrote to her children in 1896 when another daughter Sallie was on her death bed.

Rockery
Jan. 25th 1896

My dear Children:

I regret so much that I cannot be with all of you at the bedside of our dear Sallie and if she is still alive when this reaches you give her many kisses for me and say to her that the most precious gift she could leave to me would be to know that she was trusting in a Savior's love and had the blessed hope of entering that Eternal Rest He has promised to us all who love and trust Him. I too may have to cross the waters before very long, and then what a happy reunion there will be with all that have gone before and are awaiting us on the other side. And now may the richest blessings of Heaven rest upon all of you in the prayer of a true and loving mother. I am praying for you Sallie my dear child.

S.L. Hill

It seems tragic that Serena was not at Sallie's side at that time, but travel was difficult and she was unable to make the journey from her home to Lynchburg. Sallie Belle Hill died January 28, 1896.

Arthur Layne died of tuberculosis when Mother was only three years old. Mother's younger sister Alyce was born posthumously. After Mattie was widowed, she taught school and raised eight children in a house at 105 F Street on Daniel's Hill close by "Rivermont," the home built in the 1840s by Judge William Daniel, Jr. on his "Point of Honor" property. "Rivermont" is now being reclaimed from a severe state of disrepair and will be preserved as a historical site in the future. The Lynchburg suburb now known as Rivermont takes its name from Judge Daniel's house. Fortunately Mattie had considerable help from her older children. Mother once showed us a photograph of her older brother Edward standing in front of the Craddock-Terry Shoe factory, where he was working at age fourteen.

After Mattie died in 1919, Mother and her sister Alyce moved in with their older sister Louise and her husband Newton H. Shearer on Rivermont Avenue. A warm and generous lady who later played the role of aunt for me to perfection, Louise was a card-carrying member of the Women's Christian Temperance Union. When her son Newton Jr. was in grammar school, she prevailed upon him to sign a pledge never to drink alcohol and kept it in a frame on the mantel piece. I don't think it has worked. It was in Aunt Louise's living room that my mother and father were married in 1923. Although Mother did not have an opportunity to go to college, she became an avid reader and was probably the most literate of the siblings.

## THE GREAT DEPRESSION

While we were living on Englewood Avenue the recession of 1929 and the resultant Depression descended on our community. By 1932 limited finances brought on by the Great Depression dictated the pooling of the Thompson family's resources and my parents leased their Englewood house to tenants for a year and moved us in with Daddy's parents on Wilson Avenue. Although this was a difficult time for many, it was a great adventure for us children. My friend Taylor Poindexter, who lived around the corner from Wilson Avenue, was allowed to go to two cowboy movies every Saturday, one at the Isis Theater in the morning and one at the Academy Theater in the afternoon. I knew better than to suggest any such extravagance to my own parents and instead settled for the morning movie sessions at the Isis.

It was during the time we were living with my grandparents that I learned that boys never hit girls. This lesson was driven home by the back of a hairbrush held firmly in my father's hand. I knew the lesson must be important because that was the only time he ever administered any corporal punishment to me. I may have later over-compensated by developing a more or less innocent intimate relationship with another young girl in the neighborhood.

As the Depression wore on, it became clear that the family could not afford to own two houses, even while leasing one out. As a result, my parents moved us back into the house on Englewood Avenue in 1933. My grandparents and their three youngest daughters (the eldest had already married) moved in with us. It surprised no one that my father took his parents and his siblings into his modest bungalow of three bedrooms and one bath. It has always been generally agreed that he was the most unselfish and generous member of our extended family. Moreover, he was never heard to speak ill of anyone. I have sought to emulate his example in that regard, though with only a modicum of success. Without question his record as a gentleman still stands, at least in our family.

Since my grandfather traveled widely in selling his clothing line, he was rarely at home. Nevertheless, I cannot imagine how that house accommodated two families. I'm sure it helped that my grandparents furnished the relatively unfinished basement as a bedroom. They no doubt were surprised to find that it was also occupied by two guinea pig escapees. This cozy arrangement was all the more remarkable in view of the fact that at the height of the Depression my mother's sister Alyce and her husband Don Barlowe as well as their three daughters descended upon the Englewood house from their home in Delaware for a stay of several weeks when Alyce's husband lost his position.

In later years Mother told me that when her older brother Edward Layne ("Uncle Nip") visited us from Washington, DC, he often left the house at mealtime on the pretense that he had another engagement. Mother could not be dissuaded from the belief that he actually left out of consideration for her tight domestic budget. It is difficult today for our children and grandchildren to understand the deprivations many people suffered during the Great Depression.

During this time Eldon Rucker and Lavelon Sydnor, the latter the son of E.C. Glass High School math teacher Clem Sydnor, began dating my aunts Bess and Anna Lee, respectively. Lav was Aunt Anna Lee's fifth and sixth cousin, though we weren't aware of the kinship at the time. It would have made no difference, however, as it soon became apparent that they were made for one another. Lav was enrolled at Lynchburg College where he set a record in the 440 yard dash. He was eventually elected Clerk of the Corporation Court, a more or less sedentary position in which his fleetness served no particular purpose.

Within a year of our move the bank foreclosed on the Englewood Avenue house as a result of Daddy's having cosigned Granddaddy's mortgage note and of Granddaddy having defaulted on that note. From behind the shades of our living room windows, we watched with a sense of shame as the auction was conducted in the front yard. Foreclosures were commonplace during the Great Depression. It has been estimated that half of all mortgages in the United States were in default in 1933 and that there were approximately 1,000 foreclosures a day that year. In any event, Lynchburg appeared to fare as well during the Great Depression as any American city of comparable size and circumstances.

At the age of nine, I felt as though I had "grown up." I was no longer concerned about being short, or about not being proficient at sports, or even about not having clothes in the latest fashion. Indeed, growing up during that time had a significant effect on most young people. The experience may have produced those characteristics that prompted Tom Brokaw to dub us the "Greatest Generation." Though, if I had had an opportunity to speak with Mr. Brokaw before he published his book, I should have suggested that the generation of the founding fathers may have edged us out. I for one am willing to settle for second place. In retrospect, I have concluded that any disadvantage we suffered from having been reared during the Depression did us no harm and probably built character.

## RIVERMONT

By what may have been coincidence, my grandmother's only surviving sister Carrie Lee had moved to Lynchburg with her adopted daughter Florence. Florence had married a widower named Dante Talleyrand Poitevant Stanford and they also lived in Lynchburg. There were three girls born of that marriage – Florence Lee, Aldine and Virginia. (I have recently learned that the sister of my E.C. Glass classmate Powell Dillard's father was the first wife of Dante Stanford. She also had three children by Dante Stanford - Alzada, Dante, Jr. and Jean.) After Dante Sr. died, my father, who had become disaffected with conditions at home, sought solace in the company of Dante's widow.

Doubtless some of his frustration of that time originated with his failure to realize his ambition to practice law. His succumbing from time to time to the charms of John Barleycorn was perhaps further evidence of that frustration. During those bouts, Daddy sometimes adopted an altogether different, more aggressive personality. When I was about eleven years old, Mother agreed to the divorce Daddy requested (although she later confessed that, if her parents had still been living or she had enjoyed some other wise counsel, she might have worked harder to save the marriage). I vividly remember the occasion on which Daddy told me that he would no longer be living with us. It was at a time when he had been drinking and I remember thinking, on that account, that it was just as well, though of course I didn't dare tell him so.

Sometime after the divorce, Daddy met with the priest at the local Catholic Church and signed a pledge not to drink alcohol for one year. He returned to the priest from time to time over the next five years, and on the last such occasion he took me with him. After he and the priest dropped to their knees in prayer, my father signed a three year pledge. To the great relief of the family, he never drank any alcoholic beverage whatsoever for the rest of his life. Apparently the Lord spoke to Daddy through that Catholic priest, even though he himself was a lifelong Baptist. Or perhaps it was simply that the Catholics were the only ones who offered such a special service. In either event, it was a most welcome blessing. Ever since then I have had a considerable appreciation of the Catholic church for the role it played in helping my father overcome what appeared for a time to be his nemesis.

After Mother and Daddy separated in 1934, we children moved with mother from Englewood to a duplex on Norfolk Avenue across the street from Randolph-Macon Woman's College. I transferred to Garland-Rodes Elementary School, which I was intrigued to learn was named for two Confederate Civil War generals from Lynchburg. Later that same year my grandfather J. Frank Thompson died of a heart attack while staying at a hotel in Elkins, West Virginia during a business trip. It was my first experience of death of a family member. I was pulling up honeysuckle in the backyard when Mother told me what had happened and I realized for the first time how much I loved him.

In spite of the challenges of such a tumultuous year, life on Norfolk Avenue proved pleasant enough. The Redmond family lived on the other side of the duplex. John and Jimmy Redmond owned two sets of paraphernalia of which we made good use. One was a lead set with which we molded lead soldiers for sale to Randolph-Macon's students at ten cents apiece. The other was a chemistry set with which we made odorous hydrogen sulfide "bombs" in tin foil wrapping, which we tossed through open windows into the rooms of the same unsuspecting students. Once when we were accosted by the college's security guard on campus, I unabashedly adopted the alias "Billy Duke" as well as a fictitious address, without any punitive consequence that I can remember. Perhaps the name of Billy Duke still appears on their "most wanted" list. If so, I am now prepared to accept extradition.

Jimmy and I also engaged in a decidedly immature conspiracy to lift soft drinks from the delivery truck parked behind our house in the driveway of the neighboring Piggly Wiggly grocery store on Rivermont Avenue. I am sure I achieved the height of presumption as well as stupidity when I asked a Piggly Wiggly employee if he had a spare bottle opener.

There was another malefaction of that time that I cannot blame on Jimmy Redmond. In an idle moment I cut a small piece out of a lace curtain on the front door of our apartment. When asked about it, I was too ashamed to admit that I had done such a foolish thing. It was the first outright lie of a number that eventually established my credentials as a serial liar, particularly when I thought the truth would make me appear foolish.

Perhaps, as is often true, I was motivated to show penance by going to church. Although I had attended the Fort Hill Methodist Church when I lived in Fort Hill and West End (Mother was a Methodist), I began to attend the Rivermont Presbyterian Church after we moved to Norfolk Avenue. When that church endeavored to enlist new members from among its young people, I went home and told Mother that I expected to join the Presbyterian Church in a couple of weeks. "Not if I have anything to say about it," said Mother. "You are a Methodist!" After that I began to ride the bus back to Fort Hill every Sunday.

During the year that we lived on Norfolk Avenue, I embarked on my first paying job selling subscriptions to a new magazine called *Liberty*. I traveled virtually the entire length of Rivermont Avenue, managing to sell only two or three subscriptions. It's a good thing I didn't chose peddling as a career.

## WEST END

Mother's sister Alyce had separated from her husband in Delaware and she and Mother decided to combine their resources and rent a house big enough to accommodate both families. In 1935 we moved from Norfolk Avenue to 500 Westwood Avenue in the West End. The house on Westwood Avenue was near the Lynchburg College campus and is now adjacent to it. Our two families lived together comfortably for the next two years. My cousins Joan, Dottie and Fay Barlowe became like sisters to me.

Mother and Aunt Alyce were always very close. A friend named Midge Gagne of Miami, Florida wrote a poem about them in 1972.

### THE BEBANS

Two sisters from Virginia whose family name is Layne
Tell of tales when they were younger and ways that they raised cane!
And we listen rapt for hours while their faces dance with glee,
Telling stories on each other that never quite agree!
They call each other "Beban", for reasons all their own
And which of them is older? The truth will ne'er be known!
Though "Beban"1 is shorter, "Beban"2 is not so tall
And each one will insist that her sis is best of all!
"Now you're the smartest Beban, I've known that all along
I've hovered in your shadow while you led the happy throng."
"Shush, Beban, why do you persist in such a lie!
'Twas you attracted many beaus and heaven knows not I!"
So the Bebans chide each other; it's the basis of their love,
Their tempers rise together, settle gentle as a dove.
The world, perhaps, is out of step, but the Bebans are in stride,
And the secret of their sweet success is......
                                        THEY'RE SOCIETY-FIED!

That was at a time when "amateur hours" were fashionable, following the example of Major Bowes' radio program. When my brother Chick was four years old, Mother taught him to sing some of the popular songs of the day. Their favorite was "Stardust." Chick won several local contests. In fact, he became so accustomed to winning that, on what was perhaps the only occasion that he did not, I had great difficulty in helping him understand why he should not go forward to receive the prize. Another time, he brought the house down when, acting in a church Christmas drama, he looked into the Christ child's manger and exclaimed, "There's a light bulb in there!"

Chick was a very sensitive youngster. When I took him with me to the movies to see a cowboy film which was accompanied by a serial feature of the nature of "The Perils of Pauline," I often had to coax him back into his seat from the floor when the hero or heroine appeared to be at some physical risk. When he started kindergarten at Thomas C. Miller, Chick was, like many youngsters in such circumstances, somewhat intimidated by the prospect. Mother did what she could to reassure him and even walked with him to school the first day. How he managed it was a mystery, but he actually got back home before she did. She continued that exercise for several days but each day Chick soon returned to the nest. She finally gave up and let him stay at home until he entered the first grade a year later.

While Chick was winning talent contests, I was reading Ellery Queen mystery novels. My siblings and I visited the Fort Hill branch library regularly and transported a load of books from there to Westwood in my little red wagon. Mother wasn't quite sure whether Ellery Queen novels were appropriate reading fare for me. In any event, she thought I spent too much time "with my nose in a book." On more than one occasion I heard her exclaim "Why don't you put that book down and go out to play with the other boys!" Upon which I went out for a few minutes to shoot marbles or flip baseball cards with George Ports or one of the Thompson boys who lived down the street. Reading was my greatest source of pleasure, however, and I soon returned to my book.

One outdoor pursuit I do remember involved an air rifle that I somehow acquired. I regret to say that in learning how to use it, I shot a robin foraging for worms on the ground. Of course, being young, I did not fully appreciate the consequence of my act until I held its lifeless body in my hand. I immediately lost my appetite for hunting any of God's creatures – with the possible exception of house flies. I don't, however, purport to have achieved the ethical sophistication of Dr. Albert Schweitzer who is said to have reprimanded Adlai Stevenson for killing a mosquito. "That was my mosquito!" is the form the reprimand is reported to have taken.

While living in the West End, I attended Mrs. Nowlin's sixth grade class at Thomas C. Miller School. One of the highlights of that year was my drawing Evelyn Morrisette's name in the supposedly secret Pollyanna game for the exchange of presents at Christmas. I failed to resist the temptation to tell her so and was soundly reprimanded by Mrs. Nowlin for breach of the rules. If Evelyn had not been so pretty, I probably shouldn't have succumbed to the temptation! I gave her a kewpie doll of the gaudy plaster kind that I had won at the Fairground. I continued to see something of Evelyn after we both graduated to Robert E. Lee Junior High School where she starred in school operettas. She had a lovely voice. By this time I was thirteen years old and dealing with my own emerging sexuality. Mother was thirty-five and I was concerned about her dating. Somehow I summoned the nerve to tell her that I wished she would dress and look more like the gray-haired mothers of my school friends! She took it as well as could be expected, but I bite my tongue whenever I remember it. It was only a year or two later that (according to my siblings) I adopted the practice of walking several steps behind the family when we were going somewhere because I wasn't sure I wanted to be identified with them. Apparently I suffered from all of the emotional ills that beset the average teenager.

### LUCADO PLACE

Mother married Philip G. Grose in 1937 and moved to Greenville, South Carolina. In the circumstances, it was a wise decision and I affirmed her wish to make a fresh start. Chick, Bobbie and I then moved in with Daddy who was living with Nanny on Lucado Place near downtown. The game of musical houses had now come full circle! It was Nanny who saw me through the remainder of early adolescence. Soon Daddy married Florence and rented an apartment adjacent to Nanny's. My siblings and I enjoyed excellent relationships with our step-parents and our step-sisters. Both of our parents handled the situation with characteristic grace and always spoke well of each other to us children.

After we moved to Lucado Place, I was once again called upon to do "trial by battle" with certain of my contemporaries in the new neighborhood – this time with Scott West who lived on Church Street and Jack Broyles who lived on the other side of Rivermont Bridge. Brother Chick was my second in each contest. As with Billy Dooley some years earlier, I employed the only offense that I knew: I got my arms around their necks and choked them until they gave up. I never again achieved a greater stature in the eyes of my brother.

Among my most memorable teachers at Robert E. Lee, where I attended junior high school, were Mrs. Mahood, Miss Mary Ware, her sister Miss Helen Ware, Mr. Jack Horner and Ms. Celeste Wilson. They all extended themselves to me in a fashion that soon led me to appreciate my school work as far and away the most important aspect of my adolescence and set the pattern for future study. I often think of the fact that the outstanding women who taught me at Robert E. Lee and E.C. Glass High did not have any real opportunity to practice medicine or law or enter the ministry, as many do today. It was certainly unfair. But they were a great credit to the profession they had chosen and I should be the last to suggest that teaching is not among the noblest of professions.

I still blush to remember the day I went to Mrs. Wilson's room to complain that my friend Ida Thomas had been given a semester grade one point higher than I. Ida and I studied together since she too lived on Lucado Place, and we often compared grades. I reminded Mrs. Wilson that I had received higher test grades than Ida during the course of the semester. Unfortunately, in placing my books on her desk I managed to turn over a bottle of ink. I can still hear the echo of exasperation in her voice as it rose in volume, "Get out of here Sydnor Thompson before I skin you alive!"

The highlight of my career at Robert E. Lee came when one of my female classmates and I were designated to ride on the E.C. Glass High School "Education" float in the 1936 Sesquicentennial Parade. We sat together at the feet of a "goddess of education" with open books in our laps. Peyton Winfree, Jr., Jack Horner and Jack Evans, all of whom eventually befriended me, were active in the Sesquicentennial Celebration, which marked the 150th anniversary of the founding of Lynchburg by John Lynch in 1786. It was a huge, if somewhat chauvinistic, success!

## HARRISON STREET

Daddy and Florence moved the family that had resulted from the merger of their households to a rental house at 1001 Harrison Street. I was attending E.C. Glass High School by then and was, fortunately, old enough not to be called upon to do "trial by battle" in the new neighborhood. I recently revisited the house on Harrison Street with my son Brenny, who enjoys such reminiscences, and I found that it is apparently still a rental house. I was saddened to see the exterior in dire need of fresh paint in sharp contrast with the other houses in the same block.

As a teenager, I often spent Sunday afternoons at the C&O Railway traffic office with Daddy, who regularly handled the paperwork for trains that came through Lynchburg on the weekends. One Sunday he and I walked to the Academy Theatre after work to see the film "Lost Horizon" starring Ronald Colman. It was the only movie he and I saw together other than Al Jolson's "Sonny Boy" and it is on that account almost as unforgettable for me.

## E.C. GLASS HIGH SCHOOL

In 1939 the E.C. Glass High School building on Park Avenue wasn't big enough to accommodate four years of high school. As a result, I didn't move to E.C. Glass from Robert E. Lee until I was promoted to the second half of the sophomore year (ninth grade). As had been true at Robert E. Lee Junior High, my life revolved almost entirely around school. Ms. Addie Eure, Ms. Mary Spotswood Payne, Ms. Wallace, Mr. Clem Sydnor, Mr. L. H. Davis and Mr. Blake Isley were among my favorite teachers there. Mr. Isley seated students from front to rear in each row, and from left to right rows, according to the success they enjoyed in class recitations. It was competition in its most severe form. I don't know what modern child psychologists would say about it, but insofar as I can recall, no one ever suffered a nervous breakdown.

I cannot refrain from recounting a story often told about Mr. Clem Sydnor. Perhaps it is apocryphal but, because I knew him, my money is on its being the gospel truth. It seems he was walking between E.C. Glass High School and his home on Wise Street when he encountered an acquaintance with whom he spoke at some length. When taking his leave, Mr. Sydnor asked the acquaintance which way he (Mr. Sydnor) had been walking when they met. When the acquaintance indicated that Mr. Sydnor had been walking in the direction of the high school, the latter is said to have remarked, "Then I have had lunch." Mr. Sydnor, who taught me Algebra II, gave me the only "100" semester grade that I received during my high school career. While I may have answered his exam questions correctly, it is doubtful that I enjoyed a complete mastery of the subject. I am rather inclined to think that he either unconsciously took account of our distant kinship, or else he gave me that grade in a fit of absent-mindedness.

Mr. Sydnor has many descendants living in Lynchburg today, some of whom are among its leading citizens. One of his grandsons, Walker Sydnor, president of Scott Insurance, has been of great assistance to me in planning our Sydnor family reunions. He is currently the chairman of Lynchburg College's Board of Trustees. Thanks to his generosity and that of other Lynchburg Sydnors, especially my Uncle Lav's brother Kendall Sydnor, an auditorium will soon be named for Clem and his wife Rochet at Lynchburg College in a new "Centennial Hall."

My principal extracurricular activity in high school involved the *High Times* newspaper. Jack Evans was the faculty advisor for the *High Times*. In my senior year I had rather hoped to be named editor-in-chief, but Mr. Evans saw it differently. At first he named five students as co-editors – Lois Lichtenstein, Ceevah Rosenthal, Frances Watts, Bob Ramsey and me, all of whom, he said, were being considered as candidates for the post of editor-in-chief.

A few weeks later Mr. Evans announced that the mantle had fallen upon the shoulders of Bob Ramsey. We other candidates were designated "managing editors." I don't know how or why it happened but a few weeks later Mr. Evans named me as co-editor-in-chief with Bob Ramsey and, of course, I was quite pleased. Bob and I divided the duties of the post, putting the paper to bed each Thursday at a printer's office in Rustburg. Bob never had an opportunity to realize his potential. He died young as a fighter pilot missing in action in the Korean War.

Because I was engaged in a number of school activities I was occasionally mentioned in the *High Times* news stories. One day Mr. Evans pointed out that my name had been appearing with some frequency in the paper's headlines. I sought to reassure him by saying that I had nothing to do with the headlines, that

Lois Lichtenstein was the headline editor. Without batting an eye, Mr. Evans responded, "I don't care who writes them; if your name appears in one more headline in this paper, we'll be looking for another co-editor." Suffice it to say, it didn't.

There were certain advantages to my position on the *High Times*. For instance, it was while I was working there that I interviewed actress Greer Garson. She was staying at the Virginia Hotel in connection with the introduction of one of her movies at the Paramount Theatre and I was given the opportunity to conduct an interview. I remember that she was most gracious and quite aristocratic in her bearing. It was the first time, though not the last, that I should use my role as a journalist as an excuse for meeting a celebrity.

Another of my pastimes at E.C. Glass was dramatics. I played the Ghost of Christmas Past in "A Christmas Carol," Box in "Box and Cox," the Sire de Maltroit in "Sire de Maltroit's Door" and the mummy in "Mummy and the Mumps." As a consequence, I am proud to report that I "got it for best actor" in our graduating class. Ms. Mattie Craighill Nicholas was the faculty member who directed our plays. She was a grand lady and an excellent drama coach. Mr. C. M. ("Uncle Charlie") Abbott, a history teacher, played Scrooge in "A Christmas Carol" and was superb.

My closest male friends at E.C. Glass were Philip Read, James Stone, James Watson and Dick Murphy. None of us stayed in Lynchburg in later life, though I ran into Dick Murphy when we both enrolled in the class of 1950 at Harvard Law School. He now practices law in Columbus, Ohio. Elliott Schewel and Buddy Suttenfield were also in my high school class. Their fathers were on the City Council. Elliott was a popular cheerleader and I envied him the company of those sprightly female cheerleaders. He has since served in the Virginia Senate and is unquestionably a man of parts. Buddy liked Kitty Davis and persuaded me to take her to the Senior Dance at the Oakwood Country Club because he had already invited someone else and he wanted to dance with her. I was glad to have a date.

Mary Jane Black, whose pretty face was crowned by a tiara-like shock of flaming red hair, lived only a half block away from me on Harrison Street. She was a fine singer. I sought to ingratiate myself with her by asking her to become the movie reviewer for the *High Times*. She discharged her responsibilities admirably. Unfortunately our relationship never developed beyond the platonic, despite my secret designs to the contrary. In fact, I don't think we ever even went to a movie together.

In my senior year I undertook to date several cheerleaders, especially Elizabeth Krebbs, Kitty Cosby and Sally Ramsey. Sally, Bob Ramsey's sister, was the best at letting me down easy. She always told me that she "unfortunately" had other plans that day but insisted that I call again. I took her at her word four or five times until I finally got the message. I did, however, actually wangle a date with Elizabeth. We spent the afternoon strolling in the Garland-Rodes Park one Easter Sunday and I was ecstatic. I gave her a modest corsage of yellow roses, financed by dear Aunt Bess. Elizabeth was a cellist, as was Mary Alex Jordan, whom I dated the summer after graduation. (It seems at that time I was partial to singers and cellists.)

My subsequent lack of success in running for political office (twice) was presaged when Joe Gantt beat me out for Senior Class president and Bobby Ellett did the same in the contest for president of the Student Council.

As graduation approached I applied for a Fowlkes Scholarship, which paid full tuition for four years of study at the University of Virginia. As class valedictorian, graduating with the highest scholastic average in the recorded history of the school, I thought I should have a good chance of getting it. However, William Garbee and Clyde Ward, two students who had graduated from E.C. Glass a year or so ahead of me and who had been attending Lynchburg College in the interim, also applied. William Garbee was a walking dictionary and Clyde Ward stood high in his class and had also been editor of the *High Times*.

The interviews were conducted at the country house of Judge Aubrey Strode, who was the chairman of the selection committee. William Garbee won the scholarship. I later discovered that he became the president of the English Speaking Union, Richmond Branch, which I considered to be highly appropriate in view of the vocabulary that he had brought to bear upon the committee in the contest for the Fowlkes Scholarship.

I have since met William's brother Robert Garbee, a Lynchburg architect who married Polly Barksdale, my Sydnor fifth cousin twice removed. We meet annually at the Aspen Music Festival, and my wife and I recently enjoyed a visit with them at their summer home on the Outer Banks of North Carolina. I have learned that Robert is at least as smart as his brother. He has to be to keep up with Polly. Polly and my E.C. Glass classmate Shirley Moorman keep me abreast of what is happening in Lynchburg.

I now recognize that the Lord may have been at work in denying me the means of attending the University of Virginia. Dr. Frank Bryant, who ranged across the nation looking for prospects for Syracuse University, visited E.C. Glass that spring and offered me a full tuition scholarship. It was an offer I couldn't refuse. I matriculated at Syracuse University in September 1941 where in time I met the extraordinary woman who became my wife.

Our class graduated from E.C. Glass in June 1941. According to all reports, it has been one of the most faithful classes of all time, having recently celebrated its 60th reunion under the outstanding leadership of Shirley and Lewis Moorman and Doris and Calvin Falwell. Candor requires me to admit that both of my former political rivals, Joe Gantt and Bobby Ellett, have also served the alumni committee in exemplary fashion! Although the committee announced that it did not expect to schedule any more reunions, Elliott Schewel saved the day by volunteering to have everyone come to his home for the 75th reunion! I can hardly wait!

At the invitation of the reunion committee, I prepared some verses for the class in a somewhat similar vein to the talk delivered at the Jones Memorial Library:

### A REMINISCENCE FOR THE E.C. GLASS CLASS OF 1941

I

We gather here who daily seek to mend
the ravages of three score years and ten.
For we who 60 years ago were spry
now peer through multi-focal lens and try
with all the strength our age-dimmed eyes allow
to recognize the wrinkled cheek and brow
of each classmate who shouts a warm hello.
The one so hailed prays heav'n that he may know
that person who now looks expectantly
for signs of recognition, though it be
unlikely that on this erasèd slate
he'll find the name of that now balding pate.

II

But no more talk of aging or old-timers,
ague or gout or imminent Alzheimer's.
We're here to celebrate our mere survival
and drink today to memory's revival.
So let us now recall those days gone by
when none of us believed we'd ever die,
when drugs were used to comfort those in pain
and no one even heard of crack cocaine,
when teachers ruled the class with iron hand
and even heterosexual acts were banned,
when E.C. Glass was white as falling snow
and girls were taught to keep house and to sew.

III

In Isley's class we did a mate unseat
when we performed some mathematic feat.
And often risked our academic necks
to bring to berth that teacher's prize – the check (√).
We nursed a Coke at Walgreen's corner drug.
At Senior Dance we learned to jitterbug.
Recall the Isis which, like we who're here,
seemed not to know its entrance from its rear;
and next to it the Tavern's beans sublime
where sat a hundred guests "ten at a time";
and football games with rival Roanoke High
when young boys cheered to glimpse young Kitty's thigh.

Could we who knew ten years of Great Depression
who worked 'til dawn to master a profession,
have ever dreamed or held the expectation
that we'd be called "the greatest generation"?
Today we feel all those relentless years
and once again are brought to verge of tears
to view the fulsome paunch, the balding pate,
the wrinkled brow, the somewhat wrinkled mate.
But still we jog each morn at early light
and strain at bench aerobics every night
in vain attempts to outwit Father Time
and live to laugh at next reunion's rhyme.

### Epilogue

Yet each of us remembers those sweet years
and savors them with joy that's mixed with tears,
for, all in all, we know — by any test,
the Class of Forty-One outshines the rest.

October 13, 2001

In the summer after I graduated from E.C. Glass, I took a position with Craddock-Terry Shoe Company at its Ninth Street jobbing office. Through the good offices of my father's sister Helen, who worked there, I was hired to work in the mailroom. My superior was a middle-aged gentleman named "Red" who smelled of sen sen and hair tonic. The combination was apparently intended to camouflage the lingering smell of a libation he had enjoyed the night before, although they did not altogether succeed in that regard. On my first day on the job, Red sent me to the basement to ask the janitor for the "little red wagon" I was to use to carry the mail to the post office. I soon learned from the janitor's broad smile that there was no such wagon!

## THE LYNCHBURG NEWS

After my freshman year at college, I returned to Lynchburg for what proved to be my last extended stay there. It was the summer of 1942 and World War II had started.

My step-sister Florence Lee's husband Jack Coleman was the manager of a local freight company called Brooks Transportation. Jack gave me a job loading trucks that carried freight to other cities. I weighed about 115 pounds at that time and soon earned the nickname "feather ass" from my fellow-workers. I fought those boxes for a couple of weeks before getting a job that was more suited to my slender stature. Probably because of my experience on the *High Times*, I landed a job at *The Lynchburg News*. My beat was primarily writing church news and editing articles from correspondents in nearby small towns. The *News* had been editorially supportive of the Democratic Party for many years, though it was, like the city itself, quite conservative.

Mr. Irvine was the managing editor and Peyton Winfree, Jr. was the city editor. They both answered to the publisher Mr. Powell

Glass, who was the son of Senator Carter Glass. It was a Glass family newspaper, as was the evening paper, the *Daily Advance*, of which Carter Glass, Jr. was the publisher. Mr. Irvine was of the old school of journalism – gruff, and indisposed to suffer fools gladly. I got off on the wrong foot when he had to call me down for whistling in the office. Unfortunately I had not yet learned that George Washington included a prohibition against whistling in public in the list of "Rules of Civility and Decent Behavior" that he adopted as a boy. Nevertheless, Mr. Irvine suffered this fool reasonably well and I came to like him. Peyton gave me my assignments and I got along especially well with him.

Mr. Powell Glass was on the City Desk one day when Peyton was out, and he published over my byline a feature story I had written about railroad cars having to be refurbished and brought back into service because of the war. Needless to say, I derived considerable satisfaction from finding that byline in print one morning. Apparently Peyton had squirreled the story away in the City Desk and Mr. Glass found it. Anyhow, that was the extent of my career as a newspaperman. It was a grand experience. All that and scrumptious apple pie a la mode at the White House Restaurant after the paper was put to bed at midnight. What more could a fellow ask for?

### LEAVING LYNCHBURG

Daddy left the Chesapeake and Ohio Railway in 1947. He was 46 at that time and had aspired to succeed H. G. McCausland as General Agent for the C&O in Lynchburg. Unfortunately, then president Robert Young mandated that no one who was older than 45 years of age could be appointed a General Agent for the Railway. Upon hearing this news, Daddy resigned and the family prepared to leave Lynchburg for Charles Town, West Virginia.

The occasion for Daddy's return to his native state was an invitation to join his younger brother Joe (Joseph J. Thompson) in a retail appliance business there. The two brothers were always close and Uncle Joe welcomed having Daddy as a partner. Uncle Joe had been quite handsome as a young man and very popular with the opposite sex. The word in the family was that when he was visiting Mother and Daddy in Lynchburg in the mid '20s, he and a young girl named McWane had eloped. Uncle Joe had barely reached his majority and the marriage was quickly annulled. Following the annulment, he made a previously unscheduled visit to Paris at the expense of his erstwhile father-in-law. Uncle Joe was later happily married to Louise Burleigh of Harper's Ferry, West Virginia and had two lovely daughters, Joan and Nancy.

Daddy's move to Charles Town ended our family's twenty-five year residence in Lynchburg.

That is the Lynchburg I remember – with affection.

# CHAPTER 2
## SUMMERTIME AND THE LIVING WAS EASY

Summer has always been my favorite season. To this day I relish the warm summer sun when others complain of it. I have concluded that it is reminiscent of the security I felt in my mother's womb.

### "THE COUNTRY"

There were two kinds of summer vacations that I experienced as a boy in the 1930s. One was a visit to my mother's Aunt Delia Bailey at her farm on the James River near Waugh, Virginia, about twenty miles from Lynchburg. Aunt Delia and Uncle Walter had a farm of several hundred acres that extended from the riverside well into the woods behind their home. We approached the farm (known to me as "the country") by automobile and crossed the river to our destination by rowboat - after shouting for Cousin Teddy Bailey to bring the boat over to us. There was no such thing as a life preserver, so Teddy had our lives in his hands. I had learned that Mr. LaRue, a friend of my grandmother Mattie Layne, had drowned in the James River, so I always held my breath while we were crossing. To this day, I'm not much of a swimmer. I've never even learned to tread water, though some day soon I intend to learn.

Along with tobacco, Uncle Walter grew corn (and every other vegetable common to the traditional American truck farm) in the "bottom land" next to the river. There was a wonderful field of watermelons that I sometimes raided in the company of one of the boys who lived there. Why we were motivated to break them open and eat them at the temperatures they reached in the hot sun I'm not clear, particularly since Aunt Delia frequently served watermelons to us after cooling them in the spring near the house. It must have been a case of "boys will be boys."

During my earliest visits, my companion was a small boy of six or seven who was the illegitimate son of a black woman who kept house for the Baileys. I regret to say that he was called "Nig." Together we usually got into enough devilment in a week to give Aunt Delia plenty of cause for concern. Nig disappeared from the scene a few years after graduating from mere devilment to burning down barns. Years later I learned that he had spent some time in the penitentiary, though I do not know on what account. The strong possibility exists that it was arson, of course.

My sidekick on later visits to "the country" was a white boy named Bernard who was about my age. As was common in rural Virginia, Bernard had been more or less indentured to Uncle Walter by his parents, who had more children than they could care for. One summer Aunt Delia gave Bernard and me the task of drowning a sack full of newborn kittens in the river. We agitated over it for several hours until someone came to find us and relieved us of the

22

assignment. I grieved for those kittens for several days. Aunt Delia was a good church woman (we went to a small country church every Sunday that I was there), but I suppose she simply couldn't allow the house to be overrun with cats.

In retrospect I realize that Aunt Delia's life must have been quite a hard one. Besides getting up with the chickens to milk the cows, she worked with little respite until nightfall. When I saw her some years later in Lynchburg, she was bent nearly double, perhaps as much from years of performing the chores incident to farm life as from severe arthritis. It was an ironic contrast to the life my grandmother Mattie Layne had painted in such optimistic colors in the letter she wrote on Delia's wedding day (see page 8).

## WASHINGTON, DC

The other type of summer vacation that I enjoyed began when I was a little older. During the summers between 1935 and 1938 Mother arranged for me to visit in the homes of her brothers Henry Layne and Edward (Nip) Layne in Washington, DC. Their families were most hospitable, and I prized my time with them.

Uncle Henry regularly demonstrated the keenest sense of humor of any of my relatives, which was one reason I looked forward to those visits. Over the years he had acquired a number of apartments in the District. Emergency rent controls prohibited his being able to collect a profitable rental from his tenants, but he maintained a sense of humor about that too. The word in the family was that he would appear at the tenant's door in his overalls to repair the plumbing only to reappear a few hours later dressed to the nines, including his customary homburg, to collect the rent. Both Uncle Henry and Uncle Nip were balding. It was from Uncle Henry that I learned how to train the remaining strands of hair over my scalp, a skill which I have recently had occasion to develop into an art form.

Uncle Henry's son Harry, who was about five years my senior, drove a magnificent new Ford convertible and treated me to every Jeannette McDonald – Nelson Eddy movie that was shown during that period. We usually topped our visits to the local movie houses off with a chocolate milkshake at the nearest drugstore.

Uncle Henry's wife Della was an aficionado of the morning radio serials that were the forerunners of today's TV soaps. We listened together to "My Gal Sunday." In the afternoons I tuned in the radio broadcasts of the Washington Senators baseball games. When the team was playing away from home, the plays were transmitted by teletype to the Washington announcer, who then undertook to dramatize the teletype message by simulating an actual broadcast. In retrospect, it was truly a comical scenario.

I also stayed with Uncle Nip and Aunt Marg at their home, which Aunt Marg called the "Caravansary." (It was a frequent pit stop for relatives visiting the Capital City.) Their son Edward Jr. ("Nipper") and I tramped all over the city, making frequent visits to the National Zoo, the government buildings and the Presidential memorials on the mall in front of the Capitol. We climbed the stairs of the Washington monument (884 more or less) on more than one occasion and, in our youth, thought little of it. The amusement park at Glen Echo was another of our favorite diversions. Nipper eventually became a first-rate trial lawyer in Bethesda, Maryland but unfortunately died young in an automobile accident when he was returning home late one night from the District.

## GREENVILLE AND CHARLOTTE

As I have already said, in 1937 Mother married Philip G. Grose who was originally from Harmony, North Carolina. Philip worked for Raylass Stores in Lynchburg along with Mother's sister Alyce, who introduced them. Soon after they met, however, Philip was transferred to Greenville, South Carolina. They continued their long distance courtship for several months until Mother eventually accepted his proposal of marriage (which came by mail) with all that it entailed. This included leaving us in Lynchburg to live with Daddy at Nanny's house. Within a year Mother had a son, Philip Grose, Jr., who soon proved a great joy to all of us and in time has made us very proud.

After Mother moved to Greenville, Bobbie, Chick and I made the trip south on a Southern Railway train every June after the semester ended, well supplied with comic books and other literary fare of similar quality. We spent most of the summer and all of the major holidays with Mother and watched as our brother Phil grew to appreciate our company and we his. One of our greatest pastimes was teaching him to recite the state capitals at the tender age of six. On his own, he learned reams of big league baseball minutiae by the time he was seven and is a master of the subject to this day.

My stepfather was soon transferred to Spartanburg at a salary that was not, in Mother's judgment, commensurate with his newly-acquired family responsibilities. They had just moved into a new public housing project when Bobbie, Chick and I came for our summer visit. I stayed only about a week because that was the same summer that I worked at Craddock-Terry Shoe Company. I was there long enough, however, to conclude that the Grose family's fortunes were at low ebb. As my brother Phil tells the story, in September of 1941 Mother sent my stepfather to Charlotte with instructions to find a job and a house for the family before returning to Spartanburg. Much to his credit he accomplished that mission in spades, securing a position in the piece goods department of Belk Stores and renting one of the few available houses in the city. Mother and young Phil followed in a few days on the front seat of the moving van.

# CHAPTER 3
## GO NORTH YOUNG MAN

In early September 1941 my father saw me off to Syracuse University from the Southern Railway Station in Lynchburg. As was his custom, he stood outside the railroad car and waited for the train to leave. I greatly enjoyed the fact that he always saw me off that way.

Syracuse University, located in Syracuse, New York, was originally founded as a Methodist College in the late 1800s. In time it shed its Methodist connection and grew into a great university offering many academic disciplines to a student body that numbered 7,000 by 1941. If I had not been so glad to be there I should have been somewhat intimidated by its size. Today it is much larger, of course.

Upon my arrival I was assigned a room in a house just off campus at 101 University Place. The house had belonged to an elderly lady named Mrs. Sibley, who had apparently deeded it to the University, retaining the right to live on the rear of the first floor for her lifetime. My roommate was Warren Jackson from Mt. Vernon, New York. I considered myself lucky in that he and I got along exceptionally well from the beginning. Warren liked to be called "Stoney" (short for Stonewall), but ironically was rarely accommodated in that respect. He was a good student, enrolled in the forestry school, and had a low-key personality. Unfortunately, he suffered a bout of colitis in the first semester. I awoke one night shortly after the school year began to hear him groaning in the bunk above me. I went with him to the hospital, where he underwent an emergency colostomy. When I visited him in the hospital, I had to be careful not to say anything funny because it hurt him to laugh. He had to drop out of school, but we renewed our friendship a year or so later when he returned to campus.

Years later Stoney visited my home in Lynchburg when I was on furlough during the war, and became enamored of my stepsister Virginia ("Jinny"). When I returned to Camp Shelby after my furlough ended he stayed on with the family for some weeks, apparently in order to press his courtship. As is occasionally true in such matters, including some within my own experience, his ardor sometimes prompted him to overstep the bounds of reason. Apparently he became jealous of the attention shown Jinny by other suitors, causing the family some embarrassment. My brother Chick recalls one occasion on which Stoney crawled out of a second story window, shimmied down a downspout, and purported to slash the tires of the car which Jinny's date had parked in front of the house. Chick insists he was an innocent bystander.

Eventually Daddy asked me to write Stoney and suggest that he should make other arrangements if he intended to stay in Lynchburg – as he had no doubt become aware of Stoney's infatuation. Shortly thereafter, Stoney left Lynchburg. Years later I learned that he had moved to Alaska and was working as Fire Control Chief in a forestry unit. He organized and supervised fire fighters in twenty-four districts there. We lost contact when he changed his address and my correspondence was returned unopened. I hated that because he had been a loyal friend and I liked him very much.

One of my first classes was with Dr. Rhine who taught English. He had a passion for the subject of semantics. Our text was written by S. I. Hayakawa, the educator who eventually became a United States senator from California. Dr. Rhine delighted in asking us such questions as "What does it mean to say 'the United States declared war on Germany?' Who or what is the United States? Who or what is Germany? What does it mean to 'declare war'?" At the time, that seemed a foolish way to spend a full semester of study but in retrospect I suppose it was a worthwhile enterprise. We sometimes speak too freely in such abstract terms when greater precision would be helpful.

The other course I remember from my first year at Syracuse was Speech. My teacher was Dr. Milton Dickens, who assured me that except for one vowel sound my southern accent was acceptable. The exception was in the words "out" or "shout," which I had always pronounced very much like the two "o's" in "moot." I understand that such pronunciation also exists in some sections of Canada. He suggested that if I could pronounce "out" like the "ou" in "loud," my southern accent would pass muster. I adopted his suggestion, of course. I later made a speech about the life of General Robert E. Lee, whom I had long admired. It seemed to me that those Yankees should learn something of our Southern icon.

As a consequence of my taking that speech course, I was appointed to the freshman debating team. Early on we visited Rochester University for an intercollegiate debate. The question was "Should we reorganize the League of Nations after the war and give it more power?" Unfortunately I had to debate the negative side of the proposition, which was contrary to my personal view of the matter. While I didn't appreciate it at the time, it was good preparation for what would some day be expected of me as a lawyer. In the course of my argument, I used the word "lamentable." After the debate, our coach said "I prefer that you not use big words when a smaller one will serve just as well - especially since you may mispronounce the word." The coach was right, of course. While there are times when complex words are appropriate, they are often unnecessary. But, I had not mispronounced the word!

When I was recruited to attend Syracuse University, it was understood that I should earn my meals by waiting table at a men's dormitory. To that end I served three meals a day at Sims Hall. Most of the other waiters were athletes, but not all of them. Two of the exceptions were named Sam and Bill. Before long they began ribbing me about my southern upbringing and the slow pace at which I waited tables. One might say they ganged up on me. Another student waiter named Rudy undertook to rescue me from time to time, with varying degrees of success. On his recommendation I finally learned to ignore them and they tired of the game. But they left their mark and I can thank them for having helped me build a little character.

On the whole, my being a southerner actually worked to my advantage in terms of gaining friendships among my fellow students. For example, I was elected to represent my freshman house in the Men's Student Government. In the spring term, I was asked to nominate one of the upperclassmen as Speaker of the House and agreed to do so. While I was on my feet, describing his qualifications for the office I forgot his name, which I had failed to write in my notes. I continued to describe his virtues at length, both real and imagined, until I finally remembered his name. I learned a good lesson there.

When I turned 18 years old in February 1942 the upperclassman who was the manager of the dining hall took me with him to the Rainbow Lounge in the Syracuse Hotel. The entertainer in the Lounge at that time was a singer named Alice O'Connell, who was a sister of the popular singer Helen O'Connell. Alice was an absolutely gorgeous blonde and I was dumbstruck with admiration. Her husband traveled with her, which was a good thing. Not that an awestruck teenager could have given him any competition.

Early on in the first semester I participated in fraternity rushing even though I knew it was unlikely that I could afford to join one. I was invited back to a local fraternity called Sigma Beta, which has since become affiliated with the national fraternity Alpha Tau Omega. The brothers seemed to like me and I liked them. They waived the initiation fee until I could afford to pay it and I became one of seven pledges to Sigma Beta that year.

In general my association with the fraternity was one of the most satisfying aspects of my freshman year, despite the rather rigorous hazing we experienced during "Hell Week" in the spring. First we were abandoned several miles out of town after dark without any transportation or wherewithal; then we were kept awake for the balance of the night after we finally made our way back to the fraternity. We were shocked with electrical wires and had raw oysters tossed into our open mouths after hearing the sound of someone preparing to expectorate. As a grand finale, at daybreak we suffered numerous whacks across the derriere with paddles that we had to carry with us. When, in response to a demand to describe "any sexual experiences you have had," I confessed to having once fondled the "mammary glands" of a schoolmate, my tormentors were inspired to renew their paddling with vigor.

When I visited the university several years ago, I found the fraternity house in need of a good deal of work. Situated between two handsome sorority houses on Walnut Avenue, its physical shortcomings were all the more apparent. Recently, however, the extraordinarily dedicated faculty advisor Dr. Steven Chamberlain has begun the process of rescuing ATO from the termites. Another loyal alumnus, Charles Johnson, who shares Dr. Chamberlain's dedication, actually painted the exterior of the house himself. Thanks to their example, my own interest has now been stimulated to the point that I have agreed to participate in a five year financial plan that we hope will put the house in good physical order.

In addition to joining the fraternity, I decided to go out for a sport. That spring, I was selected as a coxswain for one of the freshman crews. My responsibilities were to steer an eight-man shell and to count cadence so that the oarsmen would row in rhythm. I was also expected to call out the number of any oarsman who was not in sync with the others. It soon became evident, however, that they did not appreciate having their numbers called out. In fact, a few raised the issue with me after we returned to the dock. There wasn't much room for diplomacy. And they were all big guys!

My only qualification for the position was my slight stature, since I had never done any rowing of any kind and could barely swim. I was taking quite a risk because, if a coxswain wins a race, the oarsmen throw him into the water. Fortunately, or maybe unfortunately, my career as a coxswain was short-lived and I was never thrown into Lake Onondaga. One day, during practice, I steered the shell onto a jagged rock which was concealed just below the surface of the water and it tore a hole in the bottom of the shell. I decided to seek another medium for athletic stardom.

My freshman year ended with a bang (or perhaps I should say a whimper) when I decided to run for president of the sophomore class. Several of us put together a slate. Agnes ("Aggie") Shoffner, a Phi Mu, was our candidate for secretary and John Weiss, a football player, was our candidate for treasurer. We conducted an active campaign, making speeches in the freshman residences on various issues we had fabricated and plastering the campus with posters. I placed second in a four-man contest and the rest of the slate did about the same. A Phi Delt named McTiernan won. My excuse is that he was a basketball and baseball star - apparently my brief career as a coxswain did not measure up. Aggie and I have remained good friends and kept in touch through the years. We both still play tennis and when the court's temperature is over 90°, I can usually beat her.

My second year at Syracuse University was interrupted by the draft board but was not otherwise eventful. By then, I was more or less marking time waiting to be drafted and my grades suffered accordingly - especially in the second semester. I gave up my job at Sims Hall and instead earned my meals at the University Hospital, where my classmate Bill Stapleton, who was from Holyoke, Massachusetts, and I washed trays. He was a member of Delta Kappa Epsilon, which was probably one of the strongest fraternities on campus. We spent a lot of time together that year.

Bill and I were both interested in drama and we auditioned for roles in two clubs – Boars Head (drama) and Tambourine and Bones (musicals). Bill got a role in "Mr. Roberts" and I got a role in a musical called "High on a Hill." Joyce Crabtree, a drama major from Radford, Virginia, wrote the script, which was quite funny. The theme concerned a feud between two mountaineer families named Gandy and Botts. I played Grandpa Botts. "Well, it's like this, jedge. The Botts ain't to blame. The folks that done it are the Gandys by name," I proclaimed in a sing-song approximation of an Appalachian accent. Janet Hayes played my daughter "Dodie Botts" in a Romeo and Juliet kind of plot and Bill played a member of the Gandy clan.

I stayed on in Syracuse during Christmas vacation that year and worked at the Onondaga Men's Shop as a salesclerk. The fraternity closed for the holiday but I prevailed upon the brothers to let me stay there, even though the furnace was to be turned off. It proved to be one of the coldest Decembers in Syracuse history and, despite piling mattress on mattress, I nearly froze to death. When I was not working at the Men's Shop, I made the rounds of every warm refuge I could find before going back to the fraternity for the night. I am not sure I would do it again, but the money I earned that December represented a substantial portion of the financial resources I would need until I was drafted into the Army about two months later.

Bill Stapleton and I left Syracuse for the armed services at about the same time. (We also returned at about the same time after the war ended.) Once, when we were flush and having dinner at the Varsity Restaurant, I noticed that Bill had nearly finished his meal but hadn't touched his roll. I asked him if he intended to eat it. His reply was characteristic. "You look like you want it more than I do, Syd, so help yourself." It reminds me of the lines Sir Philip Sidney made famous in 1585. As he was raising a canteen to his parched lips during a battle in the Netherlands, a dying soldier begged for water. Sir Philip gave up the canteen with the words: "Take it. Thy necessity is greater than mine."

Bill and his family were deeply religious. He attended mass regularly and his brother Edward became a priest, serving throughout poverty-stricken communities in the South. I was particularly impressed by Bill's determination to avoid sexual relations until he married, as I rarely encountered such a principled ethic among my contemporaries. Bill was all that I could have hoped for in a college chum and our friendship has weathered the test of time.

# CHAPTER 4
## UNCLE SAM'S CALL

As I left the library at Syracuse University on the afternoon of December 7, 1941, I came upon a group of students who were listening with rapt attention to a radio on the library steps. That is how I learned of the Japanese attack at Pearl Harbor on what was, in the words of President Roosevelt, a "day that will live in infamy." It was an event that would significantly affect my life, though I had little appreciation of it at the time. I was seventeen years old.

Just over a year later my number was called in the draft and I was instructed by the U.S. Selective Service Commission to report for a physical examination at the Syracuse, NY Induction Center. Along with other draftees, I stripped to the skin and proceeded along the line of doctors until I came to a group conducting heart examinations. One doctor held his stethoscope to my chest and listened intently. Then he asked me to bend over and touch my toes. After I did, he again applied the stethoscope to my chest. He called upon me to repeat that exercise several times until he finally called another doctor over and asked him to listen to my heart. By that time I had become quite concerned. Not only had my heart sunk, it had also skipped a few beats.

As the second doctor checked my heart, the first doctor asked "Doesn't he have a heart murmur?"

"I don't think so," replied the second. "He just has a thin chest."

"You think? All right. Move on, son, and good luck."

I was passed to the next station. "Thank you, Lord," I thought with relief. I had avoided being classified as 4-F! While I had no burning desire to enter the fray, I certainly did not want to have to report to my family and friends that I had been found physically unfit for military service. Apparently, I was not fully self-sufficient. To this day what other people think is still quite important to me.

### BASIC TRAINING

By March 17, 1943 I was on a train headed for Camp Callan, near San Diego, California, to report for basic training in a 40 millimeter Coast Artillery Anti-Aircraft Battalion. Camp Callan had been built as a basic training center on the cliffs of the California coast. (The camp no longer exists. I am told it is now the site of a celebrated golf course called Torrey Pines on the PGA tour.)

Short and stocky, Sergeant Shepherd was perfectly cast as the cadre sergeant for basic training and he sought to intimidate us from the moment we arrived. He badgered us, beleaguered us and shouted at us from dawn to dusk. A nice looking fellow who could be well-spoken when he chose to be, had I met him in civilian life I should never have imagined that he was capable of such gross behavior. But of course that was his assignment at Callan. As a tough cadre sergeant, he was phenomenally successful.

At daybreak on that first morning, I fell out for reveille and set off to run the obstacle course with the other men in our battalion — crawling through pipes and under fences, climbing over walls, running through a field of automobile tires, jumping water-filled trenches, et cetera. That morning I dragged myself in among the also-rans near the end of the line. I had never had occasion to move my 118 pounds at any such speed!

While I did not distinguish myself on the obstacle course, there were two trainees who did. One, named Tippett, was in C Battery with me and the other, named Petersen, was in B Battery. It soon became general knowledge that Petersen finished the course first every morning and that Tippett finished second just behind him. It was also rumored that Petersen was dating a Hollywood starlet on weekends.

Over the next few weeks Sgt. Shepherd undertook the awful task of whipping us into a disciplined fighting force. We took long marches carrying heavy shoulder packs and rifles, climbed steep cliffs at the Pacific Ocean's edge, and learned to fire the Springfield '03 rifle. Having never fired anything other than my air rifle, I was surprised to qualify for the "sharpshooter" medal with the Springfield. Fortunately, I haven't had cause to fire anything since the war. During that training, we also simulated firing the 40 mm anti-aircraft gun at a sleeve that was being pulled by an airplane. It was a good thing we weren't firing live rounds!

I remember one particular morning when we were standing in ranks for a rifle inspection. We had been warned it was coming and so we had cleaned and re-cleaned our rifles as diligently as we could. The captain took my rifle, closed one eye and looked up the bore with the other. Then he said to Sgt. Shepherd, who was following one step behind him, "This is the most remotely clean rifle I have seen this morning." With some difficulty, Sgt. Shepherd undertook to conceal a look of surprise mixed with admiration before he moved on. To this day I am satisfied that he did not understand the captain's appraisal of the condition of my rifle, which was just as well.

One of the more difficult tests to which we were put was the "infiltration course." There we crawled under barbed wire while fifty caliber machine guns were fired over our heads. The word was passed that a trainee had been killed a few weeks earlier because he didn't stay low enough. You may be sure that this information had the necessary *in terrorem* effect, regardless of its veracity.

Some trainees were eventually selected as "gadget" non-commissioned officers to lead their fellow recruits. I was named a platoon sergeant in Battery C and was given an arm band with three stripes to identify my rank. Petersen, now cast in the "gadget" role of battalion commander, strutted like a drum major at the forefront of the battalion.

Along with my new responsibilities, I was surprised to develop a remarkable degree of energy that I had not known before. Not only did I have no difficulty in carrying my pack on the frequent marches, which grew longer and longer, but I found myself urging other members of my platoon on and encouraging those who fell behind to close ranks.

I was even more surprised when, in the last week of basic training, I managed to place third on the obstacle course - just behind Petersen and Tippett. As luck would have it, it was the only time in three years of Army service that I was given any command responsibility. I think there is a moral lesson there – for me as well as for the Army. It seems that at any age the confidence of one's superiors (and peers) is a powerful motivator.

Toward the end of basic training our battalion was cast in a war film that was being shot in southern California – "Guadalcanal Diary." The film starred Preston Foster, Lloyd Nolan and Bill Bendix. We marched along the beach with our barracks bags on our shoulders, representing an army unit that was relieving the marines who had captured the island. Petersen was, of course, the only man in the battalion who was given lines to speak: "Hey, buddy, what's it like out there," he shouted to the marines who were about to board a ship. After Bill Bendix's noncommittal "You'll see," Petersen added, "See you guys in Tokyo."

Tippett and I and four other men in our battery were eventually designated to apply for Officer Candidate School. We took turns drilling each other in close march on the parade ground. We were also dispatched to headquarters in the evenings to take a trigonometry course. Presumably that study bore some relationship to the math one should master in order to set the gauges for firing the 40 mm anti-aircraft guns.

We were finally interviewed by an OCS board as basic training was coming to an end. In making out the application, we were told to list three OCS schools that we should like to attend – in order of preference. I listed them in the following order: artillery, infantry, and transportation. I was surprised when the first question put to me was, "Why do you think you qualify for transportation OCS, soldier." I replied somewhat hesitantly "My father works for the C&O Railway." "Your father is not before this board," my questioner snapped back. From then on it was uphill sledding.

## ARMY SPECIALIZED TRAINING PROGRAM

While my application for OCS was pending, a new program called Army Specialized Training Program (ASTP) was announced. Although the program encompassed many languages that were more directly related to the war effort, the Army offered Spanish on the theory that Spain might eventually join the Axis powers because of Franco's Fascist bent. Having taken Spanish in college, I undertook to qualify for foreign language study. I applied and was selected. The man who assigned me to study at Syracuse University must have either had a kind heart or a keen sense of humor. Within six months of the day that I left Syracuse to make the world safe for democracy, I was on my way back to make the world safe for the Spanish language.

The ASTP assignment served to prevent any possibility that I should have to participate in the D-Day Invasion of Europe. Had I gone to infantry OCS in July 1943, I may very well have been among those who were called upon to land on the Normandy beaches on D-Day in June 1944. And this memoir might never have been written.

# CHAPTER 5
## YOU CAN GO HOME AGAIN

After I arrived back at Syracuse University in the summer of 1943, I began an in-depth course of study in Spanish. Our curriculum included not only the language but also Spanish history, geography and culture. Two of my teachers were Señora Berta Montera and Dr. Homero Seris, the former originally from Cuba and the latter from the Madrid University faculty in Spain. Dr. Seris had been in Madrid during the Spanish Civil War in the 1930s and regaled us with stories of how the "Republicanos" or "loyalists" had fought bravely but had eventually been forced to surrender to the superior forces of Franco's Fascists. He hadn't quite forgiven us Americans for not coming to the aid of the Republicanos. Of course, I should have reminded him that Ernest Hemingway and a number of other idealistic Americans did not stand idly by. But he was a splendid old gentleman of great scholarship and I admired him greatly.

Along with Spanish, I studied voice privately with Professor Frederick Haywood of the Crouse College faculty. He was primarily concerned with teaching me to breathe from my diaphragm. His lessons still serve me well, as my current yoga teacher calls for that same approach to breathing. Having become interested in vocal music, I also enlisted in the Syracuse University Chorus, which was preparing Handel's "Messiah" for performance in early December 1943. I sang in the bass section and enjoyed it immensely. (Unbeknownst to me, my future wife, whom I had not yet met, was singing in the soprano section.) The chorus was so big that it filled half of the seats in the Crouse College concert hall. Dr. Lyman was our conductor and Donald Dame of the Metropolitan Opera was the tenor soloist. I was delighted with both of them and with the opportunity to learn the "Messiah." "And the glory, the glory of the Lord shall be revealed," I sang with great enthusiasm. I suppose it is nearly everyone's favorite oratorio. I haven't sung it since then but I still thrill to every performance of it.

There was a shortage of space sufficient to accommodate several thousand ASTP students at the university, so we were housed in the gymnasium for the first three months of our stay. Eventually I was transferred to a makeshift "barracks" that had formerly been a private residence on Euclid Avenue. Because several students had tragically died some time earlier when a mobile unit on the campus caught fire, we were required to take turns at guard duty inside the house throughout the night in three hour shifts. Guarding against an ordinary residential furnace fire seemed to me to be the worst sort of make-work.

Having returned to Syracuse, I began to spend a great deal of time with Douglas Courage, whom I had met on campus before I left for the Army. Doug was a big, hail-fellow-well-met extrovert who lived within walking distance of the campus. His father was an Episcopal priest, as was his brother Max, and his brother Bert was an excellent amateur heavyweight boxer. They were all grand to me.

In time Doug introduced me to a young woman with a view to double-dating on a picnic at Pine Lake. Doug hinted that this might be an opportunity for me to learn to probe the mysteries of physical intimacy. In candor I must report, however, that when the time came to test his hypothesis, I proved unequal to the task. I later came to appreciate that the difficulty probably arose from the fact that I had bent immediately to the ultimate goal without the appropriate preliminaries. In any event, my education in such matters was delayed indefinitely.

Doug had a splendid baritone voice and he taught me how to harmonize several of the popular rounds of the day, including "With All My Heart" and "Tell Me Why." Neither Doug nor I played the piano, so we often imposed on piano students in the practice rooms at Crouse College to help us work on our vocal pieces. On one such occasion in January 1944 we entered a room in which a young piano major and scholarship student from Carlisle, Pennsylvania, was practicing. Her name was Harriette "Hattie" Line and she was quick to oblige, playing our songs while we practiced. I found her delightful!

Hattie had transferred from Dickinson College in her hometown in order to earn a music degree, and was studying with Elvin Schmitt, who had recently transferred to Syracuse from Oberlin College. Schmitt had married one of his students at Oberlin, which was enough in that day to prompt his having to leave. I learned later that when Dean Butler told Hattie that she would be studying with Schmitt, she expressed her delight at being assigned to study with "that good-looking teacher." Butler made the mistake of telling Schmitt what Hattie had said (no doubt in lighthearted banter) and, perhaps because of his experience at Oberlin, he was very hard on Hattie in her first year. Although it was difficult for her then, she now believes that this made her work harder and thus become a better pianist.

After meeting Hattie that first time, I began seeking her out in the Crouse practice rooms. It was like playing at Frank Stockton's "the Lady or the Tiger" when I opened each door. If I made a wrong choice it was not a tiger I found, of course, but the wrong pianist. I eventually tired of this game and summoned the courage to call her at the Chi Omega sorority where she lived. After that, we went bowling, attended concerts and went to the movies. We saw a touring company perform "La Traviata," in which Ethel Barrymore Colt, a daughter of one of the celebrated Barrymores, sang Violetta. It was the first time that I heard the beautiful baritone aria "Di

36

Provenza Il Sol." We also heard the Chilean concert pianist Claudio Arrau in recital. I undertook to make an impression by using my newly-acquired Spanish to say, "me da mucho gusto conocerle" when I shook Arrau's hand after the recital. Hattie appeared to be more impressed than Arrau, which was, after all, what I had in mind.

Unfortunately, our courtship was cut short when the Army decided it needed cannon fodder more than it needed linguists. The ASTP program was unceremoniously shut down in mid-March of 1944 and I received notice that I was being transferred to the 69th Infantry Division in Camp Shelby outside of Hattiesburg, Mississippi (certainly a remarkable coincidence in names). Knowing that Hattie's birthday was coming up on March 27, I arranged with a local florist to deliver a gardenia on her birthday. In Lynchburg gardenias were favorites. When I left Syracuse, Hattie was standing on the Chi Omega front lawn waving good-bye as we marched to the train depot.

One final note on this brief but fateful encounter: three years later Hattie's mother showed me a letter Hattie had written her in the winter of 1943-44. In it she had said "I went out last night with a soldier named Syd Thompson. I never had so much fun but I don't think I would marry him." How's that for presumption? I hadn't even asked her.

# CHAPTER 6
## CAMP SHELBY

At Camp Shelby, I had the extraordinary good fortune to be assigned to the 879th Field Artillery Battalion rather than to one of the 69th Division's infantry regiments. Perhaps that was because I had received basic training in the Coast Artillery. I was assigned to C Battery, under Commander Captain Lamar McLaughlin from Oklahoma. He was a tall slender fellow who kept his own counsel. Rarely did he speak to the battery in ranks. He left that to First Sergeant Richard Greene, who was of just the opposite temperament. In fact, Greene was highly voluble. He saw his responsibility as that of representing the enlisted men in their relationship with the battery's officers, and he did just that.

Within a day or so I was assigned to the wire section. It was our responsibility to lay telephone wires across the countryside to provide the means of directing the firing of the four 105 millimeter howitzers which constituted the battery's ordnance. Fortunately we were not called upon to climb poles or trees but laid the wire on the ground. We also learned how to operate radios, though we should rarely have occasion to use them in combat because of concern that the enemy might intercept our communications. Our section leader was Corporal Bill Harr, who was a lawyer from Ohio. Although somewhat excitable, he was on the whole a good leader.

We were on maneuvers in the DeSoto National Forest (bordering Camp Shelby) when we learned of the D-Day invasion of the European Continent. The news was both frightening and welcome: in spite of the many casualties suffered, we knew that it also might mean that we were closer to the end of the war.

There were about a dozen men in the wire section. I was immediately drawn to John Melanson who hailed from Long Island, New York and, like me, had attended a couple of years of college. When we were allowed passes to go into Hattiesburg, John and I often went together. Since Hattiesburg was a small town of about 18,000 souls, there were probably as many soldiers at Shelby as there were residents of the town. That's a heavy burden to put on any community. But they accommodated us well.

On one of our visits to town that spring, while classes were still being conducted at Mississippi Southern College (now Southern Mississippi University), John and I introduced ourselves to two young women who were playing tennis on the campus courts. One of them was Doris Rhea Curry, the daughter of the college's treasurer, Mr. B.W. Curry, who lived only a block from the campus. We treated the girls to a soda at the Student Union, where I managed to make a lasting impression by choking on a Nehi orange soda. After I recovered, we walked Doris Rhea home and met her family, including two sisters named Jean and Janet. Jean was only a year or so younger than Doris Rhea and John soon teamed up with her on our frequent visits to the Curry homestead.

I was delighted to learn that Doris Rhea was a voice student who also played the piano. Before long we were trying our hand at duets of the kind that Nelson Eddy and Jeanette McDonald had made famous, like "Rose Marie" or "Wanting You." She sounded somewhat like Jeanette, but I didn't sound much like Nelson. When I could get downtown from camp, I sang in her choir at the Methodist church. I had also begun to appreciate serious orchestral music and in my spare time I often visited the listening room at the public library. Tchaikovsky's "Romeo and Juliet Overture" was an early favorite. In a sense it was the vehicle by which I traversed the bridge between vocal music and orchestral music. It is still one of my all-time favorite pieces.

The Currys' next door neighbor was Brigadier General Robert V. Maraist, the commanding general of the 69th Division Field Artillery. He was second in command to General E.F. Reinhardt, the commander of the Division. John and I occasionally saw General Maraist in his front yard when we were on our way to the Currys' home. On one such occasion I snapped him a smart salute when he was relaxing in a lawn chair. He just waved. In the circumstances I suppose my salute wasn't called for, but I certainly didn't want to take the chance of offending the artillery's commanding general!

My friendship with Doris Rhea and her family was the most satisfying aspect of my time at Camp Shelby. They extended themselves to me most hospitably. That fall, when I learned that I was scheduled to go overseas, I gave Doris Rhea my fraternity pin. It seemed the proper thing to do and she accepted it graciously. It was good to know that there was someone like Doris Rhea who would correspond with me and who would miss me if I never returned from the Great Adventure.

The 69th Division entrained for Camp Kilmer in New Jersey on October 31, 1944. A few days later we were encamped at Kilmer, virtually in the shadow of the New York City skyline. The next few weeks were spent marking time, waiting to ship out. We finally departed for England on December 1, 1944, aboard a Liberty ship called the *Le Jeune, a* former German luxury liner rumored to have been caught in a South American port at the opening of hostilities and then converted into a U.S. Army troop vessel.

# CHAPTER 7
## OVER THERE

When our ship was a day or two out of New York, the public address system confirmed that we were en route to Southampton, England and a loud cheer went up. That's what we had wanted – service in the European Theater rather than the Pacific. We zigzagged in convoy across the Atlantic to avoid German U-boats and arrived safely at Southampton on December 12, 1944. The 879th Battalion and the 880th Battalion soon entrained in typical English private railroad compartments for the city of Reading where we were transported by truck to a British military facility called Brock Barracks. Brock Barracks had, in earlier days, accommodated British troops but had more recently quartered American troops of the 99th Division before that division left for the Continent.

We remained at Brock Barracks for about a month, awaiting orders to ship to the Continent. Occasionally we went out on maneuvers on the moors just to keep our hands in, but for the most part our time there was spent without significant activity. Eventually I was designated, along with several others from our battery, to act as a route marker for the battalion's trip to a practice firing range. Sergeant Arthur Lopez was in charge of our detail. He and I had occasionally sparred at the Camp Shelby gymnasium and had become friends. The day before our trip to the practice range, Sgt. Lopez told me he had identified a village pub about 100 yards from the corner where he was going to let me off. He invited me to meet him at the pub for a drink of what he declared to be the best scotch whiskey ever made, Haig and Haig's pinch bottle. I had never drunk any scotch whiskey and had certainly never drunk anything alcoholic before noon, but it sounded like a great adventure so I agreed to meet him there.

On the way back to my post from the pub I realized that I had not left in time to return to my position as route marker before the battalion arrived. Colonel Allen, the battalion commander, and the entire battalion drove past me while I was still walking along the road. It turned out to be the only time I got in trouble during my entire army career. When Lieutenant Wazny later called me on the carpet for deserting my post, I explained that I had answered a call of nature, which was incidentally true. I failed to advise him that I had also answered the call of Sgt. Lopez and a drink of scotch whiskey. I was confined to barracks for a week and considered myself fortunate to have avoided a more serious punishment.

Pubs were not the only diversion available to American troops. The British arranged several social events for us while we were at Brock Barracks – to which a number of young Reading women were also invited. One evening there was a gala dance scheduled while I was assigned guard duty at the entrance to the Barracks. I soon ascertained that one of our female visitors was entertaining several GIs, one at a time, in the back hall of a neighboring building. She was a tall, rather garishly made-up redhead who had been dubbed "Regimental Red" for reasons that you might imagine. Fortunately I was not so foolish as to try to join in the frolic.

I did, however, participate in a somewhat similar experience on another occasion when I was assigned with another man to police a motor pool in Reading. Two young English girls joined us for coffee and doughnuts in the afternoon and stayed the night in a small building on the premises where cots had been provided us. At one point during the night I heard heavy breathing coming from the other cot. For my part, I merely took advantage of the opportunity to become intimately acquainted with the upper anterior portion of the female anatomy.

On Christmas Day that year, John Melanson and I were entertained by an elderly English couple named Hull who had volunteered their home in a program designed to entertain young men who were far from home. Mr. Hull had received the British Empire Medal from King George VI for work he had done in aeronautical engineering. After dinner we listened to the radio Christmas message of the King, somewhat haltingly delivered because of his slight stammer but nonetheless appreciated by our hosts and ourselves.

While some of us were enjoying a scrumptious holiday repast, about two thousand men from our 69th Division were dispatched as replacements to the front lines in Belgium. The Germans (under General von Runstedt) had counterattacked and driven our troops back into the Ardennes Forest in what has come to be known as the Battle of the Bulge. Fortunately, our artillery battalion was not seriously affected since most of the replacements were infantrymen.

# CHAPTER 8
## How I Was Deployed Just in Time to Win the War

The men of the 879th Field Artillery Battalion were alerted that we would be leaving our quarters at Brock Barracks at midnight on January 20, 1945. We were finally going into combat. After a short drive to the city of Portland on the channel coast, we loaded onto LSTs bound for France. The trip across the channel was hampered by bad weather, but we eventually arrived at Le Havre, which had been hard hit by the war. Traveling parallel to the Seine River, we moved in truck convoy through a series of French towns toward the Belgian border where we began to see evidence of the contest that had raged there in recent weeks.

We were told that we should be relieving the 99th Infantry Division in the Siegfried Line at the German border. The 99th had gone into the front line in early December 1944. On December 15 it had borne the brunt of General von Rundstedt's surprise counterattack, suffering horrendous casualties. Entire units of the 99th were taken captive by the Germans. Indeed, on December 17 virtually the entire B Battery of the 285th Field Artillery Observation Battalion had been herded into a field near Malmedy, Belgium, and unceremoniously shot in cold blood with a 50 caliber machine gun mounted on the rear of a truck. Those who survived the slaughter did so by escaping into the woods. It was one of the most blatant war crimes of World War II. Had we arrived two months earlier, it would have been our division that von Rundstedt struck.

American forces had launched a counterattack in January 1945. With the help of the Second Infantry Division, which was sent to its rescue, the 99th reclaimed the lost ground just days before we relieved them. As we traveled to our destination, we saw corpses of men and animals strewn over the Belgian countryside. Many were frozen, some in extraordinarily distorted positions. It was a fitting introduction to the violence that is war and the reality of what was about to happen finally dawned on me. It was stomach-wrenching. Soon we began to see "*minen*" (mines) signs in the fields to the right and left of the roads, mute testimony to the danger that members of the wire section were to face in laying wire through the countryside.

On February 11 the 879th Battalion's C Battery took its position in the line of battle, which more or less coincided with the Siegfried Line. We had become a part of Gen. Courtney Hodges' First Army. In relieving a field artillery battery of the 99th Division, C Battery actually moved into its gun emplacements. I was assigned with Lieutenant Karl Kramer, the battery executive officer, and his driver Bob Aylesworth, to a foxhole from which the exec issued firing orders to the 105 millimeter howitzer crews. While we were setting up our equipment, the sound of a terrible explosion rent the air nearby and in a few minutes an engineer from a supporting outfit, who was helping to clear a gun emplacement of mines, was carried past us on a stretcher and dispatched to a field hospital. He had stepped on a mine. I don't know whether he survived.

We remained in those gun emplacements for two weeks, firing at the enemy across the valley on instructions from the forward observer. It was his responsibility to observe the explosion of shells from our guns from the front where he could see the enemy lines and send word by telephone or radio to correct their vertical or horizontal range (*e.g.*, "up 200, left 100").

I received my first assignment to accompany a forward observer to the front on February 19. Lieutenant John Desmond headed the team and Jim Root, another wireman, went with me. We moved into an empty pillbox the Germans had evacuated before we arrived. Just before dawn the next morning, I left the pillbox to answer the call of nature. Because I did not expect to go far, I did not wear my helmet or carry my rifle. I was barely out the door and into the trench at its fore when a rifle shot whistled past my ear, apparently from a German patrol. I quickly withdrew to safety, of course, and waited until dawn to venture forth again. I still sometimes reflect on the fact that my bare head was once in the crosshairs of a German rifle. That errant bullet has caused me to feel that my last sixty years have been a gift.

The wire section was soon called upon to lay wire along the road to other units in the vicinity of the Village of Buschem. During the entire time that we were holding our position in the Siegfried Line we were besieged by cannon fire from German 88s, generally referred to as "screaming meemies" because of the sound they made coming in overhead. The sound was eerie and frightening. We later learned that this would be the most severe winter northern Europe had suffered in many years, and because of the heavy snows our feet were always cold. Many suffered frozen toes, and there were severe cases of trench foot, especially among the infantrymen. The mud was so deep that our jeep was hardly able to move forward and from time to time it had to be pushed by the entire crew. A photograph of our Battery C wire section and its jeep appeared in the 69th Division's official Pictorial History published in Germany on July 20, 1945. On the same page there is a picture of my friend Corporal John Runden, surveyor, cutting another soldier's hair. John was an academic before the war and returned to teaching French in college after the war. We have maintained a stimulating correspondence in recent years.

Our patrols reported that the Germans had begun to withdraw toward the Rhine. The 69th Division jumped off from the Siegfried Line on February 27, two infantry regiments abreast with our artillery supporting them. We moved forward toward the Rhine

River on a line between two small towns called Gescheid and Honningen.

On March 2 I was assigned to go forward again, this time as the only lineman with Lieutenant Wazny's forward observation team. That night I was called upon to go out alone to repair our telephone lines because we had lost contact with our guns. Venturing forth, I had several concerns: *"minen"* (mines) signs generously sprinkled the countryside I was traversing in the dark and an artillery barrage pounded the sector from time to time. I also realized that an enemy patrol may have cut the wire and could now be lying in wait.

At one point in the mission I came upon an American patrol and worked my way around them before I was able to identify them as friend or foe. In fact, it was not until I heard them speaking English that I knew for certain. Later, when my father asked me to tell him about some of my war experiences, I regret to report that, in order to make the story more compelling, this American patrol was magically transformed into a German patrol. Invited by him on another occasion to tell the same story, I forgot my earlier embellishment and described it as an American patrol, remembering the inconsistency after it was too late. To his credit and my relief, my father never changed expression or mentioned my dissembling. In any event, I returned to the pillbox from that nocturnal adventure unchallenged and unhurt.

Outside of one of the villages we came upon a German artillery emplacement containing the bodies of two young German boys in uniform. They could not have been more than fifteen years old. As representatives of the "Home Guard," they had died bravely in defending their village. Organized by the Germans for the first time in October 1944, the Home Guard consisted entirely of young teenagers and old men.

By March 5 we had assembled at Schmidtheim and were held there for several days while units ahead of us dealt with the initial crossing of the Rhine River. As we approached the Rhine we learned that the 12th Armored Division had captured the Ludendorff Bridge intact and a bridgehead had been established on the east side outside the town of Remagen. Our artillery battalion was temporarily assigned to Patton's Third Army in support of the bridgehead, and I again went out with the forward observer. I climbed the tower of a nearby church and was able to see the bridge while it was still standing. Ten days later the bridge crumpled into the river as a result of the Germans' frustrated efforts to implode it, but they were too late to prevent the Americans from crossing. I later heard that the German officers who had botched the job were court-martialed and condemned to death when their superiors learned that the Americans had succeeded in crossing the bridge before it was imploded.

From Remagen our artillery battalion moved south to the city of Coblenz where we crossed the Rhine on a hastily constructed pontoon bridge, stopping on a hillside in the neighboring town of Valendar. From the time we crossed the Rhine River we began to stay the night in German homes, at times evicting the owners and at other times sharing their homes with them by moving them to another floor. In Valendar I watched as a pretty young blonde woman and her female companion struggled up a hill with buckets of water. Although we were under instructions not to fraternize with the German civilians, John Melanson and I could not resist offering to help them. In the course of carrying the water to a house at the top of the hill, I asked if John and I might pay them a visit that night. They agreed. After dark we set out for our appointment. We had gone only about one hundred yards when we were challenged by a sentry. Not being in a position to explain our mission, I manufactured a story about my having lost my wallet and we returned to our beds, greatly frustrated. Hopefully the girls were frustrated too.

You may well wonder how I had managed to communicate with the young women as we climbed the hill. Although I never studied German in school, the Army had provided us with a small booklet setting out basic German phrases such as "haben sie heis wasser, bitte?" ("Do you have any hot water, please?"). I soon acquired a familiarity with basic German words and phrases. A member of our battalion named Sheldon Schleimer had been born in Germany and he was also quite helpful to me. In time I was acting as interpreter for other members of the battery who had legitimate reason to converse with the German citizenry, taking over houses, et cetera.

In that capacity, I was assigned to help register local citizens in a small German town. Another man from our battery, who spoke no German, was assigned to work with me. When two young women came into the building to register, I began to converse with them. They were justifiably amused by my attempts to speak their mother tongue and together we laughed heartily from time to time. Suddenly my colleague grabbed me by the collar and shouted in my face, "Stop making fun of me." I was shocked, of course, and tried to assure him that we were not talking about him. It cost me the relationship, however, as we never spoke again. It also taught me a lesson about speaking in a tongue that others present do not understand.

From Valendar the division began a rapid advance across Germany as the Germans fell back. Infantrymen rode on tanks and in trucks to expedite the advance from Bad Ems to Giessen and from Giessen to Kassel. The ultimate outcome was now evident to all. The Germans were retreating en masse and they were surrendering by the thousands. It was just a matter of time. Although the infantry regiments continued to run into some opposition, the shooting war was just about over for the men of the 879th Field Artillery Battalion.

As the 69th Division continued to move eastward near the city of Weimar, it relieved the 80th Division, which had liberated the Buchenwald Concentration Camp on April 11. Buchenwald had been one of the more populous concentration camps, incarcerating thousands of African, Austrian, German, Croat, French, Yugoslav and Polish refugees, some British and American prisoners of war, a few Nazis who had fallen from favor, and tens of thousands of Jews. At one time the camp is reported to have held 84,000 prisoners, though most of them had died or been moved eastward before our arrival. Our commanders required the citizens of Weimar to tour the camp and witness the horrors there first hand, including a great many corpses that had not yet been incinerated. Some 69th Division personnel were selected to visit the camp but I was not among them.

I did, however, tour the Dachau concentration camp in southern Germany months later. It was the first concentration camp the Germans built. Buchenwald had been built on the Dachau model by the notorious Heinrich Himmler deputy Theodor Eicke, who was also the commander of the SS Totenkopfdivision (Death's Head Division) until his death in Russia in 1943. Dachau was more horrendous than I can possibly describe – the so-called "shower rooms" in which victims were gassed, the lamp shades made of human skin, the mountains of personal belongings left by prisoners, the ovens in which victims bodies were cremated.

There was a time when I did not understand how the German people could have allowed six million Jews to be rounded up by the Nazis and exterminated in concentration camps. Although those Germans with whom I spoke denied knowledge of the Holocaust, I have no doubt that many were eventually aware of what was happening. By the time they learned the truth, however, they would have been powerless to intervene. Hitler and Himmler were in control by then so it would have been very difficult for ordinary citizens to object without risking their own lives. It is appropriate, however, to ask if earlier events like "Kristallnacht" should not have prompted immediate objection from the populace before it became too late. In fact, an earlier attempt by the Nazis to institute a public program to euthanize mentally incompetent Germans was temporarily discontinued following protests from the German church. In the end, the Holocaust was the price Germans paid for a totalitarian government. Unfortunately a greater price was paid by their hapless victims, who were deceived into thinking that they were being transported to work camps rather than being systematically exterminated in gas chambers. Certainly the "Final Solution" was the most heinous crime committed against humanity by so-called civilized man, and one must stand aghast at the ease with which

Himmler's SS deputy Reinhard Heydrich (sometimes known as 'The Butcher of Prague") obtained unanimous support for that policy at the Berlin Wannsee Conference in January 1942.

I was greatly saddened when I received the news of President Roosevelt's death on April 12, 1945. It put me in mind of Lincoln's assassination at the close of the Civil War. In a very real sense President Roosevelt was himself a victim of the war. By the time of the Yalta Conference, most of the conferees recognized that the demands of war had left him a mere shadow of the man who first launched us on the road to victory. Winston Churchill wrote his wife Clemmie from Yalta that President Roosevelt appeared so weak that he doubted he had long to live. His concern proved to be well-founded.

As the war drew to a close, we advanced rapidly through a succession of villages, including Sehlis, Pfersich, Schönbach and Holleben. By this time, the Luftwaffe was flying very few sorties. Their gasoline was virtually exhausted. From time to time, some German units stood and fought bravely to cover the general retreat. They mounted strong defenses against units of the 69th Division in Weissenfels on April 12 and again in Leipzig on April 18. On April 19, 69th Division forces liberated prisoners at Leipzig-Thekla, a Buchenwald labor sub-camp. The 69th Division has been recognized as a liberating unit by the Holocaust Memorial Museum in Washington, DC, and also by the U.S. Army Center of Military History.

Approaching Leipzig, the 879th Battalion was diverted northward to the vicinity of the city of Halle. Our C Battery was bivouacked in the village of Benkendorf on the Saale River. We were housed in a splendid *schloss* that had been owned successively by the von Zimmerman family and Baron von Gablenz, neither of whom was in residence when we arrived. One of the locals told me that von Zimmerman had been required to give up his interest in the property because of his Jewish ancestry. On May 8 we learned that the Germans had surrendered and the war was over. The news was strangely anticlimactic, as we had known for weeks that the end was near.

We remained in Benkendorf for several weeks and it was there that my dilettante efforts at learning German paid off in spades. I made the acquaintance of a pretty young Magdeburg woman named Liselotte Wachtmann who was then living in Halle but who regularly visited her aunt Frau Elly Siedentopf in Benkendorf. In a short time we became close friends. She told me about her boyfriend who was a prisoner of war in Russia and who had served in the Waffen SS elite forces. She called him "Schnappi." When I left Benkendorf, Liselotte and I agreed we should try to meet there again in five years. By that time, however, it was somewhat impractical for me since I had married, graduated from law school and was on my way to post-graduate studies in England.

In lieu of a visit, my wife and I sent Liselotte several care packages when we were at law school. Liselotte's plight at that time was quite pitiful, of course. We corresponded with her for several years and learned that she did eventually marry Schnappi. We also learned that his name was actually Hans-Jürgen Maurer. They were to have a child in November 1951 but we lost contact before the child was born. I recently undertook to locate them on the internet and learned that a Hans-Jürgen Maurer in Germany has written a book called "Love and Marriage" ("Marriage is loving together, not just living together"). I have not yet been able to determine whether he is Liselotte's "Schnappi," but I haven't given up trying.

While I was stationed in Benkendorf, Lieutenant Wazny and I had to go to battalion headquarters one day, though on different missions. He asked me to drive him there and I explained that I didn't know how to drive. Contrary to Army regulations (an officer had to be chauffeured by an enlisted man), he drove the jeep to headquarters and I went along as his passenger. Later, as we were leaving battalion headquarters, Major Charles Kessler, the battalion S-3, was playing catch in front of the building. "Do you think you could drive this jeep out of the parking lot, if I tell you what to do?" asked Lieutenant Wazny. "I'll try," I responded. On his instructions I turned the key and began to release the clutch as I applied the gas. He handled the gears. Major Kessler must certainly have arched an eyebrow or two as he returned Lieutenant Wazny's salute while the jeep lurched forward as if it were suffering some kind of mechanical spasm. Fortunately it did not stall. When we turned the corner, Lieutenant Wazny took over the controls and we both breathed sighs of relief.

Another memorable event occurred when Captain McLaughlin had us form ranks on the grounds in front of the *schloss* to award bronze stars to several members of the battery. I was surprised and pleased that my friend John Melanson and I were among those so honored. A copy of my citation appeared in *The Lynchburg News*:

"For heroic achievement, Private First Class Charles S. Thompson, working with an Artillery Forward Observer Section, with utter disregard for his own safety, faced murderous fire from many artillery, mortars and small arms in order to repair telephone lines vital for the direction of fire of the artillery supporting the action."

I was known as "Sydnor" in Lynchburg, so it is unlikely that anyone who read the account was aware that I was involved. The same is true of the World War II monument at Ninth and Church Streets in Lynchburg - where I am listed as "Charles S. Thompson, Jr." among Lynchburg's World War II servicemen. I have drawn some satisfaction from having received the award because it attests to the fact that my superior officers believed I had met the test of a good soldier.    No doubt my having successfully driven Lieutenant Wazny out of the battalion parking lot within eyeshot of Major Kessler was a major factor in qualifying me for the award.

Because the 69th Division did not go into the line until February 1945, its casualties were not high.  No one in C Battery of the 879th Field Artillery Battalion was killed in action.  We did not altogether escape without fatalities and injuries, however.  One of our wiremen lost a leg and at least one other member was temporarily relieved of duty for what was euphemistically characterized as "battle fatigue."  Another was accidentally killed by his own weapon just as the war ended.  In addition to those individual casualties, a number of men in two of the 69th Division infantry regiments were killed en masse in tragic accidents.

One such accident occurred on February 20, 1945, when the division was preparing to jump off from the Siegfried Line.  Fifty-one men from A and B companies of the 273rd Infantry Regiment were killed when satchel charges were accidentally fired in a house they were occupying in the town of Miescheid, subsequently igniting flame throwers and eventually hand grenades the men were carrying in their breast pockets.  At about the same time, forty men of the 271st Infantry Regiment who were being briefed in a bunker were killed when one of them accidentally tripped a hidden wire.  The Germans left many such "booby" traps when they withdrew.  In all, about four hundred 69th Division soldiers were reported to have been killed in action and about 1,200 to have been wounded.

As with most divisions, it was the infantrymen who suffered eighty percent of our casualties, although they represented a much smaller percentage of the men in the Division.  It underlined for me again how fortunate I was to have been assigned to the artillery.

The 69th Division's greatest claim to fame is the fact that it was the first American unit to meet the Russians, who were advancing from the east as we advanced from the west.  Representatives of our Division met the Russians on April 25 at Torgau on the Elbe River just east of Leipzig.  The meeting triggered a grand celebration.  Champagne flowed freely.  The celebrants also drank a great deal of vodka, or *spierta* as the Russians called it.  *"Tovarich!"* (Comrade!) was the common cry.

Because the three principal allies, Great Britain, the Soviet Union and the United States, had agreed that the Soviet Union should occupy Thuringia, we soon withdrew to the west.  The Germans and the people of Eastern Europe, especially the refugees, were keenly disappointed when that plan became known.  They had hoped the Americans would remain and were terrified of being occupied by the Russians.

Throughout my service with the 69th Division I had one exceptionally satisfying bit of good fortune: serving in the wire section with John E. Melanson. John was in every sense a classic "war buddy." Many of the experiences that I have described occurred in his company and he and I enjoyed each other's complete confidence. While we were at Camp Shelby, John and I learned the song "East of the Sun." It was often sung as a duet in which each line is followed by another line of "chatter" sung by the second member of the duo: "East of the Sun (bathed in the brightness) and West of the Moon (you'll be singing a song) we'll build a dream house (a righteous path) of love, dear; near to the sun in the day (we'll be jumping) near to the moon at night (you'll be with me). . ." is more or less the way it goes. We entertained ourselves and innocent bystanders with heartfelt renditions of such songs at the drop of a hat.

After the war, John and I stayed in touch, and in 1993 we both attended the 69 Division Reunion on the 50th anniversary of the Division's having first been commissioned in Camp Shelby. Jim Root (who changed his name to Jim Jones after the war), John Runden, Don Masterana, Bob Stern and Frank Kruger, all from C Battery, also attended. It was a grand occasion! In honor of the reunion, I wrote some verses that were published in the 69th Division magazine:

### REMINISCENCES ON THE 69TH DIVISION

#### I

Today we raise a glass to celebrate
the 69th Division's glorious fate.
Recall Camp Shelby – oasis of the South?
Where Mississippi chiggers filled their mouth
with Fighting 69th Division skin.
The greatest red bug feast that's ever been!
Recall the pretty maids of Hattiesburg
by whom our young romantic hearts were stirred?

#### II

Recall the nights our Don Juans made their bed
with Reading's generous Regimental Red.
Recall the blue of vamping fraulein eyes
that tempted purest hearts to fraternize.
Recall the day we forged the Russian link
and saw the ebbing Nazi fortunes sink.
So now we may relive that distant time
and toast it once again in beer and rhyme!

John and I met again at the Division's 60th anniversary reunion in St. Louis in August 2003. Of the 600 or so original members of the 879th Field Artillery Battalion, we were the only two who attended! After beating me soundly at tennis at the 1993 Reunion, John had suggested I should work on my backhand and second serve if I wanted to play him again. I accepted the challenge in 2003 and he beat me again, but it was in a 7-5 tiebreaker. I have served him notice that he must play me again at the 70th anniversary reunion in 2013. I'm still working on the backhand, but I've just about given up on my second serve.

# CHAPTER 9
## THE BREMEN ENCLAVE

In late June 1945 those of us who did not yet qualify for discharge (based upon points acquired for time in service and computed at a higher rate for service in combat) were transferred to the 29th Division in Brake, Germany on the Weser River in the Bremen enclave of the American zone. About half of C Battery made the trip. John Melanson was not among them because he had earned enough points to be discharged. Because I had accumulated only 54 points, I was assigned to the 227th Field Artillery Battalion, a 155 millimeter howitzer unit.

On arriving in Brake I was posted for a time with other transferees in the home of a Lutheran pastor named Kirchner in the village of Kirchhammelwarden. He and his wife had lived there with their children for several years. Maria, who was about 20 years old, and somewhat favored Ingrid Bergman, was the only child living at home. In time I came to appreciate that Maria was a splendid young woman. She was gentle and kind and musically trained. She performed Mozart's lullaby "Schlafe, mein Prinzchen" on the piano for me with great feeling.

After the Kirchners were allowed to reclaim their home and I had been transferred to a nearby barracks in Lemwerden, the family invited me back from time to time for a meal. They served eel from the river (I managed to choke it down), tomatoes and fresh German bread. Obviously they were living on short rations. Maria and I corresponded for a while after I returned home and I eventually learned that she had married a Lutheran minister named Hansalbrecht Steffen. For a time he served a Methodist church in East Germany but he later returned to West Germany. They had two children – Hans-Martin born in 1947 and Irene Maria born in 1949. My wife and I sent them several care packages, for which they thanked us profusely, but we haven't heard from them since 1949. I recently traced them to Bremerhaven but learned that they had left there in April 1950 for East Germany again.

## WARTIME JOURNALISM

From the time the 69th Division went overseas, I had been C Battery's reporter for a newspaper that was published sporadically by the 879th Battalion. It was called *Combatears* and was eventually produced on a German printing press. I'm not sure it achieved as high a caliber of journalism as even a high school newspaper but at least it was something of a bridge back to civilian life. My most noteworthy journalistic achievement of that time was an editorial on the San Francisco Conference at which world leaders were negotiating the establishment of a United Nations to replace the moribund League of Nations. My editorial ended with a clarion cry:

"How much must the world suffer before we learn the lesson of complete internationalism." After that issue was printed and distributed, General Reinhardt recalled all copies and we were instructed not to publish any more political opinions. Of course, I should have hardly expected freedom of the press in the U.S. Army. It would appear that we still have not learned the lesson to which my editorial referred.

After I was reassigned, I was appointed to the staff of the 227th Battalion newspaper, called the *Lilac Times*, and I continued to write a column for my battery. I was also eventually assigned responsibility for a program called Information and Education (I and E). I inherited the post when Joe Glider, the I and E officer, went home to be discharged. Joe was a lawyer from Philadelphia whom I visited after the war. In connection with that assignment, I attended a seminar in Oberammergau, Germany, the purpose of which was to train us to act as an Army of Occupation. We were regaled with discussions about the meaning of the war in which we had recently been engaged and the prospects for establishing a democratic society there in the future.

While stationed in Oberammergau I made the acquaintance of the Lange family who had for many generations practiced the principal handicraft for which Oberammergau was known – sculpting crucifixes from linden wood. I bought a crucifix there and cherished it for years. The Lange family also provided many cast members for the world renowned "Passion Play" which was presented every ten years. A woman who had played Mary, the mother of Jesus, once entertained me at dinner. She told me that when she was cast as the virgin mother, she was required to give up smoking and drinking alcoholic beverages. Apparently such constraints did not extend to fornication. Although "Mary" was unmarried, she had conceived a child in an SS camp under a program the Nazis had designed to provide the fatherland with healthy children on whom to build the country's future. SS men were thought to have the proper genes with which to perpetuate the Aryan race.

I wrote about my trip to Oberammergau in the *Lilac Times*:

Many of the Passion Play actors have been offered highly remunerative contracts with professional theatrical companies (including Hollywood) but the original charter of the drama forbids participation by its cast in any other Thespian work outside of the Oberammergau drama.

The principal industry of the village is wood-carving, a sculpture of the Crucified Savior being their specialty.

The natives still wear the old-fashioned garb of their forefathers, including "a feather in their cap." It is said that, when the Americans first came through Bavaria in their push from the Rhine, one GI was so impressed with the dress of a particularly old gentleman sporting a long beard, that he gave vent to his enthusiasm with an exclamatory, "Je - sus Christ!"

The town of Garmisch-Partenkirchen, where the Olympic winter games have been held from time to time, was only a short distance away and I managed to make my way there to meet one of its residents – Dr. Richard Strauss, the renowned composer. I arrived at Dr. Strauss' home in uniform and with my carbine – which I usually carried while in Germany. Although I didn't have an appointment, a maid asked me in when I told her that I wanted to interview Dr. Strauss for an army newspaper. The carbine may have helped convince her. The good doctor played the piano for me and described an oboe concerto he was composing for an American soldier. He gave me an autographed photo of himself and asked if I could get some gasoline for him, but I'm afraid I had to disappoint him. His sister finally came in and hinted that the interview was over. I never wrote an article about that visit but I gave an account of it in talks I made to several Lynchburg clubs after the war. And I have had more than one occasion to invite a fellow aficionado to "shake the hand that shook the hand of Richard Strauss."

In August we learned of the Allies' victory in the Pacific. For the first time we were able to breathe easily in the knowledge that we should not have to go to the Pacific. I later learned that the 69th was one of the divisions originally scheduled to deploy to the Pacific after a thirty day leave. Dropping the atomic bomb in Japan may have been a controversial decision for some, but it saved many American lives, perhaps mine among them.

The following month I discovered a notice posted on the battalion bulletin board advertising that opportunities for study in certain European universities were being offered to the men of the 29th Division. The program, called Training Within Civilian Agencies (TWCA), was touted as a means by which our European allies were to repay the United States for lend-lease aid in the early years of the war. One of the positions offered was at St. Andrew's University in Scotland. I applied for it and was miraculously accepted. It was to be the second time that the Army sent me back to college.

On the day before I was scheduled to leave for Scotland, I came down with a sore throat and a very high temperature. The doctor immediately diagnosed my ailment as Vincent's throat angina. Sympathetic with my plight, he put me on a regimen of penicillin shots for twenty-four hours and confined me to a cot at Battery Headquarters. The next morning I was driven to the airport and took a flight to London. I shall always be grateful to the doctor who cleared me for that flight. My time at St. Andrew's University would without a doubt prove to be one of the greatest experiences of my life.

# CHAPTER 10
## ST. ANDREW'S UNIVERSITY

From London, I flew to Prestwick Airport outside of Glasgow and took a train to Edinburgh, traveling from there to St. Andrew's. The oldest of the Scottish universities, St. Andrew's was founded in 1410 as a college for ministers of the gospel. By the time I arrived in 1945, it had grown to become a first-class university consisting of a number of faculties offering many academic disciplines. At 600 scholars, however, the student body was still quite small.

I was welcomed to the campus and assigned to St. Regulus Hall, a dormitory for men presided over by the "warden" and his wife. This was to be my home for the next three months, known there as the Michaelmas term. (The school year was divided into three terms of three months each. I was to attend only the first term.) On locating my room I learned that I should have two roommates, Jerry Campo and Jerome Murnick, both American soldiers assigned under the same TWCA program that had tapped me. In all, there were about thirty GIs assigned to St. Andrew's from various divisions in Germany, many of whom were billeted at St. Regulus. One of them, a man named Charlie Weeks, had coincidentally also studied at Syracuse University.

The other principal men's dorm was St. Salvator's ("Sally's") which is adjacent to the university "quad," or center of campus. I understand that Prince William, the elder son of the Prince of Wales and heir to the throne, is now a student at St. Andrew's. The word is that the University first cleared the entire top floor at Sally's for him, but I understand he now shares an off-campus apartment with three other students. In fact, the more recent word is that he is expected to become engaged to one of his housemates there. He is apparently doing all he can to lead the life of an ordinary student. The British media have agreed to honor that plan by not plaguing him. Doubtless his having enrolled at St. Andrew's was occasioned at least in part by the royal family's desire to cement relations with Scotland at a time when the Scots have been expressing a desire for more self-government, a degree of which they have actually achieved.

St. Andrew's is a highly picturesque little town, steeped in tradition. Every Sunday after chapel we walked down along the wharf, as St. Andrew's students for centuries past had done to bid farewell to the bishop who spoke at chapel and then returned to his residence across the firth in Dundee. It was a grand tradition and we performed it with enthusiasm, even though the bishop had stopped coming long ago.

### ACADEMICS

I enrolled in three liberal arts courses at St. Andrew's: Political Science, Economics and Moral Philosophy. Professor Nesbit taught the first two courses and Professor Knox the third. Professor Nesbit was an ardent admirer of Adam Smith's theory of laissez faire and he often showed his disdain for the views of John Maynard Keynes. Professor Knox was an older gentleman who taught the ethics of David Hume. Both professors were classic in every sense, as were their views of their subjects. I once caught a glimpse of the notebook from which Professor Knox read his lectures and the pages were dog-eared from many years of marking the place he had stopped reading.

There were a few cultural differences that we Americans had to adapt to, both in class and on campus. In class, for example, we soon learned that one does not interrupt a lecturer at St. Andrew's University. Instead one listens attentively for pearls of wisdom. I fear that the American guests may have honored that custom in the breach – at least at the beginning. The British students did sometimes register their opinions by stamping their feet when they approved of something, or by sliding their feet across the floor when they disapproved. Of course, none of the students presumed to express disapproval of their professors' opinions while I was present. On campus, I was immediately struck by the scarlet robes worn by all students, though as a soldier I was required to remain in uniform and was thus denied this colorful privilege.

### BOXING AND THEATER

In addition to my studies, I participated in two extracurricular activities at St. Andrew's. The first, boxing, was not exactly an unmitigated success. Because I still weighed only 120 pounds, I was relegated to sparring with men who were much heavier. On one such occasion a fellow named Gordon, who outweighed me by 25 pounds, stuck a straight left jab in my face. We boxed with eight ounce gloves, rather than the sixteen ounce gloves used at American colleges, and the blow broke my nose. I spent the next two weeks in the Dundee Royal Infirmary with a hematoma of the nasal septum bleeding into a nose bandage. Thanks to Gordon's straight left, I never had the opportunity to box in an intercollegiate contest in Scotland.

Unfortunately, my experience in the University Mermaid Dramatic Society was no more successful than my boxing exploits. I auditioned for a one-act play, "In the Summer Perhaps," that had been written by a St. Andrew's student. It was a suspenseful drama, dealing with an underground organization in Paris during World War II and I was cast as an American soldier who had managed to join the team of conspirators in their hideout. As I stood next to a door, I was to deliver the line "There is someone coming up the stairs." When I heard my cue on opening night, I leaned over the footlights, arched an eyebrow, leered at the audience and recited the line in a hoarse stage whisper. The audience roared with laughter and I realized that I had utterly destroyed the mood of the scene.

# New Friends

While I was at St. Andrew's I established four close relationships among the English students enrolled there. All four – Ian Redhead, George Poston, Fiona Graham and Sylvia Clark – became lifelong friends.

## Ian Redhead

The staff at St. Regulus served afternoon tea to the resident students every day at 4 p.m. On one of my first afternoons there, I sat next to a radio listening to a Rachmaninoff Symphony. One of the British students sat down in a chair nearby and, after introducing ourselves, we sat quietly and listened to the Symphony to the end. That's how I met Ian H. Redhead of Newcastle. Everyone from Newcastle is called "Geordie" in other parts of Britain and Ian was no exception. Since the U.S. Army required that every soldier use his first name for identification and my first name is Charles, I was known as "Charlie." Soon "Geordie" and "Charlie" became close friends. Not only did we have a common interest in music but we learned that we were kindred spirits in many other respects as well. It is fair to say that Ian eventually became one of my closest friends.

Ian invited me to visit his family in Newcastle after the term ended on December 15 and I spent several days there before Christmas. His father was in the advertising business, to which Ian's brother Sam eventually succeeded. They entertained me royally, including taking me to dinner one evening at a local hotel. After dinner Ian's father offered me my first cigar. I carefully removed the cellophane wrapper but left the label on the cigar, whereupon Mr. Redhead leaned over and quietly suggested "In this country we remove the label too." I'm afraid I had seen too many Edward G. Robinson films.

Ian later graduated from Dundee University as a medical doctor and became an outstanding specialist in communicative diseases. Years later when my family was en route to Vienna, Austria, they spent ten days at the Redhead home in Peterborough, England. We have returned the compliment by having them in our Charlotte home.

## George Poston

George was the son of two medical doctors from Oldham outside Manchester. He and Ian appeared as two of the principals in excerpts from Gilbert and Sullivan's "Pirates of Penzance" under the auspices of the University drama program. Both of them wore my GI medals on their costumes. George went on to attend the Medical College at Dundee, like Ian, and later returned to the Manchester area to practice medicine. He was a good friend and I always admired his savoir-faire.

Years later Hattie and I visited George's family in Oldham at a time when his father was in his last illness. Dr. Poston had been among those evacuated from Dunkirk in the early months of World War II and we were privileged to hear him describe that extraordinary drama. George's son Graeme, who is also a medical doctor, trained for a time in a Galveston, Texas hospital - where he visited with our son Sydnor III who was pastor of a church near there.

## Fiona Graham

I met Fiona Graham at one of the social events staged by the University soon after I arrived on campus. We became friends and had tea several times before my boxing reversal occurred. While I was convalescing, she took the time to visit me in Dundee, which I especially appreciated.

Fiona's father James W. Graham was a dental surgeon in Bournemouth, whom I met when I visited the Graham home in January 1946 (during the time I was waiting to be shipped back to the United States and after Fiona had already returned to St. Andrew's from Christmas vacation). Her father was a gentle spirit and her mother Jessie was a real live wire. Jessie could not understand how I could eat a salted egg and jellied toast in the same mouthful.

I also met Fiona's younger sister Jean, who would later matriculate at St. Andrew's University. Jean eventually married Stanley Maitland, whom she met at St. Andrew's. A Polish count, Stan had become an expatriate after Hitler invaded Poland in 1939. His name was actually Stanislas Pininski but he had changed his name to Maitland after seeing that name on a legal publication in the University library. Stan's son Peter returned to Warsaw some years ago and reclaimed the name Pininski and the title that goes with it. (Stan joined him there in 2001 after Jean died.) Peter wrote a book entitled "The Stuarts' Last Secret: The Missing Heirs of Bonnie Prince Charlie," published in England in 2002, establishing to the satisfaction of the critics who have reviewed it that his father and he are direct descendants of "Bonnie Prince Charlie," the Stuart pretender to the British throne. In a May 25, 2002 review from *The Spectator*, Hugh Massingberd wrote:

> After all, as everyone who has dabbled in the history of the ill-fated royal house of Stuart knows, Bonnie Prince Charlie had a daughter, Charlotte, who, in turn, bore three children, but the line expired in 1854 with the death of her only son, Charles (a singularly unlucky name, incidentally). Of his two sisters, as James Lees-Milne wrote in *The Last Stuarts* (1983), "nothing is known". It has always been assumed that both died childless.
>
> But – and it is a very big "but" – in this painstakingly researched book, Peter Pininski now proves to surely the most skeptical pedant's satisfaction that though the elder sister, another Charlotte, died unmarried and without issue in 1806, the younger grand-daughter of Bonnie Prince Charlie, Marie-Victoire, born in 1779, married the Polish nobleman the Chevalier de Nikorowicz and had a son, Antime. Antime's daughter, Julia, married Count Leonard Pininski – the author's great-great-grand-father. Hey presto!

Such bald facts make it all sound simple. In reality it was anything but, on account of the secrecy and concomitant cover-ups that attended the whole affair. For as Bonnie Prince Charlie had forbidden his daughter – for the tidiness of the Jacobite cause – either to marry or to get herself to a nunnery, Charlotte's three children by Prince Ferdinand de Rohan had to be brought up incognito. In order to establish the documentary evidence, Peter Pininski had to trawl through archives all over Europe. The result is an astonishing achievement by an amateur historian.

On one of our trips to England Hattie and I had lunch with Jean and Stan at Rules, which was established in 1798 and is the oldest restaurant in continuous operation in London. During lunch, Stan related a remarkable story about his aunt's husband General Bor Komorowski, one of the leaders of the heroic Warsaw uprising against the Germans in 1944. Taken captive when he negotiated the surrender of Warsaw, General Komorowski was eventually released in an exchange of prisoners. He later became commander in chief of the free Polish armed forces in London. After the fall of communism in Poland, his ashes and those of his wife, having been originally buried in England, were re-interred in Warsaw in 1994 with full state honors.

When I was attending a legal seminar in London in the early seventies, I called Fiona, who was then recently widowed, to ask her to have a drink with me. (She has since married Charles "Toby" Carpenter and moved to Spain.) Fiona and I met that evening at a local pub near her place of business prior to my attending a ceremonial black tie dinner at Lincoln's Inn Hall. We caught up on the last twenty years' events over a couple of glasses of sherry and I then took a taxi to Lincoln's Inn. When I entered the hall, an old gentleman dressed in "Beefeater" attire stood just inside the front door. In need of a restroom, I asked him where the toilet was. He looked rather puzzled, as though he had not understood me or was hard of hearing. I then repeated my question in a louder voice, emphasizing the word "toilet," whereupon he swallowed hard, turned toward the hall and shouted to a receiving line about ten feet away "Mr. Toilet"! Rather than trying to correct the misunderstanding, I quickly went through the receiving line under that sobriquet. No doubt the doorman concluded that if I had to go through life bearing that name, he was going to see it through for me without apology. When I returned from England in the early morning hours a few days later, I related the story to Hattie, who was in bed. She could not stop laughing for hours, but finally fell asleep just before dawn!

In time all of the members of the Graham family befriended me and my family and those friendships have become far more important than I could ever have imagined. Hattie and I have visited Fiona, Jean, their sister Doreen and their progeny often, though I have never been able to entice any of them to travel to our home in the United States.

In the early 1990s we attended the four o'clock wedding of Jean and Stan's daughter Vickie in the village of Branscombe on the English Channel. All of the men in attendance wore morning coats and all of the women wore hats. When Hattie asked one of the guests if this was customary for an afternoon wedding, he pointedly responded "it depends upon who is getting married."

## Sylvia Clark

I met Sylvia Clark when I joined the chapel choir at St. Andrew's. Ian Redhead arranged for me to audition for Cedric Thorpe Davie, their outstanding choirmaster, and I shouted a couple of verses of "Onward Christian Soldiers" into his ear. I'm satisfied that he accepted me out of appreciation for the role the American Army had played in the victory in Europe, rather than the quality of my voice. Sitting behind Sylvia in the choir, I remarked to Ian on how small and delicate her hands were and asked him to introduce me. It wasn't long before I asked her to have tea with me at the Cross Keys tearoom.

As a wartime evacuee, Sylvia had lived with a family in Canada where she adopted several Canadian styles, including wearing white socks with saddle shoes. She made that style popular upon returning to her home at the Village of Galleywood in Essex County, earning the nickname "Socks." Not long after we met, I invited Sylvia to a Saturday evening "hop" where we danced the Dashing White Sergeant, the Highland Fling and the Eightsome Reel. At one dramatic point while our arms were linked, she lost her footing, but I pulled her to her feet before she reached the floor. It was a physical feat of which I am still proud.

By the time the term ended, Sylvia had invited me to visit her family in Galleywood. Her father Leslie Clark was an agriculturalist who frequently lectured on the British radio. Her mother Thurza was an absolute dear. All of the members of the family played various musical instruments and they often held musicales in their home – usually small chamber music concerts. They were particularly fond of Wagnerian opera. I wrote to my father after visiting the Clarks:

> Sylvia met me at the door and took me in to introduce me to a family I shall never forget. It is impossible for me to tell you about it in a letter. I'll just have to wait until I see you. They are really some wonderful folks though. There is just her mother and father and one sister – though the house is nearly always full of guests. All of them are exceedingly well-read, intelligent, and musical sans ostentation or affectation. All four play the piano very well. Her mother is a gifted violinist – teaches occasionally now. Her father is a master of the cello and Sylvia is apt to outstrip him on the same instrument. The sister, aged 14, is already a member of a London ballet company and shows considerable promise. She does pirouettes all over the house, as well as up and down my back.

While I was with the Clarks on Christmas Day their friends Charles and Sonia Frend visited and we played charades according to the English style. In that version a mystery word is hidden in a short drama enacted by one team and the other team undertakes to discover it. My team chose the word mistletoe and lost when the other team guessed it!

Charles Frend was a movie director with Ealing Studios. In later years, when Hattie and I returned to England for further study, he gave us a private showing of his film "Scott of the Antarctic." A first-rate documentary, it recounted the story of Captain Robert Scott's 1912 Antarctica exploration, which ended in tragedy for him and key members of his crew. After we saw the movie, Charles took us on the set of another movie that was in production. They popped open a whole case of champagne bottles in trying to get just the right shot for the camera. After a time they began putting the corks back in the bottles until they got it right.

## SIR DARCY WENTWORTH THOMPSON

The most extraordinary person I met at St. Andrew's was Sir Darcy Wentworth Thompson, who taught zoology. It was generally acknowledged that he was the most erudite and the most popular professor at the university. His father had been an outstanding classical scholar and, in addition to being the leading zoologist of his day, Sir Darcy was himself a master of Latin and Greek.

Knighted by King George V in 1937, he was a man of great stature with a head that looked as much like the head of an anthropomorphic God as Michelangelo's painting on the ceiling of the Sistine Chapel. Someone told me that Sir Darcy had once been invited to appear on the British equivalent of the *Information Please* radio quiz program, but he demurred with the comment that it was bad taste "to sell one's brain" in such a commercial endeavor. It reminded me of a comment attributed to Petrarch, the great fourteenth century Renaissance figure, when he declined to adopt his father's suggestion that he should study law. "I could not take making a merchandise of my mind," he said. Obviously I have had no such reservation.

I recently discovered a reference to Sir Darcy in Stephen Jay Gould's book "Dinosaur in a Haystack." Gould, a brilliant Harvard paleontologist, paid Sir Darcy the ultimate tribute by referring to him as his "earliest intellectual hero, along with my father and Charles Darwin." Neither of Sir Darcy's two children ever married. One did, however, write a splendid biography of her father's life. In honor of this extraordinary figure, my wife and I named our first child, a daughter born in England in 1951, D'Arcy Wentworth Thompson. I should like to think that our sharing the same surname is more than mere coincidence but I have as yet been unable to establish a connection.

While I was in Scotland, I did learn that the Thompsons were originally a sect of the Campbell of Argyll clan, whose seat is in southwestern Scotland. In time, however, I was advised that I should be careful about mentioning my connection to the Campbells. It seems they had set upon and slain a large number of the McDonald clan in 1692 at what came to be known as the Massacre of Glen Coe. Fortunately I didn't meet any McDonalds.

### DEMOBILIZATION

My stay in England after the term at St. Andrew's ended was, to say the least, without the Army's express approval. Our orders were to return to our units in Germany but no date had been specified. Operating on the theory that no one would mind if I spent the Christmas holiday in England before returning to the Continent, I visited the Redheads in Newcastle and the Clarks in Galleywood, as I have already mentioned.

In fact, I may have come very close to wearing out my welcome with the Clarks. After New Year's, I made a reservation to return to Brake, Germany. Having reluctantly said my good-byes in Galleywood, I took a train to Heathrow Airport for the flight to Germany. By some extraordinary good fortune the airport was socked in with a heavy fog and no planes were flying that day. I had the unmitigated gall to return to the Clarks' home in Galleywood. Moreover, I then borrowed money from Mr. Clark to tide me over. After that, I called the airport every day (well, it may have been every other day) to see if the fog had lifted. During the interval, I read in the European edition of the *New York Herald Tribune* that my 54 points had now earned me the right to a discharge and that I was entitled to report to a U.S. Army Center in London to book passage home!

Along with hundreds of other happy GIs, I shipped out for New York aboard the *Augusta* on February 3, 1946. I shall never forget the thrill I felt at seeing the Statue of Liberty as we entered the New York harbor. I have seen it many times since then but it has never been a more welcome sight than when I came home from the war.

I had not written to my parents for the two weeks at Christmas during which I had remained generally incommunicado. In fact, none of the letters that I had written from St. Andrew's in November had yet reached home. When my father didn't hear from me, he contacted the American Red Cross to find out what had happened after I left the university. Weeks later I learned, much to my embarrassment, that the Red Cross had contacted the Clark family in their search for me. Apparently I had written my father at some point and asked him to send money to Mr. Clark to pay my debt to him. When Daddy wired the money to Mr. Clark, he asked the Red Cross to follow up on it. Perhaps he thought I was being held at ransom, though $30.00 should have seemed a bargain for my release.

Mr. Clark, who must have been somewhat nonplussed, wrote to the American Red Cross:

26th January 1946.

Dear Mr. Salsbury,

Re; Thompson, Charles S. Jnr.<br>32847522.

I am so sorry that there should have been any anxiety over Charles Thompson. He has been on a course at St. Andrew's University Scotland and there met my daughter who brought him down with her at Christmas time to spend the holiday with us here.

* * * * *

We had a letter from him dated 19th Jan. in which he said his tentative sailing date was 28th January so it may well be that his folk will soon get the best possible news of him – in person.

Our family felt very privileged to have Charlie with us for the holiday and to make such close acquaintance with one who seemed to us to epitomize all we expected of a Southern Gentleman.

What a nice thing to say! Salsbury sent the letter to my father.

After I disembarked in New York, I went directly to a separation center in Fort Meade, Maryland, and was discharged from the Army on February 15, 1946. When I arrived in Charlotte, my homecoming had to compete with my fifteen year old brother Chick's recent announcement that he was planning to become a professional boxer when he reached eighteen. He had been taking boxing lessons at the YMCA and doing some sparring there. I recall sitting with him for some time, trying to persuade him to plan for college instead. Eventually he did change his mind, but it was nip and tuck for awhile.

## RETURN TO HATTIESBURG

Soon after I arrived home I left for Hattiesburg to visit Doris Rhea Curry. Although our correspondence had become somewhat sporadic during the fifteen months that I was in Europe, I was still anxious to see her.

During the following week, Doris Rhea and I attended Mardi Gras in New Orleans and had dinner at the Court of the Two Sisters. One must see Mardi Gras to believe it. Inhibitions are thrown to the winds. Ours were not, of course. Doris Rhea stayed with her aunt. When Doris Rhea and I were at the station waiting for the train that would take me back to Charlotte, she handed me my fraternity pin. Both of us had yet to complete our education. As there appeared to be little prospect of our seeing each other again soon, I was not really surprised. It was as though we were turning a page and starting a new chapter.

Many years later John Melanson and I called Doris Rhea from the 69th Division's 50th reunion in Rochester to see how she and her sister Jean were getting on. In the years that followed my last visit to Hattiesburg, she had obtained a graduate degree in music and taught school. Still later she and her husband visited my family in Charlotte, resulting in a veritable fusillade of pleasant reminiscences. She and her husband have now adopted the nomadic life that accompanies ownership of a RV.

# CHAPTER 11
## RETURN TO SYRACUSE – AGAIN!

That spring I once again made the familiar train trip to Syracuse from Lynchburg, by way of Washington, DC and New York City, to make arrangements to return to the campus for summer school. I applied to the housing office for a position as resident advisor and was eventually hired for the summer session.

One of my first acts upon arriving on campus was to call Hattie Line at the Chi Omega house. It was March 27, 1946 and she was then in her junior year. Exactly two years had elapsed since I marched past her sorority house en route to Camp Shelby. "You are calling on my birthday! You remembered," she exclaimed when I called. "Of course," I replied, "Happy birthday, Hattie!" It was as grand a coup as I had ever achieved with the opposite sex. I visited her at the Chi Omega house for a brief reunion, finished enrolling for the summer session and returned to Lynchburg. Hattie has always insisted that she hardly recognized me because I was no longer in uniform, had a broken nose, and had lost much of my Southern accent.

When I returned to campus in June 1946, I was assigned to a freshman house at 759 Comstock Avenue as a resident advisor for the summer session. I would continue in that position through my senior year. My most vivid recollection of my time at Comstock Avenue is suffering my only experience of passing out from indulging too freely of alcohol. Warren Jackson had returned to the campus by then and he and I were visiting in a women's faculty residence when I very foolishly undertook to chug-a-lug a water glass full of some kind of whiskey. The next thing I knew I was in my bed and Warren was swabbing my forehead with a wet towel. I was one sick fool! Fortunately the school's housing authority never heard of the incident or I should probably have been fired. It wasn't something they should have expected from a resident advisor.

By negotiating with the College of Liberal Arts, I received full credit for the sophomore semester from which I had been drafted in 1943, thirty and one half credit hours for the seven months of ASTP, and nine credit hours for the three months at St. Andrew's University, constituting me a second semester junior when I returned. I resumed my studies at the Maxwell School of Citizenship, primarily under the tutelage of Dr. Earl Ketcham, Dr. A. A. Beyle and Dr. Spencer Parratt, with a view to fulfilling the requirements for a major in Political Science. I also continued my study of voice with Frederick Haywood. By that time, I really enjoyed singing and I had joined the chapel choir - with Hattie's encouragement.

I did not, however, resume participation in the affairs of my fraternity. Somehow, after three years in the Army, fraternity life did not attract me, nor did the other extracurricular activities I had enjoyed before the war. Studies were my principal concern. In fact, the only extramural activity I pursued in my last year at Syracuse was boxing. My hospitalization at St. Andrew's had done little to squelch my interest in the sport. But again, my attempts did not prove especially fruitful. Coach Roy Simmons offered me an opportunity to box for the Junior Varsity against Army, but the match was during the week of final exams, so I was unable to accept the challenge. I did manage, however, to win the intramural medal at 120 pounds. The only other candidate within my weight class didn't show up for the match.

## COURTING HATTIE LINE

Hattie and I had exchanged a letter or two after I left for Camp Shelby and then we more or less went our separate ways. During the interim she wore the fraternity pin and class ring of an Air Force flyer who was later killed in action in Germany. But Hattie also stayed on campus for that summer session and we more or less picked up where we had left off two years earlier. By the fall semester we were seeing each other rather frequently.

Early in the semester, however, Hattie invited Jimmy Hunter, a friend from Dickinson College, to a dance at the Chi Omega house. (In later years Jimmy became an outstanding hand surgeon in Philadelphia. He developed an operation for correcting a finger injury that actually carries his name – the Hunter rod.) I decided I needed to meet my competition and so went to the kitchen door at Chi Omega and asked someone to tell Hattie I was there to see her. She appeared somewhat surprised to see me but she brought Jimmy to the door so that I could meet him. He was a tall good-looking medical student and I liked him. If anything, that meeting served to whet my appetite for the courtship. Fortunately, I had the advantage of him, of course, as I was living in Syracuse and he wasn't. Believe me; I made the most of that advantage.

Nonetheless, during the fall semester I occasionally saw a student from Brunswick, New Jersey whose name was Shirley Kew. One of Hattie's sorority sisters saw me with Shirley at a local restaurant in early 1947. Because we had been seeing so much of each other, Hattie justifiably had the impression that she and I were going steady. When she learned I was seeing someone else, she gave me my walking papers! Within a very few hours, however, I appeared at the Chi Omega house with a dozen roses, a box of Whitman chocolates and a declaration of eternal fealty. That was the last of Shirley Kew.

I gave Hattie my fraternity pin in the spring of 1947. I prevailed upon my fraternity brothers to bring the cannon that the fraternity had owned for many years (the brothers fired it whenever the Syracuse football team scored a touchdown, which wasn't very often in those days) to a point behind a hedge in the yard of the DKE house next door to Chi Omega. I then called Hattie to the front door and we serenaded her and her sorority sisters. Just as the final note sounded, one of my fraternity brothers fired the cannon from behind the hedge. The blast was so great that it blew the cannon off its carriage. It was a phenomenal happening which I am confident is remembered to this day by all those who were present. My fraternity brothers were magnificent, despite my not having been active in the fraternity that year.

Hattie had continued her studies as a piano major with Elvin Schmitt and in the intervening two years had established herself as a promising pianist. That spring, she gave her senior recital at Crouse College. It was a resounding success and the dean immediately offered her a full scholarship for graduate study at Syracuse.

For some time I had known that I should definitely go to law school when I finished at Syracuse. I had applied to Harvard, Yale and Columbia Law Schools but had not yet heard from any of them. For some time too, Hattie and I had been talking about getting married. At first it was to be after I finished law school. Later we agreed it should be after the second year of law school. Eventually we decided to get married after the first year of law school. Finally, on the night of her senior recital, when I carried the congratulatory flowers to the stage, I asked her to marry me right away. No doubt the drama of that moment, combined with our impatient hormones, prompted me to suggest the new schedule - and her to accept. Of course, that was in a day when marriage was the only acceptable solution for the normal red-blooded youngster's hormonal demands. That was true of Hattie, anyhow!

The Chi Omegas staged a beautiful reception after the recital and we seized upon that opportunity to announce both our engagement and our imminent wedding. Hattie's mother, also known as Hattie, and her Aunt Millie Kitzmiller were present for both the recital and the reception. After first expostulating, "Your father will skin you alive," Aunt Millie took Hattie out the next morning and bought her an extensive trousseau.

## AUNT MILLIE KITZMILLER

Aunt Millie was a unique individual. Her husband died young and left her more money than she could readily spend, although she did try. A large woman, with a heart as generous as her physical proportions, Aunt Millie was like a fairy godmother to Hattie. After meals at the Chi Omega house she would go into the living room and call out "Now, girls, let's play a little game." Then she'd throw two handfuls of silver dollars in the air. "You should have seen those girls scramble," Hattie reported. After we were married, Aunt Millie occasionally took us to the Mt. Gretna summer theater, preceded by dinner at the Hershey Hotel, where we ordered our favorite dessert –

Coup de Jacques. She always commandeered front row seats at the theater, even if it meant a tight squeeze for her neighbors. A shared box of Whitmans chocolates, brought along for the occasion, soon assuaged any hurt feelings among her neighbors. Charlton Heston was then doing summer stock there.

## HARRIET BRENNEMAN LINE

I had met Hattie's mother, Harriet Brenneman Line, on a visit to Hattie's home in late 1946, after Hattie and I had been dating for some time. I had stopped off in Carlisle on my way back to Syracuse after Christmas vacation. In fact, Hattie came to Philadelphia to meet my train and escort me to Carlisle. I was immediately drawn to the senior Hattie. She was very warm and very natural. In fact, I have told Hattie that it was her mother that "clinched the deal" as far as I was concerned. She doesn't mind a little teasing on that score because she agrees with me that her mother was a truly exceptional woman.

By 1922 Hattie's mother had given birth to four sons and had suffered a couple of miscarriages when she told Aunt Millie that she was pregnant again. "Drink some tea," Aunt Millie advised, hoping to spare Mother Line all that an additional pregnancy would entail. Years later, after Hattie had just played a beautiful piano recital that they both attended, Mother Line turned to Aunt Millie and said, "Aren't you glad I didn't drink that tea!"

Mother Line was raised on a Cumberland County farm that was originally the property of her great grandfather Melchior Brenneman. A few years before her death, she prepared a memoir of her youth for her children. This excerpt captures the essence of her truly remarkable person:

Dear Children:

Now I've recently passed my 89th birthday happily indeed, gaily and painlessly, and I've enjoyed the past year I believe health wise as much as any. It has been suggested to me that I should write a memoir. Just where to begin I know not. I definitely recall the doctor vaccinating me at one year of age incredible as it may sound and also lancing a spot on my neck, as to both of which I have yet visible proof so I have begun there. The next event that has registered was the moving of my grandfather Harry Brenneman and grandmother Harriet Cassel Brenneman from our large eighteen room farmhouse to a recently purchased lovely place a block distant eastward. I was delegated at the age of three to ride down with the so-called fittings on the wagon with the stones. I remember little else of that day except that carpenters were building a nice barn at the new farm. That barn today has not stood the 86 years of wear any better than I have and looks grey and tottering on its last leg. I took some of my family to visit the lovely old farmhouse and described to the owners the various changes that had occurred.

* * * * *

There are no words in my vocabulary that can adequately describe the joys of our childhood life on that farm. We entertained many friends for weeks at a time and also were visitors to friends' distant homes, but all was so simple as compared with today's bustle and noise.

66

I've not spoken of my great love for reading and the study of piano which I loved and for which I paid the exorbitant price of 25 cents per hour to my first teacher. After a little while I played an organ in the village church for services and then was asked to teach the various children of the area. When I earned $2.00 for eight hours work I was rich indeed. My father was very proud of my accomplishment. After I mastered a few Sousa marches and hymns he thought it unnecessary to pay for lessons. I then took over that burden from my teaching fees and I found a fine teacher who inspired me to do a better job and enjoy Chopin and Beethoven. They satisfied my soul until my own daughter Harriette took over and helped me with her course in music at music school many years later.

*****

Before Daddy died he said "If I am going to die I hope you will realize I've had a great life, much longer than seventy some years for I've had such a good time." There were a few dark days I suppose, but as a family I feel we were very close, loved each other dearly and were harmonious generally. You have all done us proud and after I am gone I hope there will be nothing to ever break that love that could make even a chilled feeling among you. I hope you will be a help to any one of you in distress of any kind. My old age which I so dreaded has, up to the present time been so happy, much brighter than I even anticipated and the day I'm called will be a great day for me and I want no tears.

One of my friends, who knew them both, once asked me if I didn't wish that Aunt Millie was to become my mother-in-law. I loved Aunt Millie, of course, but in my eyes Mother Line was the perfect mother-in-law. She was the most genuine person I have ever known, which comes across in her memoir. And no one else could have produced Hattie the younger.

### REACTION TO THE ENGAGEMENT

Aunt Millie was right about Mr. Line's reaction to the news of our engagement. When I wrote him to ask for Hattie's hand, I must have made use of the old rubric that I hoped he would consider me like another son. Hattie had four brothers and his reply was short and to the point. "I already have enough sons," he said. Fortunately, Hattie's mother was sympathetic, though she too had second thoughts after she returned home from Syracuse and heard the objections of other family members. Her letter to me, while somewhat apologetic, made it clear that she had been persuaded that we should wait:

Saturday A.M.
May 18, 1947

Dear Syd, Your letter to Dad was very fine and I felt very depressed after reading his in reply. We sometimes feel Dad is a bit stern and not as understanding as he might be but when the big issues are at stake it's usually been found that his judgment was best and I believe perhaps he is right this time and I wrong in encouraging this marriage. Brenneman is a most sensible son and I'm sure you and he will be the best of friends but when he too seems to see the futility of a happy marriage now I have moved to the top of the fence – and am asking you to postpone it until you are financially in a position to keep Harriette. She and you are in love so deeply I'm afraid neither of you can see straight.

*****

Thank you so much for all your consideration and kindness to us and I hope you'll not misunderstand this note. If I could offer you financial aid and could see a way clear now for you I should do so but Mr. Line and her brothers who've had experience in financial matters convinced me I am doing wrong to encourage you in marrying now. With love and my best wishes in any decision you make –

Harriet B. Line

Letters from my parents on the same subject, though ultimately supportive, expressed similar reservations:

Tuesday Night -<br>May 6, 1947

Dear Syd –

I hardly know how to write in reply to the letter I received from you yesterday. Of course, I am happy in your happiness, but I had hoped that you could make yourself satisfied with your present state until you had completed your education. However, you are a man and your decisions must be your own. Whatever you decide, you can, of course, always depend on your dad for his cooperation and love for you and your wife. From what I have heard, I am sure Harriette is a sweet girl and will make you a splendid wife. My only adverse thought is that you will both face tough going at times for the next few years. Nevertheless, if you both feel that you'd rather tackle those few lean years together than wait until you've finished law school to be married, I believe you can do it. There is no use in my calling your attention to the fact that there will be some necessary sacrifices for a while, but love often makes sacrifice a pleasure, and possibly you'll both be much happier married than waiting.

I am glad to hear of Harriette's, as well as your own determination that you shall actually become a lawyer. Not to go through with that plan would be a grave injustice not only to both of you, but also to the children you will inevitably someday have.

One thing which occurs to me, son, in connection with your plans, is that you should do everything possible to reconcile her father as well as her mother to your plan. Take them completely into your confidence on everything and do your dead level best to avoid any ill-feeling. You must never forget that they are her parents and are just as dear to her as yours are to you. For you to be antagonistic or fail (through your fault) to get along with them would cause Harriette many a heartache, and this, I know, you would never intentionally do.

* * * * *

Give Harriette my love, and both of you may rest assured that you have a father's prayers for an abundant life of many years of married happiness whether your final decision is to go ahead with your plans now or to wait.

With lots of love, I am, as always,

Your devoted -<br>Dad

Thursday -<br>May 8, 1947

Dear Sydnor.

Your letter has so completely floored me that I'm just now coming around. Of course I've known that you were falling in love but had no idea you were planning to be married so soon.

You certainly deserve all of the best, but I don't like to think of your struggling with bills, studies, etc. without a small nest egg, anyway. Of course, I know you have thought of all these things many times and have probably worked out a wonderful plan that enables you to have your cake and eat it too. You've been wonderfully sweet to tell me your plans and want my advice – Ha!! All you really want is my sanction and that you know you'll always have when it involves your happiness.

So – do as you think best and be very sure I shall stand by – whatever the decision.

* * * * *

About Harriette's father – I'm sure, dearest son, that there is nothing personal in his attitude. It's just a father's wish that his daughter should have the best, and we can't blame him for that. You must be sure that you do everything in your power to reconcile him before you marry his one and only daughter. You _must_ remember that he has a very real claim for consideration from both of you.

* * * * *

Be sure that if you decide to come home supporting a blushing bride I shall receive her with open arms.

Love to you both,<br>Mother

I find the letters very touching. They still nearly bring me to tears. I think it especially noteworthy that both of my parents independently urged me to try to reconcile Hattie's father to the marriage. Unfortunately, it did not prove to be possible. Mr. Line died of cancer during the first year of our marriage, so I never really had the opportunity.

### J. HARVEY LINE

Mr. Line was a rather extraordinary gentleman in a number of ways and certainly deserves further description. He had graduated from Dickinson Law School in Carlisle (now affiliated with Penn State University) at the turn of the century. After he finished law school, he and Mother Line were engaged for nearly ten years before he felt financially secure enough to take on the responsibility of a bride. Perhaps that is why he thought Hattie and I were pushing the envelope to marry while I was still in law school. After they were married, he and Mother Line moved into his mother's home where they lived for several years until they had their first child. When she was leaving that house to set up house for Mr. Line and herself, she told her mother-in-law that she was looking forward to having her own home, to which her mother-in-law replied, "Why, I offered Harvey the house on West Street the day you were married." When asked what she had said to Harvey about it, Mother Line said "I never mentioned it." Mr. Line had his way in most things.

The stories the family tells about Mr. Line are legion. For example, when their children were still quite young, Mother Line took them to First Lutheran Church faithfully every Sunday while Mr. Line lay abed. One Sunday Mother Line did not get up to go to church and when Mr. Line asked why, she said she just didn't feel like going that morning. He immediately dressed and took the children to Sunday School. Mother Line was quite resourceful in making her points without precipitating a confrontation. Indeed,

69

thereafter Mr. Line attended the Sunday School himself with such regularity that in later years when he was not feeling well enough to attend, he sometimes had his son Henry mark him present in order to preserve his perfect attendance record. Mr. Line is reported to have read through the Bible seven times. He got a good start when his mother gave him a penny for every chapter he read when he was young.

Mr. Line was quite independent in his lifestyle and strong in his opinions. For example, he did not approve of his mother-in-law's remarrying at age 66 after her first husband died. In fact, Mr. Line refused to allow her new husband in his home for the twenty years during which they were married, although Mother Line may have occasionally sneaked him into the house for lunch when Mr. Line was not at home.

The most extraordinary story I ever heard about Mr. Line, however, was told me by Mother Line, and in it he eventually comes off rather well. It seems that Mr. Line had become quite ill and had been hospitalized when he was about seventy years of age. When he began to feel better, he asked his wife if there was anything that she would do differently if she could live her life over again. "I don't know what got into me," she later reported, "but I said 'Yes, I don't believe I would have married you.'" "What do you mean? Why wouldn't you have married me?" he cried in surprise. "Because you are not nice to my friends," she replied sincerely enough.

A few days later, Mr. Line had returned home from the hospital and was engaged in his usual pastimes of listening to the radio, playing solitaire and smoking a cigar in the living room when Mother Line's best friend "Aunt Nannie" Liggett came to the door. When she rang the doorbell, Mr. Line jumped up from the card table and ran to greet her. "What in the world has got into Harvey?" Mrs. Liggett asked when she joined her friend in the kitchen. According to Mother Line, her only regret was that she hadn't volunteered that information years earlier, but of course he hadn't asked her the question.

In the short time I knew Mr. Line he was pleasant enough, even allowing me to participate in a pinochle game with his sons at the Mountain Club despite my innocence of the rules of the game. That certainly is a factor in his favor when you consider that I insisted on being the son that he didn't think he needed.

## ONE FINAL HURDLE

Mr. Line was not the only person concerned about Hattie's decision to marry. Within a day or so after our betrothal was announced, Hattie told me that her piano teacher Elvin Schmitt wanted to see me. He had great hopes for her music career, and I knew that he was disappointed that she was getting married. I also knew that Hattie admired him greatly, and I was as interested in satisfying him that she was not making a mistake as I had been in satisfying her family. Of course, I assured him that I intended to support Hattie in her profession.

I had a good relationship with Elvin. In fact, I was confident enough of our relationship that I had earlier asked him to let up on his criticism of Hattie's playing just before her senior recital. I wanted to build her confidence. How is that for presumption? As a consequence of that good relationship, Elvin gave us the best piece of advice we received when Hattie and I were married. I don't know what experience it grew out of, but his counsel was "Don't be possessive of each other." That counsel has served us well and we have sought to pass it on to our children.

Hattie and Elvin remained close friends and we visited the Schmitts years later when they were living in Barcelona, Spain. We recently made a modest gift to Syracuse University in Elvin's memory.

### THE WEDDING AND HONEYMOON

Hattie and I were married on campus at Hendricks Chapel on June 2, 1947, immediately after attending our graduation ceremony. The altar flowers for the baccalaureate service were still in place for our wedding and our friends from campus turned out in force. Dean Charles Noble, whom I had come to know well and whom I greatly admired, conducted the marriage ceremony. It had been in his company at Sunday evening sessions that we brash youngsters had presumed to challenge various orthodox Christian doctrines, including the Virgin Birth, the Trinity and the theory of Atonement. Hattie's roommates Elly Spooner and Patricia Younkins were her attendants and my friends Doug Courage and Elmer Owen shared the responsibilities of best man. One of the guests had to remind me to smile as we were walking down the aisle after the ceremony. I must have been contemplating the seriousness of the responsibilities of which our parents had so recently reminded me!

Hattie decided to go to a gynecologist a couple of weeks before our marriage to be sure that she did not suffer any physical discomfort on our honeymoon. Of course, Aunt Millie, a classic traditionalist, was mortified when she learned of Hattie's intentions but fortunately that did not deter us. Following the ceremony, we promptly set out for the honeymoon suite at the Biltmore Hotel in New York City, which was made available to us at the ridiculously generous price of six dollars a day. After several days in New York, we left for our respective homes where we were prepared to do penance to the extent required of us.

Soon after we arrived in Charlotte to visit Mother, I took Hattie to meet Eddie and Elizabeth Clarkson at their home "Wing Haven." I had met the Clarksons during the war at a reception at the Charlotte Country Club following a concert to which soldiers were given free tickets. They had developed their garden as a refuge for birds, and Elizabeth had become an expert in ornithology as well as gardening. Eddie gave Elizabeth dedicated support in both fields of endeavor and in fact, they told us that they often gave each other bricks and plants for their birthdays.

They were immediately drawn to Hattie and invited us back to dinner that evening. As we sat on their patio looking out on a beautiful pink crepe myrtle at the far end of the garden, Hattie counted forty hummingbirds at the feeders. I was delighted that she was so pleased with the Clarksons, and they with her. Elizabeth had studied organ at the New England Conservatory in Boston, where Hattie was about to enroll. They were a perfect match. Within a short time of their meeting, Elizabeth arranged for Hattie to give a recital for her friends on the Steinway piano that Eddie had bought her as a wedding present.

### BACK IN SYRACUSE

Back in Syracuse after the honeymoon trip, we needed a place to stay while we awaited our move to law school. Doug Courage had become engaged to Laura Holzworth, whom he had met at Elmira College and who hailed from Buffalo. He and Laura were married about two weeks after Hattie and I and they invited us to stay with them in the house they had just purchased at 109 Century Drive in Syracuse. Suffice it to say, we accepted "with pleasure" and moved in before they did. The four of us had a great time together in those early months of marriage and we'll never forget their generosity.

Daddy and Florence came to Syracuse to visit us while we were living on Century Drive that summer. Neither Hattie nor I had ever done any cooking. Hattie's only specialty was seven minute icing and mine was chocolate fudge. At the time our budget was also quite tight. Hattie bought some short ribs and cooked them at great length for the occasion. There was very little meat on the ribs in the first place and what there was of it was cooked nearly to a cinder. Daddy and Florence never mentioned it, of course. It was rather a shame because that proved to be the only time we ever had the opportunity to entertain them.

While we remained in Syracuse awaiting Law School, I enrolled in the graduate school of political science, continuing to study under the same professors with whom I had been working as an undergraduate. I was also employed as an instructor to teach a first year political science course at the Maxwell School of Citizenship. I taught two six-week terms and in the first term I barely managed to stay a few pages ahead of the students. When they asked a question to which I didn't have a ready answer, I replied, "We'll be getting to that in due time."

The final exam was made up of both true-false and essay questions. Very foolishly I used the same true-false questions the second term as I had the first. One of the second term students who had been doing poorly in the course evidently fell heir to a copy of the true-false exam from the first term and turned in a perfect paper. After some considerable soul-searching, I graded the essay portion of the exam closely and gave him a C in the course. Another excellent example of my learning the hard way!

Meanwhile, Hattie enrolled in the graduate school of music and continued to work with Elvin Schmitt. She was learning Rachmaninoff's Second Piano Concerto and practiced it daily in order to get ready for a performance with the Buffalo Symphony Orchestra. Unfortunately, that didn't work out because the conductor George Szell became ill. They substituted Phil Spitalny and his all-girl orchestra!

In late June a letter arrived from Harvard Law School. I opened the letter with bated breath. Happy day! I had been accepted in the Class of 1950, to matriculate in September 1947. So much for graduate school study at Syracuse. And so much for Yale and Columbia Law Schools. We were off to Cambridge, Massachusetts!

# CHAPTER 12
## <u>HARVARD LAW SCHOOL – A DREAM REALIZED</u>

Ever since my first year at Syracuse when my intention to study law had become firm, I had hoped to attend Harvard Law School. It was then reputed to be the best law school in the country, as it is today.

Hattie and I had learned before we left Syracuse that there was a shortage of residential quarters for Harvard law students. We saw the reality of that situation for ourselves when we were assigned furnished quarters in the Hotel Brunswick on Boylston Street in Boston. We had a room with a lavatory and a tin-lined shower in one corner. The furniture consisted of a bed, a sofa and a standing lamp. We had to eat all of our meals out. We set out the next day to find better living quarters and within a short time located a basement efficiency apartment at the foot of Beacon Street, in the house of a family named Gold. The head of the family was an old gentleman who had played vaudeville with Georgie Jessel.

Although the apartment was quite attractive, the Boston address was not convenient to the law school across the river in Cambridge, so we moved to a first floor apartment at 352 Harvard Street in Cambridge. Our landlord, Mr. Estabrook, made his home on the second floor, as did Blaine and Lucy Evans. Blaine was a fellow first year law student from Idaho. During the year we often played bridge with them in our room, setting the alarm for about thirty minutes in order to assure plenty of time for studying. Blaine and Lucy once suggested going to a movie after the bridge game and we rather hesitantly agreed. When we went to their door to pick them up, they reported that they had reconsidered and decided that Blaine needed to study instead. He and I were both greatly intimidated by the demands being made upon us that year. I'm not sure we ever did get to a movie with them, but we certainly enjoyed their company.

Within a few days of our arrival in Cambridge, Hattie undertook to find a job. She soon went to work as a file clerk at the Harvard Coop. On her first day she was talking to one of her fellow workers when the office manager told them that they were not permitted to talk while they were filing. Hattie resigned on the spot. Within a few days she found a post as a receptionist at the Veterans Administration Offices on campus, where she worked for the remainder of the year. There she met Midge Bohrer whose husband Mason was a year ahead of me in law school. We became close friends almost immediately and have remained so ever since. They became the catalysts for a small group of graduate students to socialize. Mase had a car and he took Hattie and me to the gatherings, driving with such abandon that I usually became car-sick before we reached our destination.

At Harvard, I was assigned to Section II (there were about 170 students in each of three sections). In my first course, Property I taught by Benjamin Kaplan, we were seated alphabetically. Ted Stevens, now a United States Senator from Alaska, sat on my left and Tom Weary, later a Philadelphia lawyer who chaired our fortieth reunion, sat on my right. Contrary to everything I had heard about Harvard Law School, our professor did <u>not</u> tell us that one of the three of us would not return next year. I was almost disappointed. It was clear that it was an outstanding class. Don Zimmerman sat on Tom Weary's right and he very quickly impressed me as brilliant. In our private conversations, Don appeared to have an answer for every question Professor Kaplan had asked, and often mentioned corollary points that the question suggested as well. I felt utterly intimidated. He proved to have writing skills that matched his verbal skills, garnering grades that placed him high in the class.

The first case we discussed in Kaplan's class was *Pierson v. Post*, an early nineteenth century New York case which established the principle that in order to gain ownership of a wild animal, one must reduce it to possession. (A hunter who shot a fox that ran off after it was wounded could not recover the fox from one who later found it and actually took possession of it.) It was my introduction to a mode of study known as the Socratic Method and I fell for it hook, line and sinker. Instead of telling us how the court had ruled or what the law was, the professor asked us how the court should have ruled and what the law should be. Some class members were left quite baffled in the process. I'll never forget that first class at Harvard. It was everything I had hoped for.

Professor Warren Seavey taught us Torts in the first year. Seavey was a past master of the Socratic Method, and primarily on that account he was my favorite of all the teachers I had at Harvard. Austin Wakeman Scott, who taught Judicial Remedies, was also quite stimulating and was almost as intimidating as my fellow-student Don Zimmerman. Scott had a wonderful way of slapping the top of his balding head with both hands when he was disappointed with a student's recitation.

Throughout the first semester the professors called on us to state the facts and the holdings in the cases that had been assigned us, a la the popular Hollywood movie "Paper Chase." They made no record of our performance and gave no tests during the course of the year until the final exam. It was the most frightening system imaginable – having to wait until the course ends before learning anything at all about how well one is doing. In January we took our final exam in Criminal Law since it was only a one semester course. My grade was an A and I was delighted. Hattie and I celebrated by having sundaes at Schraffts' Restaurant.

During that first year our class was given a newly devised test, a version of which eventually became the national LSAT examination. The objective of the experiment was to compare the scores we should make on that test with the grades we should make in law school as a means of validating the examination, *i.e.*, seeing if the results would correlate with the degree of our success in law school.

In early April, I began to review the year's work in the courses in which we had not yet been examined – Property, Torts, Contracts and Judicial Remedies. It wasn't long before I realized that I had started too late. I didn't come close to finishing the review. I should have started in October, which I determined to do the next year. Final exams in those two-semester courses were held during the first week in June. I earned a B average and was ninety-first in the class of 519. Frankly I was disappointed because I knew that only the top twenty-five or so (those with "A" averages) would be asked to join the staff of the Harvard Law Review, the principal honorary.

After our first year at Harvard, Hattie and I spent the summer working as companions to Willard Helburn and his wife Margaret at their apartment overlooking the Charles River on Memorial Drive in Cambridge. We learned of the position through the law school employment office. Mr. Helburn had been in the tanning business and usually spent much of the year in New Zealand where his tanning factory was located and where the sheep that provided the hides were raised. He had, however, recently suffered a stroke, which necessitated their need for companions that summer. They quickly came to appreciate Hattie when she showed Mrs. Helburn how to make cream puff shells.

I didn't make so grand an impression. I had helped move the library of Harvard's theological seminary just before we joined the Helburns that summer and hurt my back carrying boxes of books. I spent the first few days with them on my back being waited on hand and foot. Shortly after I recuperated from that injury, I carried dinner to Mr. Helburn's room on a tray one night and somehow managed to drop it in his lap. He took my blunder with characteristic grace.

Mr. Helburn had graduated from Harvard College with Franklin D. Roosevelt in 1903 and dismissed the President as an "average" student; but, of course, he was a conservative Republican. His sister Theresa Helburn was a prominent Broadway producer who co-produced the New York Theatre Guild plays on the radio. Mr. and Mrs. Helburn had a summer place in Martha's Vineyard near Concord, where we accompanied them for picnics. They liked to play bridge and Mr. Helburn had a habit of striking the bridge table with his index finger to remind his partner when the dummy's hand had the lead. I have never dared try that on Hattie.

We became very fond of the Helburns and when Mr. Helburn died shortly after we stayed with them, we attended his memorial service. We walked through the woods at their Martha's Vineyard house while the Franck D Minor Symphony was being played over a loudspeaker.

## THE SECOND YEAR AT HARVARD

At the beginning of my second year of law school, I went to see Professor Scott to ask him to review my Judicial Remedies exam with me because I thought I had done better than the C he gave me would indicate. Without hesitating, he assented and drew a copy of the exam questions from his desk drawer. "Now, how did you answer this first question?" he asked. As he no doubt expected, I did not care to deal with him on any such basis and beat a hasty retreat. You would think I should have learned better from my high school experience with Celeste Wilson. At least I didn't knock over his ink bottle.

That year Hattie and I moved to 1713 Massachusetts Avenue. Our rooms were in a fine late nineteenth century house that had been converted into apartments. They were so small that when we entertained another couple for dinner, one of us sat in the kitchen, one in the living room, one in the hall and the last on a window ledge at the end of the hall, all eating from one card table. All of the building's tenants, most of whom were married, were Harvard graduate students. I studied day and night that year, determined to improve my academic record. One of the couples made a film in which each of the various families in the house was featured. Hattie and I were represented by a picture of our front door – closed. It was fair comment on the degree to which we participated in the social life there.

Hattie has always shown extraordinary discipline in practicing the piano and she customarily takes advantage of every opportunity to practice, sometimes at odd hours. By and large, our student neighbors were most understanding. In fact, she often found some of them on the stairs outside our door listening to her performance. One evening, Hattie was practicing rather late when Irwin Schneiderman, a law student who lived in the apartment just above ours, knocked on the door. In what was certainly a world record in diplomacy, Irwin inquired, "Hattie, would you mind turning the page?"

As a result of such discipline, Hattie got a job teaching piano at Boston University, where she had fifty-six individual piano students spread over a three-day work week. One of her fellow piano teachers was Jules Wolfers, who was most hospitable in welcoming Hattie to the faculty and helping her get oriented.

Hattie then began studying piano with the Hungarian pianist Miklos Schwalb at the New England Conservatory, continuing to work with him for the next two years until we left Cambridge. Studying with Schwalb provided Hattie an opportunity to perform the Rachmaninoff Second Piano Concerto with the Conservatory's student orchestra. That alone was worth the tuition. In time she also performed in the Sunday afternoon concert series at the Isabella Gardner Museum in Boston.

In the meantime, I had applied for a scholarship and, as the second year got underway I learned that I had been awarded the Shelton Hale scholarship on the strength of my first year's grades. The scholarship had been established through the generosity of the second husband of Susan Herman in memory of her first husband Shelton Hale, who had attended Harvard Law School. She lived at 52 Pinckney Street on Beacon Hill and had a Christmas party every year to which she invited those who had held the scholarship. We learned that Alger Hiss was a former recipient of the Shelton Hale Scholarship, although he did not attend the party that Christmas. This was at the very time that he was making headlines in connection with Whittaker Chambers' charges that he had engaged in espionage on behalf of the Russians – in what became known as the infamous "pumpkin papers case."

In order to improve my standing in the class I adopted a suggestion made by our law school advisers and formed a study group with two classmates, Ken LaVoy and Philip Dunlay. Ken was also a Syracuse graduate. We met two or three days a week to review the materials and share points of view. It was the best decision I made during my law school days because we established the discipline of reviewing our course work soon after each class. Both Ken LaVoy and Phil Dunlay eventually became partners at the Root Ballentine law firm in New York City.

Ken was a member of the Pow Wow Club, one of the oldest moot court clubs at Harvard (and virtually the only one not named for a law professor), which he arranged for me to join early in our second year. Club members participated in the Ames competition in teams of two, each team being graded on its performance by volunteer judges who were either members of the judiciary or practicing lawyers. I was teamed with Jerry Andrews. Hattie agreed to type our brief so I was responsible for turning it in to the Ames office. By some terrible misfortune I misunderstood the due date and turned it in a day late, for which our team was penalized one point. When Jerry and I were graded by the judges after our oral arguments, we fell one point shy of the score of our adversaries, losing the contest on that account. But for my gaffe, I believe we should have progressed to the next round. I hope Jerry has found it in his heart to forgive me.

Unfortunately Daddy had not left the Chesapeake and Ohio Railway in time to salvage his health. The combination of train smoke and Camels cigarettes resulted in his being diagnosed with lung cancer within two years of the move to Charles Town. In a last minute effort to help, I carried X-rays of his lungs to Dr. William Reinhoff in Baltimore, Maryland, one of the first thoracic surgeons to have successfully removed a lung. I also took the x-rays to the George T. Pack Cancer Hospital in New York City. They both were of the opinion that it was too late to operate.

After the second year at Harvard, Hattie and I spent several weeks with Daddy in Charles Town and then went to Charlotte for six weeks so that I could clerk with the law firm of Taliaferro, Clarkson and Grier. Francis Clarkson, one of the partners in that firm, had issued that invitation and despite his illness, my father had insisted that I should take advantage of the opportunity.

The firm had been established in 1884 by Francis' father Heriot Clarkson who later served on the Supreme Court of North Carolina. Heriot was a leading "dry" in his day and Francis followed in his footsteps. Both of them fought against the evils of alcohol all of their lives. For them, that meant total abstinence for themselves and prohibition for their community. Francis was Eddie Clarkson's brother, but they were quite different in their lifestyles. Where Eddie loved birds and animals, Francis was an enthusiastic hunter. In fact, it was said of Eddie that he "fed birds and never turned down a drink," and of Francis that he "shot birds and never took a drink." It makes a good story, but in Eddie's case probably does him less than justice.

I enjoyed my work at the firm that summer and came to know and appreciate the other firm members – Carol Taliaferro and Joe Grier. Mr. Taliaferro was a representative of an old Virginia family that had migrated to Charlotte in the nineteenth century. He had graduated from the University of Virginia Law School in 1912 and had become Charlotte's leading expert on wills and trusts. Joe Grier had graduated from Harvard Law School in 1940 and joined the firm right after the war.

During the summer I also met John P. Kennedy, Jr. who had been studying law at the University of North Carolina Law School and was clerking with the Tillett law firm. We quickly became good friends. Little did I realize then how much time we should eventually spend together in the years ahead. John had married Barbara Whitby, an English girl whom he had met when he was a student at Cambridge University. She was the daughter of Sir Lionel and Lady Whitby, the latter of whom we came to know most pleasantly from her frequent visits to Charlotte.

In August I received word from Harvard that I had placed twelfth in my second year class, and on that basis was invited to join the staff of the Harvard Law Review. It was all I could have hoped for and more than I should have expected. I immediately called my father to give him the news. It turned out to be the last time I spoke with him.

## DADDY'S PASSING

Within a few days of that call, my Uncle Joe called to say that my father was failing fast. I cut my stay in Charlotte short and immediately left for Charles Town with my brother Chick. He had been staying with Mother for the summer and was scheduled to continue his studies at Shepherd College in nearby Shepherdstown, West Virginia that fall. When Uncle Joe met us at the Charles Town bus station, he told us that our father had died that morning. He was only 48. He had weighed about one hundred pounds at the time of his passing. I was somewhat consoled by the fact that I had been able to bring him news of the success I had enjoyed that year at law school.

Neither Hattie nor Chick agrees with me but I have always strongly suspected that the doctor and Uncle Joe arranged for Daddy to be relieved of his suffering before my brother and I should arrive to witness it. All it would have required was an increase in his dose of morphine. I could certainly understand if that were the case.

After Daddy's funeral at the Charles Town Baptist Church, he was buried in the Thompson family plot in Martinsburg, West Virginia with his mother, father and two siblings who had died as children. I don't suppose it makes any real difference but I think it is sad that neither of his spouses is buried next to him. Each was buried in a plot with her other husband. I dreamed about my father for many months after his death. In my dreams he returned to life to share a number of experiences with me.

According to Carl Jung, the most profound effect upon a child is the unlived life of a parent. Perhaps that is why I feel as though I represent my father in the here and now – or perhaps it is because I became the lawyer he hoped to be – or perhaps it is because he died so young – or perhaps it is for all of those reasons. At any rate, I am a better man for undertaking to represent him, though I do seem to forget from time to time that he never spoke ill of anyone.

Daddy really didn't have a fair shake in life, especially considering that he was such a fine man. It would be wrong, however, for me to imply that my father did not lead a full life during the short time allotted him. He was, with Florence, very happily married. In his later years he returned to live near his childhood home and joined a successful business venture with a brother who, biblically speaking, was a Jonathan to his David. And his exceptional kindness and generosity brought him the devotion of all of the members of our extended family. Who will say that such a life was not a satisfying one? Still, I cannot help but imagine what his life would have been like had he finished law school and returned to West Virginia to practice law. Of course, in that case the combination of genes that constitutes me should never have come to pass.

## THE LAST YEAR AT HARVARD

Hattie and I returned to Harvard in September 1949 for what was to be our last and, by a considerable margin, our best year there. We rented a furnished apartment on the third floor of 124 Walker Street next door to the Radcliffe College dormitory and tennis courts. Peter Moser, a law school associate, and his wife Liz lived in a first floor apartment in the same building. Liz was lighthearted and spirited. Peter was considerably more serious but equally good company. We soon became friends and often played bridge together. Pete and Liz were both from Baltimore and they returned there after law school. In recent years we have seen them from time to time at American Bar Association meetings and Fourth Circuit Judicial Conferences. Peter served as treasurer of the American Bar Association for several years and Liz recently published a book of poetry that is delightful in its sensitivity. They both still played a mean game of tennis when last we met them on the court during a Fourth Circuit Judicial Conference.

Before many weeks had passed, I was commissioned by the Harvard Law Review to write an article on the regulation of retail installment sales under an Ohio statute that had become effective in August 1949. The article was published[*] and represented many weeks of work, primarily due to fine-tuning at the hands of Leon Lipson, the note editor, who was not averse to requiring me to rewrite practically every sentence. It was a grand exercise, however, and I have always been grateful for Leon's help. Not only did he teach me to write with precision, he also helped me build character. Thanks to him I learned to suffer criticism, however picayune, with relative grace. I understand that Leon later taught at Yale Law School so I am confident that many others have benefited from his conscientious tutelage as well.

From time to time, various notables dropped in at the Law Review offices in Gannett House. One such visitor was a former professor there, Supreme Court Justice Felix Frankfurter, who, as I shall describe, eventually played a much larger role in my professional career than I could have imagined at the time. Another was James L. Landis, former chairman of the Securities Exchange Commission, who was reputed to have attained the highest academic average in the history of the law school. The possible exception was Supreme Court Justice Louis Brandeis, whose studies there predated

---

[*] 63 HARV. L. REV. 874 (1950).

the current grading system, so it is difficult to compare their records. Each of our visitors dominated the conversation to the point that it became virtually a monologue, largely because we were loath to interrupt them. Obviously we found both Frankfurter and Landis quite impressive.

As the academic year end approached, the Law Review staff undertook the task of electing officers for Volume 64. It proved to be an all-night affair. We met at about 6 p.m. on a Saturday and began discussing the qualifications of all of the staff members who were in the Class of '51 – some 25 men in all (women were not admitted to the law school until a year after I graduated). After several hours, the first vote was taken. It was decided by a majority vote where a natural break occurred in the voting and everyone below that break was eliminated. The candidates remaining were then discussed again and another vote was taken on those still in the running. This process was repeated again and again until the new president and other officers were elected as Sunday morning dawned. Jim Vorenberg was elected President of Volume 64 and in time became dean of the law school. My friend Jim Sheedy, for whom I campaigned enthusiastically, was elected Treasurer. He practiced law in Cleveland after law school.

In retrospect and not surprisingly I view the education I received at Harvard Law School as one of the most significant mountain-top experiences of my life. Both the faculty and the student body were an inspiration to me and contributed to my education far more than I could have imagined was possible. The fact that the majority of the current federal Supreme Court justices graduated from Harvard Law School is fitting testimony to the school's excellence.

In appreciation of the education I received there, I have served as an officer of the Harvard Club of Charlotte and of the Harvard Law School Association of North Carolina, as well as acting as an agent in annual fund- raisers. Moreover, I have contributed more than I can properly afford to the Harvard Law School Fund, especially in those years in which Hattie and I attended the 25th, 30th, 35th, 40th and 50th reunions. The 55th reunion is scheduled for October 2005 and I have agreed to serve again on the Reunion Gift Committee of about a dozen class members. I shall never be able to repay the school for what it did for me. It is, of course, ironic that I contribute far more liberally to Harvard, which is already quite wealthy, than I do to Syracuse. I need to correct that disparity, as I am also greatly indebted to Syracuse.

## LOOKING FOR A JOB

In the fall of 1949 we were advised that we should begin applying for jobs, since law firms often hire the following year's associates before Christmas. A number of the larger firms in the major cities actually visited the campus to conduct interviews before

Thanksgiving. Potentially successful interviewees were also invited to visit the firms on their home ground during the Christmas holiday.

In view of my academic success in the second year, Hattie and I discussed anew the question of where we might wish to live. We concluded that we should like to try our hand in one of the major cities in the east – New York, Philadelphia, Washington, DC or Atlanta – at least for a time.

My only experience in Washington, DC bears describing in some detail. I interviewed with Graham Claytor and Charles Horsky of Covington and Burling. They had both been editors-in-chief of the Harvard Law Review in the mid-thirties, and I understood them to be outstanding lawyers. During the course of my interviews there I explained to Horsky that I had promised to give a New York firm an answer to their offer within the week and should therefore appreciate hearing from him as soon as possible. He may have considered this approach a little presumptuous because when I arrived back at my apartment in Cambridge, I found a telegram from him under the door. "Please do not fail to take advantage of any offer you have received since unfortunately we are not in a position to make a decision at this time" – or words to that effect. Somehow it reminded me of my high school overtures to Sally Ramsey and her attempts at a diplomatic response.

I also interviewed with a pleasant and highly successful Harvard Law graduate named Lewis van Dusen at Drinker Biddle and Reath in Philadelphia. However, because of the attraction afforded by the New York firms' reputations, we eventually decided to limit our search to that city.

While I enjoyed meeting lawyers in other New York firms, I was immediately very much drawn to Charles Spofford and Nelson Adams, who interviewed me at Davis Polk. I accepted their subsequent offer of employment enthusiastically. Hattie and I were going to the big-time in the Big Apple!

# PART TWO
# THE NEW YORK YEARS

# CHAPTER 13
## A SUMMER AT DAVIS POLK

During my last year at Harvard, I had applied for a Fulbright Scholarship to attend law school at a British university to be designated by the Fulbright Committee. As we were preparing for our move to New York, Hattie and I received word that I had been awarded an all-expenses-paid scholarship to Manchester University Law School. We were delighted, of course, and I immediately arranged with Davis Polk to begin work there a year later than I had originally planned. (My friend Jack Roemer insists that he was hired that year only because of my delay in reporting for work.) The firm was most cooperative, and invited me to work there for six weeks in the summer before we left for England.

To that end, I went to New York in June 1950 and stayed at the 92nd Street YMCA for two weeks while I took the Bar Review course in preparation for the New York bar exam to be offered later that month. Hattie, who had gone to Carlisle for the month of June, rejoined me in July. We leased a 116th Street efficiency apartment that overlooked virtually the full length of Claremont Avenue.

I reported to Davis Polk as arranged and soon received assignments from George Brownell, Morton Fearey, Porter Chandler, Marion Fisher, Nelson Adams and Taggart Whipple. Charles Spofford had been named the United States ambassador to NATO with offices in London, so he was not at the firm that summer. Elliott Schewel's brother Stanford, who had graduated from E.C. Glass in Lynchburg several years ahead of me, was an associate at Davis Polk at that time and we enjoyed reminiscing about our common upbringing.

I also came to know and admire John N. "Jack" Irwin who was a senior associate at Davis Polk. During the summer, he invited Hattie and me for a weekend at his home in New Canaan, Connecticut. While Jack and I played tennis, Hattie spent the day with his wife Jane, who was the daughter of Thomas J. Watson, the late founder and president of International Business Machines. Jack and Jane lived in the home in which her father had resided during his lifetime. Hattie and I stayed in a bedroom that featured antique Italian furniture that almost spoke to us of its history – in Italian, of course. It was a splendid weekend. Jack later left Davis Polk to join Patterson, Belknap and Webb, the firm that represented IBM.

I researched several interesting questions that summer: (1) how long a private bank should retain cash statements and deposit ledgers, (2) whether an oil producer could avoid the jurisdiction of the Federal Power Commission by selling its natural gas reserves, (3) whether a father could be guilty of kidnapping his own child when there had been no adjudication as to custody, and (4) whether a bank could safely discourage trespassers from sitting on a retaining wall by incorporating broken glass in it. I was delighted with those assignments and immediately felt as though I had found my niche.

Some of my Harvard classmates also began working at other New York firms that summer, including Ken LaVoy, Phil Dunlay, Art Sporn, Reed Baldwin and Brian Forrow. We soon began meeting for lunch to compare notes on our experiences. Everyone appeared to be pleased with his choice and all of them, with the exception of Reed Baldwin (for reasons to be explained later), eventually became partners in their firms.

In mid-August, the results of the Bar exam were published in the *New York Times* and I was delighted to learn that I had passed. Later that same week, we sailed for England on the *SS America*. A number of friends, including John Melanson and several Syracuse classmates, came to our stateroom to see us off. Others sent telegrams wishing us well.

# CHAPTER 14
## FULBRIGHT STUDIES

The eight-day voyage to England was quite difficult for Hattie, who was three months pregnant when we sailed and immediately became seasick. After going to the dining room several times, she spent most of the trip in our stateroom. Although I managed to get her up on deck for fresh air nearly every day, she didn't stay long. As we approached Southampton, Hattie became concerned that she might not be able to disembark under her own steam. At the appointed hour, however, she managed to walk off the ship leaning on my shoulder.

From Southampton, we entrained for London where I put her up in a hotel on Queens Gate off Kensington the moment we arrived. Our room was next to the elevator shaft and she insisted that the sounds the elevator made were at the same pitch as those she had heard on the ship, which had the unfortunate effect of delaying her recovery. She spent a week recuperating before she would venture out.

As soon as Hattie was strong enough, we traveled to Galleywood to visit the Clark family. The next day we left for Manchester by train and took a hotel room while we searched for living quarters. Most of the places we saw left a great deal to be desired but within a couple of days we found what we considered to be the perfect apartment in a house called "New Farm." Located in a suburb of Manchester called Didsbury, it was owned by Esther Michael, a widow who lived there with her daughter Esmé. Mrs. Michael was an extraordinary individual, being of Jewish and Greek ancestry and having been raised in Spain. Her husband had brought her to England just after World War I and together they had operated a farm on that site until his death.

We had one bedroom with a bath and kitchenette - which was quite adequate. There was also a piano in the living room, made available for practice sessions at Hattie's call. Mrs. Michael could not have been more cordial, often providing Hattie with her own egg (eggs were still being rationed at the time; each person got one per week) when she learned that Hattie was pregnant.

Mrs. Michael celebrated her one hundredth birthday in 1995. Hattie and I attended the celebratory party in London. Unfortunately she didn't remember us but her family appreciated our coming. As is the custom in England, the Queen sent her a congratulatory telegram. In America we must be satisfied with Willard Scott's displaying our photograph on television, of course. That is the price we pay for rebelling against King George III. I read some verses honoring Esther at the birthday party:

## A Tribute to Esther Michael on the Occasion of Her 100th Birthday Celebration in London

### I

Another decade brings our pilgrims here
to celebrate dear Esther's hundredth year.
What better day than this on which to pay
due homage to our friend, of whom they say,
no honor is too great for this fair maid
whose charm and wit the seasons cannot fade.
Near half a century's passed since Esther saved
her weekly rationed egg that Hattie craved
to nourish our first-born on Millgate Lane –
an act of love most generous and humane
for Fulbright guests who daily did her pester
for this or that in Lancaster's Manchester.

### II

Young Hattie practiced long into the night
on Esther's keyboard, e'en to morning's light.
Nor even then our heroine complained
while Bach, Chopin and Shostakovich reigned.
Most happ'ly we enjoyed her cuisine
which joining with a Greco-Spanish gene
produced this paragon mamá and wife
who still with pluck and spirit clings to life.
So here's to Esther Michael and her brood
who housed us for a time they must have rued.
We'll travel any day three thousand miles
to honor you who've made us Anglophiles.

## MANCHESTER UNIVERSITY LAW SCHOOL

Within a few days of our arrival in Manchester, I registered at the Manchester University Law School. My principal professor and advisor was Professor Ben Wortley, who was also the dean of the law school. He was a specialist in public international law and had at one time represented Great Britain at the International Court of Justice at The Hague. In the course of time he wrote and published a book on the expropriation of private property by foreign governments, which became the definitive work on the subject in the English speaking world.

Professor Wortley was without a doubt one of the finest men I have ever known. Besides being exceptionally well spoken, he was a brilliant scholar and embodied the essence of gentility both in his manner and in his appearance. He immediately made me welcome to the University by showing me a degree of personal attention I could never have imagined. He also enjoyed writing poetry both in English and French, some serious and others quite whimsical. He sent me one that was short and to the point:

### SEVENTY-SEVEN

At seventy five
we may surmise
with some surprise,
that we're alive,
though friends are not.

At seventy six
New thoughts scarce mix
in one's old head.
At seventy seven
hope for heaven.

Soon after we settled in at New Farm, Hattie made contact with an obstetrician to prepare for the birth of our first child. She was accepted in the national health program so there was no expense involved. When she went to St. Mary's Hospital for a checkup, the Catholic sister said, "Now, dearie, go into the cubicle and take off your vest and knickers." It sounded like a foreign language to Hattie. After waiting in line with other expectant mothers, she was told to lie down and a curtain was dropped over her head. When she heard men talking as they entered the room, she threw the curtain aside and asked "What are they doing here"? "This is a teaching hospital and they are the medical students," the doctor replied. "Well, there is nothing unusual about me so they won't learn anything new. I'd appreciate it if you would ask them to leave," Hattie insisted. He did and they did. Hattie's modesty was salvaged. At her request, I spoke to the hospital's superintendent in the interest of accommodating her desire for privacy and happily he agreed to oblige her.

Before long, Hattie also identified a pianist with whom she would study during our time in England. His name was Iso Elinson and he was an extraordinarily talented musician. A frequent soloist with the Halle Orchestra, his repertoire, which included all of Beethoven's sonatas, was comparable to that of any internationally acclaimed soloist. In fact, at one time we hoped to arrange for him to perform his Beethoven tour de force in New York, but it didn't work out. Hattie was delighted to study with him and did so for our entire year in England.

In Manchester, we particularly enjoyed the newspaper, *The Manchester Guardian,* and the Halle Orchestra conducted by Sir John Barberolli. The *Guardian* carried Alistair Cook's report from the homeland, "Letter from America." In later years, Cook endeared himself to American television viewers as the host of one of our favorite television programs, "Masterpiece Theatre." It was from a series of those programs featuring a barrister named "Rumpole of the Bailey" that I learned to refer to Hattie from time to time as "she who must be obeyed." And for two shillings sixpence we heard Barberolli conduct Edward Elgar's "Enigma Variations." The paper and orchestra represented the intellectual and artistic strengths of the city, and we became great supporters of both.

Among the friends we made in Manchester were a delightful married couple – Marcus Cunliffe and Mitzi Solomon. Marcus, although an Englishman, was a specialist in American history and later published a compendium of sorts on the lives of the American Presidents, as well as other books dealing with American political history. I have a copy of the compendium and often have occasion to refer to it. Also, his biography of President George Washington has been characterized by Joseph Ellis, author of another recently published Washington biography, as one of the best studies ever written about what became "the Washington legend."

Marcus was a member of the Manchester University faculty. He moved to the University of Sussex in 1965 to become Professor of American Studies. Today, the Centre for the Study of Constitutionalism and National Identity is named for him there. In 1980 he became University Professor at George Washington University in Washington, DC. Mitzi, a talented sculptress from New York City, had studied with Henry Moore and her work reflected his tutelage. Characteristic of Mitzi's free spirit, they had painted their house chartreuse in the midst of a row of coal-fire smudged redbrick houses! She designed a tragicomic mask for the British Film Academy which is still in use.

We made two trips that year during the Christmas holiday. First we entrained for Newcastle to visit the Redheads, where we had a delicious Christmas dinner. During dinner, Ian, who had just finished medical school and was temporarily living at his parents' home, was called to the door. Upon returning to the table he reported that the child of a neighbor had a pea stuck up his nose. Asked if he had been successful in removing it, Ian replied "I just held his other nostril closed and had him close his mouth and blow." It was clear that Ian was destined for success as a medical doctor!

After dinner they drove us to visit some friends in the town of Washington, which we were told had been the seat of the ancestors of President George Washington. Much to our surprise we learned when we arrived that they had postponed their Christmas dinner until we arrived so that we could join them. Of course we had no appetites. To make matters worse, they served hare as the main course which neither Hattie nor I had ever eaten. We learned then that it has a distinctly pungent taste! We did the best we could with it.

From Newcastle we went on to Scotland and I introduced Hattie to St. Andrew's University. We walked over to Sir Darcy Thompson's house where we were disappointed to learn from his daughter that he had died two years earlier. It was a snowy winter's day so the town didn't show up as well as it might otherwise have done. Princess Street in Edinburgh, which I had earlier described to Hattie as resplendent in beautiful flower gardens, lay under a heavy fog. We could hardly make out the outline of the Holyrood castle on the other side of the river, where Mary Queen of Scots had lived and reigned over my Thompson forebears.

After we returned to Manchester we emplaned for Paris where we visited law school classmate Don Paradis and his wife Betty, who were living there during his service with a United Nations agency. During the visit we met their friends John and Kathy Loughran. John was on a foreign-service assignment for the State Department, which eventually appointed him Ambassador to Somalia, and Kathy was working as a model for a Christian Dior salon.

During that trip, Hattie and I took some friends to dinner at a Parisian restaurant called Lapin. There was a large wine carafe shaped like a rabbit at one end of the table. Wine poured out of the carafe from an aperture that was strategically placed in that portion of the rabbit's anatomy to which only the French would assign such a function. Assuming that the price I was being charged included the entire contents of the carafe, I urged my guests to drink up. When the bill was presented, I learned that they charged by measuring the carafe before and after the meal! Mark Twain was no doubt referring to the naiveté of Americans like me when he wrote "Innocents Abroad."

On our last night in Paris we saw the Follies Bergere. I suffered severe eyestrain from trying to see the figures of the artistes through their thin silk costumes while at the same time appearing suitably blasé. It was barely worth the price of admission!

## MOVING TO LONDON

One of my special interests as a lawyer has been Conflicts of Law (known in England as Private International Law). One of the masters of the subject was Professor George C. Cheshire who was teaching at the Inn of Court Law School in Old Hall off Chancery Lane in London. After completing their college work, law students seeking to become barristers study there in preparation for sitting for the Bar examination. With Ben Wortley's approval, I began taking an overnight train to London once a week to attend Cheshire's lectures.

As the end of the first term at Manchester approached, I talked with Hattie about the possibility of our transferring to the London School of Economics and Political Science (LSE), so that I could continue my classes with Professor Cheshire more conveniently and also enjoy the advantage of studying at the geographical center of the British judicial system. Because I was so fond of Ben Wortley, I was reluctant to suggest it to him. In keeping with her practice throughout our married life, Hattie encouraged me to talk to Ben since it was important to me. I did so and, as I should have expected, Ben was most understanding and generous in helping me to clear the arrangement with the Fulbright authorities. Once again he proved his reliability as a friend.

We moved to London in January 1951 and I enrolled at LSE while Hattie arranged to continue her studies with Iso Elinson who came to London on a regular basis. We found a furnished apartment at 1 Rosemont Court on Rosemont Road in Acton, which belonged to

Andrew and Pamela Allen. They were a very nice couple and we soon became good friends. The apartment was on the District underground line and when Reed Baldwin, a Harvard classmate, visited us there he recited the names of every stop on both the District and Picadilly Underground Lines in order and from memory. Reed had a photographic memory, which no doubt accounted for his graduating second in our class. Soon after that visit he was tragically killed in an automobile accident while driving to Vermont on a skiing trip. Art Sporn, who was also in our class at Harvard, suffered serious injuries in the same accident.

Drew, who was studying to become an architect, introduced us to one of his fellow architecture students, John Burden. John became an outstanding architect in time and our friendship has blossomed through the years. His wife Jean took Hattie to hear Dylan Thomas, the noted Welsh poet, recite poetry at an intimate meeting of the Marlborough Poetry Society in London. By coincidence it developed that Thomas' American agent John Malcolm Brinnin has figured rather largely in our life in Charlotte by virtue of my having played that role in the play "Dylan" at the Mint Museum. But more of that later.

That spring, the State Department moved John Loughran from Paris to London and we learned that Kathy was expecting a baby at the same time as Hattie. In fact, we were all at dinner with the Allens one Sunday in March when Hattie and Kathy both began having contractions. John called us at midnight to say they were leaving for the hospital. Three hours later we went to the Queen Charlotte "Lying-In" Hospital and both children were born within 24 hours of each other. (Hattie actually delivered first.) It was an exciting time!

As I have said, we named our new daughter D'Arcy Wentworth Thompson. The Loughrans named their daughter Krystyn. Both Hattie and Kathy employed "natural childbirth" in having their children, i.e., neither used any anesthetic. Kathy had heard of the technique in France where it was called the Lamaze method and Hattie learned of it in England where it was known as the Grantley Dick Read method. In each case, of course, it was named after the obstetrician who had originated it there. Hattie has delivered all of our children by that method and in recent years it has become a common practice in the United States.

## THE LONDON SCHOOL OF ECONOMICS

The London School of Economics is one of about sixty colleges that are a part of London University. Those who enroll in any one of the colleges are permitted to take courses in the other colleges in the system. I took a course in Private International Law with King's College professor Ronald Graveson, whom I came to know personally and whose case book I still use on occasion. He was especially hospitable to us, even entertaining Hattie and me in his home. I studied the history of common law with Professor Theodore F. T. Plucknett. Clad in an old cardigan sweater and well-worn leather slippers, he virtually personified the history that he taught.

On one of my first visits to University College, I saw an extraordinary memorial to the great reformer of the nineteenth century, Jeremy Bentham. He had been the head of University College in his day and I was told that his bequest to the college was conditional upon his mummified remains being dressed in his accustomed attire and kept on view in a showcase in the boardroom where the college trustees meet, no doubt in order to remind them of the principles for which he stood. In any case, it was still there, though his head had been placed in a box at his feet and a waxen head substituted for it. I didn't look in the box!

I came to know two practicing barristers quite well while I was in London: Philip Sykes of Lincoln's Inn and S. N. Grant-Bailey of Inner Temple. Each of them entertained me in fine style. Sykes took me to a Lincoln Inn's dinner, a certain number of which an aspiring law student is required to attend in order to qualify for the bar. S. N. Grant-Bailey and I visited his alma mater, Christ Church College at Oxford University, where I had the privilege of sitting next to Lord Wright, a law lord (judge of the highest court of appeals), at dinner. Christ Church is a magnificent college originally founded by Cardinal Thomas Wolsey in the sixteenth century, and the meal was presented in a great hall with much pomp and circumstance. Lord Wright had distinguished himself as one of the finest legal minds in the English speaking world. He and I discussed his opinion in the *Vita Foods* case, which had established the principle that two contracting parties may choose the jurisdiction whose law should govern their contract if that jurisdiction has some reasonable connection with the transaction. That weekend was one of the highlights of my time in England.

Francis Clarkson and his wife Cama came to see us while we were in London. I volunteered to accompany them in visiting the Tower of London and insisted that we should go up the Thames by ferry since that was the means by which prisoners had been transported there in Henry VIII's time. As we progressed upriver I began identifying landmarks. Eventually I realized that some of the landmarks didn't seem to add up, whereupon I learned that we were actually going in the opposite direction and were headed for Kew Gardens and Hampton Court. We soon relaxed and undertook to make the most of our trip but the Clarksons never stopped ribbing me about it.

We also visited the Festival of Britain. When we walked through the anthropological exhibit where various stages in the development of *homo sapiens* were represented, Francis asked "Can you imagine anyone believing that we are related to these creatures"? His biblical training came to the fore again when we visited Old Hall at Lincoln's

Inn where he immediately identified the mural at one end of the hall as "Paul before Agrippa." The mural illustrates the occasion on which King Agrippa II, after hearing Paul's statement defending Christianity, uttered the famous words, "Almost thou persuadest me to be a Christian." Francis was a dedicated Episcopal churchman and a man of great Biblical erudition.

When the term ended in June of 1951, Hattie and I prepared to sail for home. Unlike the trip over, Hattie took the voyage back to New York in stride. We even brought D'Arcy up on deck in her "carry cot" until we noticed that she appeared to be gasping for breath. Eventually we realized that the wind was too strong to allow her to breathe properly, so she remained in the state room thereafter, swinging happily in a net hammock. During the voyage, Hattie and I had time to savor the Fulbright experience for which we have always been most grateful.

I offer no apology for being an enthusiastic Anglophile. Both my heritage and my personal experiences in the United Kingdom have contributed to my conviction that English speaking people have a "special relationship" (as Winston Churchill put it). Hattie and I were charter members of the Charlotte branch of the English Speaking Union established by Mrs. Mary Dwelle and George Cramer fifty years ago and have attended its meetings regularly.

# CHAPTER 15
## PRACTICING LAW AT DAVIS POLK

Prior to leaving Harvard, Hattie had given away all of our furniture on the theory that, since we were going to work for a big New York law firm, we should soon be wealthy and would not need those old chairs, end tables, and bookcases. Of course, things didn't work out that way. Davis Polk started me at $4,100 per year, a fine salary at the time but certainly not enough to furnish an apartment. Fortunately, when we moved into Dunnolly Gardens in Queens, Hattie's mother sent a few antique family pieces from Carlisle, all of which we still have and enjoy.

A piano has always been the most important piece of furniture in our home for obvious reasons and the same moving van also brought a Steinway piano that Hattie's mother had purchased from the Sadler estate in Carlisle. It was a rare white parlor grand electric player piano and a great many reels of music also came with it. A piano tuner soon convinced Hattie that the tone would be improved by removing the mechanical apparatus, however, and she allowed him to do it. Years later we learned that Steinway player pianos are quite rare and virtually priceless. This time it was Hattie who learned a lesson that she is unlikely to ever have occasion to put to use.

Soon after we moved to Queens, Hattie was called upon to solicit contributions for the Red Cross. After canvassing our building one Sunday afternoon, she came back to the apartment in tears. Hardly any of the neighbors had come to the door when she knocked. Calling for her to identify herself, most of them shouted that they weren't interested. She collected only one contribution, and that was from the man who had solicited the previous year. We quickly learned that New York wasn't as friendly as Carlisle or Cambridge.

### NEW COLLEAGUES

I reported for duty at Davis Polk in early July. Edgar Outterbridge Appleby, a native New Yorker who had just graduated from the University of Virginia Law School, was my officemate. Another recent graduate who came to the firm that summer from Columbia Law School was Henry King. Henry went on to become the firm's managing partner in the 1980s and 1990s. Philip Potter and Bernhard von Falkenhausen joined us in 1952. Phil had finished at Harvard that year and Bernhard at Cornell. They both soon became my close friends. Phil's father Dr. Philip C. Potter was a Park Avenue practitioner of internal medicine and he took care of me when I suddenly suffered a severe pain in my abdomen one day. At Phil's request, Dr. Potter met me at the hospital. The pain mysteriously subsided under his healing hand.

Bernhard was from Essen, Germany. He told us a wonderful story about how his name had originated. It seems that in earlier times a German prince who enjoyed the sport of hunting hawks often visited the house in which the falcons were kept. He became quite fond of a daughter of the keeper of the falcons. Although he was already married to a Prussian princess, he soon consummated what was known as a "left hand marriage" with the young woman. The offspring of that second marriage were appropriately named the "Barons von Falkenhausen." Anyhow, it makes a good story. Bernhard and his wife Bettina, a medical doctor, have visited us in Charlotte and Hattie has visited them in Essen.

Gilbert Dwyer, who was still attending Fordham Law School, was hired in 1952 to work on a couple of big antitrust cases. I liked him immediately. He was at the firm for three years before leaving to make an extraordinary career as a business executive, a management consultant, an entrepreneur as CEO of several struggling companies, and as dean of a university business school. Gil seems to have had a special talent for leadership, as well as a unique gift for friendship.

I continued to be given assignments by both corporate and litigation partners, including George Brownell, Edgar Crossman, Morton Fearey, Porter Chandler, Taggart Whipple and eventually Charles Spofford, when he returned from his duties at NATO. Except for a brief period of servitude with legal investments for savings banks, the subjects of my research and legal memoranda were varied and interesting. In the entire three years that I was associated with Davis Polk, I was never assigned exclusively to any one department.

My work in legal investments for savings banks was not, however, without compensations. For example, during this time I was fortunate to meet Parker Bailey who shared our interest in serious music. He became a great admirer of Hattie, and in time arranged for her to join the board of directors of the Third Street Music School Settlement, a position which she greatly enjoyed. Robert Ward was the director of the school at that time. He and his wife Mary, who now live in Durham where he is composer in residence at the Duke University music school, have since become our very good friends. Bob has achieved considerable renown as an opera composer. A number of his productions have been staged by Charlotte's Opera Carolina, as I shall later describe.

## THE SOUTH CAROLINA SCHOOL SEGREGATION CASE

By far the most important assignment I received at Davis Polk involved working with John W. Davis, the head of the firm and, according to one legal commentator, "probably the nation's most distinguished appellate lawyer." During the First World War Mr. Davis was President Woodrow Wilson's Solicitor General, a position he held until being appointed ambassador to Britain's Court of St. James's. On his return from that assignment, he and Frank Polk, who had served as president of the American Red Cross, were then invited to join an old New York law firm called Stetson Jennings and Russell in which President Grover Cleveland had once been a partner. That firm soon changed its name to Davis Polk and Wardwell. In 1924, Mr. Davis was the Democratic Party's nominee for President, a contest which he eventually lost to Calvin Coolidge, of course.

Governor James F. Byrnes of South Carolina retained Mr. Davis to represent the State of South Carolina in the United States Supreme Court in *Briggs v. Elliott,* one of five companion public school segregation cases that, according to the U.S. Attorney General's *amicus curiae* brief, "changed the whole course of race relations in the United States." Jack Greenberg, a prominent civil rights lawyer and now a teacher at Columbia University, characterized it as "the most important Supreme Court decision of the century." A federal three judge court in Charleston, South Carolina had ruled against the plaintiffs in their attempt to have school segregation declared unconstitutional. Judge John J. Parker of Charlotte had written the majority opinion. Judge Parker was the father of Francis Parker, whom I had come to know at Taliaferro, Clarkson and Grier.

Within the year, I began writing legal memoranda for Mr. Davis on various issues relating to that case, though I did not participate in writing the first brief. (That was the work of senior associate Bill Meagher and Mr. Davis himself.) After the initial argument of the case in December 1952, the U.S. Supreme Court set the case for re-argument on certain specific questions drafted by Justice Felix Frankfurter and his then clerk Alexander Bickel who had been my contemporary at Harvard Law School. I worked directly with Mr. Davis in writing the South Carolina brief that responded to those questions, preparing the first draft of the body of the brief and the appendix dealing with the Congressional history of the Fourteenth Amendment. With a phrase or a sentence here and there Mr. Davis brought my tired legalese to life. His colorful additions virtually leapt from the page. I enjoyed the privilege of sitting next to him when he argued the case in the Supreme Court in December 1953. Thurgood Marshall appeared for the plaintiffs. Mr. Davis had every confidence that we should prevail. Neither of us had yet seen the handwriting on the wall, though we should have done so in light of the fact that several of the questions framed for argument by the Court appeared to assume a reversal.

It was clear to us that neither the Congress that adopted the Fourteenth Amendment nor the states that ratified it contemplated that it would abolish school segregation. Bickel himself later admitted as much in an article he wrote for the Harvard Law Review after the Supreme Court ruling.[*] It was Bickel's view that the Court

---

[*] 69 HARV. L. REV. 1 (1955).

effectually ruled that the meaning of the Fourteenth Amendment can change in the light of changing circumstances. Of course, that was anathema to Mr. Davis, but it is clear that it was the view that the Court eventually adopted.

Although we did not appreciate their significance at the time, two circumstances did not bode well for our cause: (1) Earl Warren was appointed Chief Justice when Fred Vinson suddenly died, and (2) Justice Frankfurter quietly set the stage to assure the abolition of segregation, including working behind the scenes with the Solicitor General's Office on the federal government's *amicus curiae* brief. When these communications later came to light, a *New York Times* editorial entitled "With All Deliberate Impropriety" was highly critical of the extra-judicial communications between Frankfurter and Solicitor General assistant Philip Elman, his former law clerk.

The Court ruled against South Carolina and against the other defendants in the companion cases in May of 1954.** Integration was simply an idea whose time had come. Nothing I had written or Mr. Davis had said could have affected the outcome. As Philip Elman later wrote,

> "The more important the case is, the more far-reaching its effects, and the more the Justices have studied and thought about the issues beforehand, the less likely it is that the quality of the oral arguments will affect the decision. . . Brown [companion to Briggs] was quintessentially that kind of case. In Brown nothing the lawyers said made a difference. Thurgood Marshall could have stood up there and recited 'Mary had a Little Lamb,' and the result would have been exactly the same."

Of course, that is not to detract from Marshall's leadership in choosing to challenge segregation *per se* and shepherding the case to the Supreme Court.

Mr. Davis refused to accept a fee from South Carolina for his work in *Briggs v. Elliott*. Governor Byrnes sent him a beautiful silver tea service inscribed "From the People of South Carolina." My colleague Stuart Marks, who saw it on view in the Davis Polk library, quipped "Shouldn't it say 'from the white people of South Carolina?'" Of course, he was right. Until I worked on this case, I had never had occasion to question the system with which I had lived since childhood. I grew up in a culture that accepted segregation as a way of life and I had never known anyone, black or white, who questioned it. I simply had not appreciated that a moral issue was involved. That is not an excuse but merely an explanation. Suffice it to say, I have quite a different view of the matter today. If Mr. Davis appeared to be insensitive to the emotional and psychological needs of African Americans, that was a trait common to many of us who shared his southern upbringing. Time has fortunately provided many of us with an opportunity to do penance.

---

** 347 U.S. 483 (1954).

It was a privilege to have had the opportunity to work in depth and at length with Mr. Davis, whom King George V characterized as "a perfect gentleman" when he served as the United States ambassador to the Court of St. James's. I agree with King George. Mr. Davis treated everyone with courtesy, including his adversaries, and exemplified the definition of a "gentleman" attributed to General Robert E. Lee:

> "The forbearing use of power does not only form a touchstone, but the manner in which an individual enjoys certain advantages over others is a test of a true gentleman."

Mr. Davis, who was known for his sartorial correctness in every circumstance, wore formal attire whenever he appeared before the Supreme Court. This included a club coat and striped trousers, dating from his frequent appearances as Solicitor General of the United States. At a time when hats were the fashion for men, he is reported to have offered a ten dollar bill to a young associate whom he encountered hatless on the elevator at 15 Broad Street, with instructions that he should remedy that condition during the lunch hour. When I later served on the North Carolina Court of Appeals, all of the members of the Court wore hats. I find that I am still somewhat inclined to that mode of dress on formal occasions. Perhaps it is a subconscious hangover from my time with Mr. Davis, or perhaps it is a recollection of my father's custom.

Years later I wrote an article about Mr. Davis and his role in the school segregation cases for the *Washington and Lee Law Review*.* There I said, "I knew him as a warm and kindly mentor who, despite his unchallenged stature as the dean of the American bar, was always quick to put me at ease." I can think of no better way in which to describe our relationship.

The fiftieth anniversary of the Supreme Court's school segregation decision, now popularly known as *Brown against the Board of Education*, was widely celebrated in 2004. My role in that celebration was somewhat ambiguous since I had represented what has come to be seen as the wrong side in the South Carolina case. I rode the course of the celebration with what I hope passed for good humor and actually spoke to the subject at a panel discussion at the Levine Museum of the New South in Charlotte. Joseph Delaine, whose father, a minister, had been instrumental in filing the action that became *Briggs v. Elliott,* was also a panelist. It was then that I learned for the first time how the Reverend Delaine had been made to suffer for his role in that contest. I am still seeking to compensate for having failed to recognize the serious plight of African Americans.

In connection with the fiftieth year anniversary, I was also interviewed by National Public Radio legal commentator Nina Totenburg. From about fifteen minutes of tape, she chose only

---

* 52 *W&L L. Rev.* 1679 (1996).

one short sentence to broadcast: my expostulating "Thank God we lost!"

## LEGAL AID ACT

For some time after I returned to Davis Polk, I continued to work on an article I had researched in England on the subject of The British Legal Aid Act. Relatively new legislation, the act's purpose was to provide governmental funding in both civil and criminal cases for those who could not afford a lawyer. My article was designed to describe the program and the cases that had interpreted the provisions of the Act. I finally finished the article in 1952, after many nights of writing into the wee hours, and it was published in the Columbia Law Review under the title "Developments in the British Legal Aid Experiment."*

I first submitted the article to the *Yale Law Review*, from which I received the following letter:

Dear Mr. Thompson:

I regret that we cannot publish your article in the Yale Law Journal. It presents interesting material from the first years of operation, but fails, I think, to tie it in with any of the major problems they were confronted with. [See Comment 59 Yale L. J. 320]. It certainly does not substantiate or conflict with the conclusion which you reach and with which I am frankly in sympathy.

Most sincerely,
/s/ Joseph Goldstein
Article & Book Review Editor

Apparently Yale felt as though the piece it had already published was the definitive treatment. I consoled myself by rationalizing that they could hardly have conceded that a Harvard man should speak the last word on any subject.

Some years later I learned that an English friend, named Everard O'Donnell, who had practiced as a barrister through the 1970s had given up his practice because the fees paid under the Act were not sufficient to enable him to make a satisfactory living at the Bar. Everard migrated to the United States for a time but is now working in Tanzania as chief of chambers for the International Criminal Tribunal for Rwanda.

At about the same time that the Columbia Law Review article was published, the Harvard Law Review commissioned me to review two books: Eric Sachs' "Legal Aid" and Emery Brownell's "Legal Aid in the United States," dealing with the subject of legal aid for the general public in Great Britain and legal aid for the poor in the United States, respectively.** One might say I wrung as much out of my new-found expertise as possible.

---

\* 53 *Columbia L. Rev.* 789 (1953).
\*\* 66 *Harvard L. Rev.* 755 (1953)

One of the most enjoyable aspects of our life in New York City arose out of our friendship with my Davis Polk colleague Edgar Appleby and his wife Allie (Alice Sandra). Edgar was from Oyster Bay, Long Island. His father, Edgar T. Appleby, had owned much of the Columbus Circle real estate that was condemned by the city for the purposes of establishing the Metropolitan Opera House and the New York City Opera. Allie was every inch a lady and one of the finest people we met in New York. She was the granddaughter of Harry P. Davison, who was J.P. Morgan's principal partner until his death in the 1920s. Davison left his "Peacock Point" estate, located on the North Shore of Long Island, to his widow "Goggie." At the time we met the Applebys, Goggie had presided over the family for decades, overseeing the compound from the comfort of her electric car. Hattie and I were fortunate to become frequent visitors.

Edgar may have been a little spoiled. I remember one occasion on which he released the brakes on a parked car in the city so that he could push it forward and make room to park behind it. When he was my office mate, he once sent word to me that he had a cold and would not be coming to work. After he had been absent for several days, one of the partners inquired about the status of a matter Edgar was working on and asked me to find out when he would be returning. When I called his home, a maid answered. I asked to speak to Edgar and was told that he had gone to Nassau to get rid of his cold. I just told the partner that Edgar had been ill and would be in as soon as he got well. I realized then that I was riding in the fast lane.

On more than one occasion Edgar took Hattie and me out on the yacht in which he sometimes commuted to the dock at the foot of Wall Street. He also invited me to play golf at Piping Rock Country Club. I probably shamed him not only with my play but with my tennis shoes as well. We also had occasion to enjoy the Davis Polk annual weekend golf outings at the Rockaway Hunt Club. The golf course overlooked the water on the south shore of Long Island and I doused golf balls on virtually every hole whenever I played there – in my tennis shoes, of course.

Edgar Appleby left Davis Polk in late 1953 and took a position with the White Weld brokerage firm. I later learned that he only stayed at White Weld for a short time because when the firm was doing a secondary issue of Libby Owens stock, it somehow prejudiced his position as a holder of stock in that company. He was given the choice of either selling his stock or resigning his position with the company, a decision that was apparently no contest for him!

Edgar's leaving Davis Polk was the occasion for my acquiring a new office mate – Bill Ketcham, who had recently returned from a leave of absence taken to work with Charles Spofford at NATO. Bill had a remarkable sense of humor. For example, he and David Lindsay, another associate who was Mayor John Lindsay's twin brother, were good friends who particularly enjoyed betting on various facts that were plainly subject to prior research. Bill would say something like "I'll bet you five dollars that in 1850 the population of Albany was greater than the population of Buffalo." "It's a bet," David would respond. On another occasion David would initiate the bet and Bill would accept it. I don't really know if any money ever changed hands, but they apparently trusted each other implicitly.

At about that time I invited three young couples who had recently joined the Davis Polk family to celebrate Hattie's thirtieth birthday by attending a Broadway play that was produced and directed by my erstwhile Syracuse University colleague Paul Crabtree (formerly named Joyce Crabtree) and starred Geraldine Page in the leading role. The couples invited were Edgar and Allie Appleby, Jack and Lane Roemer and Jacques and Lili Leroy, all of whom we especially liked. I bought the tickets, and at the last minute invited the celebrants to have dinner at a downtown restaurant before the play. They all accepted, naturally expecting me to pick up the tab for dinner as well. Somehow, that possibility had not occurred to me at the time. I summoned the resources to pay the bill by raiding Hattie's pocketbook, but for the next week or so we bought all of our groceries at Bergdorf Goodman where we were able to charge them. We had never before enjoyed such gourmet delicacies at our dinner table!

Hattie's sorority sister Sally Bennett Freeman called in 1953 to say that a place on her husband's grandmother's estate on the Hudson River was available for rent if we were interested. Were we ever! It was an old brick two-bedroom coach house with a deck overlooking an almost pastoral setting. The grandmother was Mrs. George W. Perkins who was the widow of another J.P. Morgan partner. Early in the twentieth century Perkins was one of those magnates who caught the train from his compound on the Hudson River when he went to work on Wall Street each morning. Like Harry Davison, he had died in the '20s but his widow carried on there for many years.

Sally's husband John Wheelock Freeman had been raised in a house on the compound. That house had recently been leased or sold to the British government as the residence of the British ambassador to the United Nations, Sir Gladwyn Jebb. Sally and John lived in a game house that housed the billiard room and two bowling alleys and was connected to the main house by an underground tunnel.

Hattie and I leased the coach house and settled in to our new neighborhood. Before long, we learned that Walter and Sue Blum, who lived nearby in Riverdale and were planning to move to the

Azores where Walter was being transferred on a military assignment, were looking for a good home for their four year old collie. "Belle Arbor's Duke of Swannanoah," Duke for short, was the registered offspring of several champion collies. Our laundry route man told the Blum's about our coach house and its pastoral setting so they invited us to come over to see them and meet Duke. We fell in love with Duke at first sight. He was so well trained that when they brought him to our house and had him lie down in our living room we couldn't persuade him to get up until they came back and taught us the proper commands. Shortly after Duke came to live with us, I was showing his pedigree chart to some neighborhood children and explaining that his ancestors had been champions. "Were they people?" one of the children asked. Apparently I impressed them more than I meant to do.

## THE QUANDARY

Hattie and I visited my mother in Charlotte on summer vacations during the years we were at Davis Polk and on one such visit in August 1954, Joe Grier invited me to move to Charlotte and rejoin Taliaferro, Clarkson and Grier. Francis Clarkson had recently been appointed a Superior Court Judge, so Joe felt as though there was a place for me. He pointed out that if I ever intended to return to Charlotte this was a good time to do it. Francis Parker and Bill Poe, both of whom I had met and regarded very highly, had joined the firm since I worked there in the summer of 1949, circumstances which made the offer all the more attractive.

When we returned to New York, Hattie and I wrestled with the decision for several weeks. Despite having already scheduled a debut recital at Carnegie Recital Hall for 1955, Hattie was prepared to do whatever I wanted. She had been working on a program for some time with her then coach Richard McClanahan, who was the piano teacher at Riverdale School for Boys.

I became almost paralyzed on the subject, and to help with the decision we made two lists, one of points in favor of staying in New York and the other of points in favor of moving to Charlotte. Although we were greatly enjoying the excitement of life in New York and my work at Davis Polk, I had a nagging feeling that Charlotte might afford *in situ* advantages for me and for the family over the long run. Our first son, Sydnor III had been born in May of that year at New York Hospital and we were about to outgrow the coach house. Our neighbor Kim Hartsell had driven Hattie to the hospital through New York traffic and Sydnor was born only nine minutes after they arrived. I was also troubled by the fact that I had no assurance of becoming a partner at Davis Polk - and I knew I wouldn't be satisfied with anything less.

The two lists came out about even and we still couldn't make a decision. Finally when I felt it was absolutely necessary to give Joe an answer, I suggested to Hattie that we should toss a coin. Believe it or not, we did! And that toss determined that we should stay in New York. I called Joe and told him that we greatly appreciated the offer but that we were not prepared to move at that time. He was quite pleasant about it and said that I should let him know if we ever changed our minds.

The moment I hung up the telephone, I had an overwhelming feeling that I had made a mistake. I turned to Hattie and said, "Honey, I think I made the wrong decision!" "You're kidding!," she exclaimed, "Well, then call him back!" So I called Joe back right away and he told me to come on. He must have had some reservations about having invited me after that performance, but perhaps he realized that our life in New York had been too fascinating to give up without a struggle. No doubt the Southern culture of my youth and heritage drew me back to my roots more than I understood at the time. The fact that Mother lived in Charlotte may also have been something of a determining factor. As it developed, I was able to visit her nearly every day over the next thirty years, until her death in 1985. I am grateful for that time. The truth is, I often imposed upon her for lunch and drifted off to sleep on her couch to the sound of our favorite Brahms piano concerto.

I firmly believe that Hattie's special appreciation of Elizabeth and Eddie Clarkson also played a part in her willingness to make the change. In any case, I now have no doubt that we made the right decision. But what fun we had in New York!

Mother
Helen Layne Thompson

Daddy
Charles William Sydnor Thompson

Sydnor at 3 1/2 years

Daddy as a law student at
Washington & Lee University

The wire section of C Battery,
879th Field Artillery Battalion near the
Village of Buschem, Germany
(Sydnor's head is barely visible on the right in
the back seat)

Sydnor and John Melanson
at Camp Shelby, MS

Ian Redhead and George Poston performing in
the Pirates of Penzance at St. Andrews
University, wearing Sydnor's GI medals

Hattie and Sydnor at the front
steps of the Chi Omega Sorority
at Syracuse University during
their courtship

John W. Davis attired to appear in the United States Supreme Court on behalf of the steel companies in 1952

Hattie and Sydnor aboard Warren Eginton's "Mystic Whaler" in New York Harbor, celebrating Hattie's birthday with our Davis Polk colleagues in 2003.

(l. to r.) Stuart Marks, Warren Eginton, Hazard Gillespie, Bill Ketcham, and Nelson Adams at Bill Ketcham's Brook Club in New York City in 2003

Hattie and children posing in front of a flower kiosk in Salzburg, Austria in 1966

Sydnor presiding at the 100th Anniversary celebration of the 1884 founding of our law firm and Governor Jim Hunt, who was the principal speaker

Hattie and Sydnor with Governor Terry Sanford in New Bern, NC in 1986 when the Governor was campaigning for the U.S. Senate

The principals in Grier, Parker, Poe and Thompson at the
100th Anniversary celebration of the 1884 founding of the law firm.

Eddie and Elizabeth
Clarkson and Cama
and Judge Clarkson at
the presentation of the
portrait of N.C.
Supreme Court Justice
Herriot Clarkson in
1984

Louise and Mark
Bernstein, Hattie and
Sydnor at a recent law
firm celebration

Hattie and Sydnor in period costumes for the 100th Anniversary of the founding of the N.C. Bar Association

Hattie at the piano at the height of her career as a concert pianist

Sydnor in the company of Francis Parker and Ray Farris at the time of his induction as president of the Mecklenburg County Bar Association in 1990

Sydnor in the company of (l.to r.) Bishop and Ms. Earl Hunt, Bishop Bevel Jones, and Bishop William Cannon in Nairobi, Kenya at the 1986 World Methodist Conference

Hattie and Sydnor's children, children's spouses and grandchildren at the wedding of Brenny and Karen Parker in 2004.

The North Carolina Court of Appeals in session in 1994

(l. to r.) Front row: Jack Cozort, Clifton Johnson, Chief Judge Gerald Arnold, Sid Eagles and Bob Orr

(l. to r.) Rear row: Joe Johns, John Martin, Jack Lewis, Jim Wynn, Eddie Green, Betsy McCrodden and Sydnor

Hattie and Sydnor's grandchildren

Hattie and Sydnor
with Senator John Edwards

Hattie and Sydnor
with Governor Mike Easley

The House of the Seven Gables
on Brandon Road after a snowstorm

Blundeston Hall in the Village of Blundeston, Suffolk County, England, also known as "Sydnors" from 1570 through 1832

Richard Mitchell Sydnor
Sydnor's great-great
grandfather

Dr. Charles William Sydnor
Sydnor's great grandfather

Bessie Love Sydnor Thompson
("Nanny")
Sydnor's grandmother

# CHAPTER 16
## GETTING SETTLED IN CHARLOTTE

We moved to Charlotte in September 1954. Our friend Eddie Clarkson had recently built a three bedroom ranch-style spec house in southeast Charlotte on a farm that had once belonged to the Reverend Billy Graham's family. The house was a part of a real estate venture called the "Parade of Homes," in which twenty builders each constructed a house that he was prepared to duplicate on another site for anyone who might like it. We bought Eddie's house sight unseen because it was the only one that he had for sale at the time. Eddie and Elizabeth were dear friends by any measure, and later served as godparents to three of our children.

Duke moved with us, of course, and was the perfect companion to our family until he died of cancer at eleven years of age. He was the only dog we have ever owned who was properly trained, which says more about the master, of course, than it does about the dogs.

Shortly after we moved to Charlotte, Eddie and Elizabeth began inviting us with some frequency for dinner at Wing Haven. Hattie's mother was always included when she was staying with us, which soon became quite often. One evening at dinner, Elizabeth remarked that the dinner napkins on which her initials had been embroidered were wearing out. Mother Line immediately volunteered to embroider new napkins and, once she started, worked day and night until the project was completed. On another evening the conversation turned to music, as was often the case, and Eddie remarked "All I can remember about music is the lines and spaces – a, e, i, o and u." The ladies were thrown into a fit of convulsions, of course, at Eddie's expense.

As I have said, Hattie's New York debut, to be held at Carnegie Recital Hall in April 1955, had been scheduled before we left that city. After we moved to Charlotte, she continued to prepare her program, which was presented in Carlisle under the auspices of the Carlisle Musical Arts Center before the appointed date in New York. The proceeds of the Carlisle concert went to a scholarship fund there. When we drove to New York in April, we ran into the remnant of a hurricane on the New Jersey Turnpike. Despite the weather, Hattie's recital was a great success. The *New York Times* critic Harold C. Schonberg wrote: "Harriette Line is an undoubtedly talented musician who plays clearly and delicately." All of her hard work had come to fruition, and now she had the satisfaction of knowing that she had passed muster with one of the most outstanding music critics in America.

A number of our New York friends attended, and John and Sally Freeman entertained those concert goers who could make their way to their Riverdale home. One of their bowling alleys had been raised to make a 65 foot buffet table, which was laden with food and drink. Hattie had played one of John's compositions on her program. (Harold Schonberg called it "an interesting trifle.") John has proven to be something of a Renaissance man: in addition to composing music, he has written a fascinating coffee table book about sports cars, and he eventually became an editor of Opera News, from which he is now retired. I never was able to entice John to come to Charlotte to see a Charlotte Opera production.

Soon after the New York concert, Hattie performed at the grand opening of the new Ovens Auditorium in Charlotte. She also played a program for the annual meeting of the Charlotte Music Club. Having made her mark in Charlotte's music community, Hattie now had reason to believe that her music career might in time extend well beyond the State of North Carolina. In fact, favorable reviews of her Carnegie Hall concert drew the attention of a New York agent named Max Wollheim who represented her for several years.

Hattie took time out from her career as a concert pianist to have our third child, Harriet Brenneman Line Thompson, on September 27, 1956. The only obstetrician in Charlotte who was acquainted with the practice of natural childbirth was Kingsley McDonald, who was recommended by our friend Nancy Howe. (He told us later that he once called Nancy at home on the evening after he had delivered her baby - just to make sure she was all right. She apologized for being unable to talk because she was entertaining some friends at dinner!) McDonald was also interested in hypnosis as a means of expediting natural childbirth, and Hattie agreed to try it. When he suggested to her that she was holding two large buckets of water, her arms did become quite heavy. When he told her that she was numb from the waist down, however, she did not respond. They concluded that hypnosis was not in the cards for Hattie.

She continued preparing for a delivery by natural childbirth, of course, and that's how Harriet was born. (I insisted that she be named for Hattie.) McDonald was late in arriving at the hospital on B-Day and Hattie held on for quite a while until he arrived, despite being assured by his nurse that she had "caught" many babies.

## FINDING A CHURCH HOME

Shortly after we moved to Charlotte, Hattie began to look for a church home for our family. While we were in Riverdale we had attended a Presbyterian Church, but I had been a Methodist all my life and she had been a Lutheran. Over the next few months Hattie spent Sunday mornings visiting a number of churches of both denominations while I did some light gardening. Eventually Hattie reported that she wanted me to visit Myers Park United Methodist Church. The Church had been organized in 1925 with 151 members. The sanctuary was built in 1930 and by 1955 there were 1,941 members. On her visit, Hattie had been utterly captivated by

Dr. Chesley C. Herbert, the senior minister. I attended services the next Sunday and was equally impressed. Within a week, Dr. Herbert visited us in our home on Murrayhill Road. He entertained the children with a mouse that he made by folding his handkerchief. They too were soon captivated.

After that visit, Hattie made it clear to me that she wanted to join Myers Park Methodist. I had some reservations, as I wasn't at all sure that I could pass the doctrinal test. Upon her urging, I made an appointment with Dr. Herbert and explained my concern. He told me that all I had to do was accept Jesus Christ as my savior and agree to support the church with my presence, my service and my gifts. On the strength of that interview, I transferred my letter from Fort Hill Methodist in Lynchburg to Myers Park. At the same time Hattie transferred her membership from the First Lutheran Church in Carlisle. Thus we established our church home for the remainder of our lives - or perhaps for eternity, as we have reserved a niche in the Myers Park Methodist columbarium.

Shortly after we joined the church, we made arrangements for our son Sydnor, who was still less than a year old, to be baptized. By coincidence another church member, Nancy Akers, had recently brought some water home from the Jordan River in Israel. Her grandson Jodi Akers and Sydnor were both baptized with that water. Time would tell that in Sydnor's case the baptism "took."

## THE OWNBEY CLASS

When we first joined Myers Park, Dr. Richard L. Ownbey was acting as minister emeritus, having retired from active ministry in 1946 at seventy-four years of age. He had served as senior minister of the church from 1933 to 1941 and was dearly loved. Upon his retirement, the Myers Park congregation bought him a house near the church and placed a plaque at the church describing him as "Gracious Pastor – Fearless Preacher – Gifted Author." By coincidence, Dr. Ownbey's wife Pauline was a Sydnor from Richmond, Virginia and thereby a sixth cousin of mine. They had met in 1904 in Wilkesboro, NC where he was serving as pastor.

A Sunday School class named for Dr. Ownbey had recently been organized at the church and within a few weeks of our visiting the class Carl and Kathy Hubbard, who were then the Ownbey Class presidents, came to see us. As they were leaving, Carl surprised us by asking "By the way, would you be willing to serve as class presidents for the coming year?" Apparently there weren't many candidates for the office since there were only about a dozen couples in the class. Hattie and I accepted their challenge. For the next twenty-five years, four class members took turns as teachers of the class, each responsible for one Sunday a month. They were Lou Bledsoe, Ace Walker, Bill Webb, and I. Paul Guthery also taught whenever there was a fifth Sunday in the month. We called ourselves the

"Pharisees," and often met for lunch to discuss a book we were planning to teach. One of our favorite authors was Dietrich Bonhoeffer, the German Protestant martyr, and we read his *Cost of Discipleship*, *Ethics* and *Letters and Papers from Prison*. About twenty years ago we increased the number of teachers and there are now some ten or twelve members who take turns leading the discussion. Unfortunately, the old-time Pharisees have not met in years.

Today, the Ownbey Class remains unique in its emphasis upon open discussion and use of the Socratic method of teaching. A curriculum committee selects the courses of study, which often range far a-field from the regular Methodist curriculum. The class recently celebrated its 50th Anniversary and I enjoyed the privilege of leading the attendees in reminiscing about the early years. Hattie still plays the piano for the Ownbey Class every Sunday when she is in town. One Sunday Zeb Watkins, who was in charge of music for the Luther Snyder Bible Class, asked Hattie to play for them as part of a dedication ceremony for a new piano the class had recently acquired. When she asked how long she should play, Zeb asked "How long is a tune?" She had considered playing a Chopin Ballade so she replied "About ten minutes." After a long pause, Zeb said "Well, I suppose I could call the members and ask them to come early." Hattie decided to play a three minute Chopin Etude instead.

There was a special irony in our having chosen Myers Park Methodist Church on the strength of Dr. Herbert's being the minister: shortly after we joined the church, he was moved to High Point to provide the leadership to build the new Wesley Memorial Church. We continued to see a great deal of him and his wife Libba, however, because he later moved back to Charlotte to become Bishop Hunt's administrative assistant. Years later I read some verses at his retirement dinner:

### A Toast to a Retiring Pilgrim – Chesley Herbert

I

Tonight our pilgrims gather for an orgy
to toast (with juice) a member of the clergy,
A man to whom the call came loud and clear,
who never from the narrow gate did veer,
except to hairline crack the Golden Rule
mistreating his poor wife at April Fool.
And yet our hero met his match in Libba,
nor merely as a devilish April fibber.
Her charm, transfused to Libba and to Trudge,
has opened doors that Ches could never budge.

II

For two score years our hero's held the key
to churches known afar o'er land and sea.
But what is most revealing to impart
is this – he's held the key to every heart
that's crossed his path from Manteo to Murphy
A man for others as befits Christ's serf – he.

So lift again your juice of red tomato
to honor God and man's inamorato
For truly Chesley Herbert came the closest
of all to Methodist apotheosis.

Ches had a marvelous sense of humor. In his last illness, he asked two fellow-clergymen who were visiting him to sit on opposite sides of his bed. "I want to die as my Lord did," he said, "between two thieves."

## LAME DUCK LAWYER

Because we moved to Charlotte in the month of September, I was not eligible to take the North Carolina Bar exam the following August, which was when it was next offered. Bar rules required that applicants live in North Carolina for a full year before being permitted to take the exam. That meant I would not qualify until August 1956, twenty-three months after I moved to Charlotte. Practicing in North Carolina without taking the exam was not an option as the rules of comity required five years of practice in New York and I had significantly less than that.

Joe Grier offered to go with me to visit the members of the Board of Law Examiners in the hope that they might waive the residence requirement and allow me to take the exam in August. Together we visited Judge Varser in Lumberton and Tom Leath in Laurinburg, by which time it became evident that no waiver would be forthcoming. As a result, I signed Joe Grier's name to every instrument I drafted for the next two years. When Joe's fifty years at the Bar were celebrated at a Bar luncheon in 1991, he did me the honor of asking me to speak for him. I confess that I remarked at that time that those instruments were the best legal documents to which Joe's signature was ever affixed. He had the good grace to laugh heartily.

I was finally admitted to the North Carolina Bar in 1956. I prepared for the examination by studying notes that Keith Smith Green had taken several years earlier in Claude Love's Bar Review Course and generously made available to me. Within a few weeks of my admission to the Mecklenburg Bar I was called upon to appear before Judge Basil Boyd in the Recorders Court on behalf of a client of the firm who was charged with a misdemeanor. Perhaps because he realized that this was my first appearance in his court, Judge Boyd made a point of telling me that my argument was as good as any he had ever heard, whereupon he found my client guilty!

## THE TRIUMVIRATE

In the late 1950s two men who would soon become my close friends came to Charlotte to practice law. The first, Mark Bernstein, visited our offices shortly after graduating from Yale Law School in 1957. Our firm was not in a position to hire another associate, so I suggested to Mark that he should talk to the Frank Kennedy firm. Kennedy's firm had recently merged with the firm of Covington and Lobdell, and they hired Mark on the spot. He worked there for several years until moving uptown to form a new firm with Myles Haynes, William E. "Dub" Graham and Lloyd Baucom. I am sure the Kennedy firm subsequently regretted letting him get away.

Mark and I crossed swords in court on one occasion when he represented a dry cleaning establishment for whom our client had formerly worked as a route salesman. Our client was in apparent violation of a covenant not to compete contained in his employment contract. Judge Harry Martin, then a Superior Court Judge (he later served on the North Carolina Supreme Court), heard the matter and ruled in our favor. That fact has produced much banter between Mark and me over the years, including his tongue-in-cheek assertion that his client wanted him to hire me to assist him in another case after that.

Clarence "Ace" Walker had gone to New York from Duke Law School. He eventually chose to take "the road less traveled," as I had done, and moved to Charlotte in 1959 to join the same Kennedy firm that had hired Mark. Ace has been a great strength to them, specializing in a public utility practice. He was eventually elected president of the North Carolina Bar Association. We had a great deal in common and he and Mark and I soon became fast friends, working together for various civic organizations – most notably the Democratic Party and the Charlotte Symphony Orchestra Society.

## INTRODUCTION TO NORTH CAROLINA POLITICS

While it is true that I attended a couple of meetings of the Young Republican Club in New York with some of my Davis Polk colleagues, I never felt comfortable because I often disagreed with the point of view of the speakers. I am a Democrat by inheritance, but more importantly, I am a Democrat by conviction. I favor the Democratic Party because, in my view, it is the party whose principles of government better serve the interests and welfare of the entire citizenry. I voted for Harry Truman when I cast my first presidential ballot in 1948 and have strayed from the Democratic ticket in a presidential election only once since then, under circumstances that I prefer to leave under cover of discreet silence.

I can understand how one might subscribe to the ideological views reflected in the Republican Party platform and thus support Republican candidates. For a time until it disbanded, I attended meetings of a unique organization of North Carolinians – both Democrats and Republicans – which called itself the "Society of Fools." Members traveled across the state to hear speeches that were of political interest to both parties, and we all got along fine. It was fashioned after the model of "The Other Club," which was a select group of active Conservatives and Liberals established in England in the 1920s, and to which Winston Churchill remained loyal all of his life. In this day of bitter partisanship, I miss that stimulating civil discourse. However, I do not understand how anyone acquainted

111

with the issues raised by the major parties could choose to "vote for the man (or woman)" as though he or she were running in a vacuum. I have many friends who say they do just that, but in my opinion the issues involved in an election are too important to be resolved in what amounts to a high school-like popularity contest.

End of sermon.

My friend, and fellow Democrat, John P. Kennedy, Jr. ran for the North Carolina House of Representatives in the summer of 1958. His was the first campaign in which the triumvirate, Bernstein, Walker and I, joined political forces and John became our champion. In a door-to-door, "grass roots" campaign a dozen or so volunteers went out after work that summer, canvassing targeted neighborhoods until dark. Afterward, we met at someone's home for a spaghetti supper. That method worked well and John was elected. Two years later he ran again, conducting the same kind of campaign and with the same result.

## GERRYMANDERING THE NINTH CONGRESSIONAL

The North Carolina legislature, which was controlled by the Democratic Party, revised the boundaries of the Ninth Congressional District in 1962, based upon the 1960 census. In an effort to unseat Republican Congressman Charles Raper Jonas, who by that time had been elected five times, the legislature drew the boundaries of the Ninth District to include Anson County where another incumbent Congressman Democrat Paul Kitchin lived. Shaped like a dragon, the new district extended all the way from Lincoln County, Congressman Jonas' home, east through Mecklenburg County to Moore and Lee Counties.

Seeing an opportunity for a Mecklenburg County native to make a difference in the Democratic primary, John P. Kennedy decided to challenge Paul Kitchin. I enthusiastically supported his decision and agreed to serve as his campaign manager. Charlie Smith, who had been serving in the public relations department of First Union Bank, was hired as the head of John's paid staff. John and I spent a great deal of time campaigning up and down the length and breadth of the newly-formed Ninth District. In that pursuit we visited Richmond County to seek the support of two key Democrats: Sheriff Raymond Goodman and North Carolina Board of Transportation member L. C. "Elsie" Webb. We located Mr. Webb in the back seat of a big black Cadillac parked in a square in the center of town, which was where he usually conducted business. Both Sheriff Goodman and Mr. Webb agreed to help John, who went on to carry Richmond County. We apparently failed to identify enough "back seats" in other counties, however, because John lost the primary district-wide.

## SCHOOL BOARD POLITICS

With the encouragement of Governor Luther Hodges, the North Carolina legislature began to consider a means by which the impact of *Brown v. The Board of Education* might be softened in local schools. The resultant "Pearsall Plan," so named for the legislator who proposed it, contemplated that the school board would make the initial assignment of the student to a particular school and that the student might then request a transfer if he was not satisfied. Although several prominent leaders in the state, including Senator Irving Carlyle of Winston-Salem, opposed this suggestion, the Pearsall Plan was nevertheless enacted by the state legislature.

During the time the matter was being considered, Kitty Huffman invited me to speak on that subject to an ecumenical organization called Church Women United at Dilworth United Methodist Church. I took the position that the Pearsall Plan was not the answer and that it was futile for the state to take a measure that was so blatantly designed to defeat the purpose of the United States Supreme Court's decision. The Plan was eventually held unconstitutional.

## THE CHARLOTTE SYMPHONY ORCHESTRA

In addition to church and politics, another of our early interests was the local symphony orchestra. The Charlotte Symphony Board of Directors resigned en masse in 1957 and the orchestra effectively disbanded. The crisis arose out of a serious financial predicament that was exacerbated by a dispute between the orchestra members and its conductor James Christian Pfohl. In an effort to save the Symphony, the Charlotte Chamber of Commerce assumed responsibility for appointing a new board. At the suggestion of my friend John P. Kennedy, Chamber President Tom Robinson appointed me to the new board. Bud Coira, also a lawyer, was named president.

One of the first actions of the new board was to retain the services of Esther Waltenberger, who had been serving as the orchestra's manager when the old board disbanded. Esther was a dedicated devotee of good music and she willingly accepted our offer despite a substantial reduction in her salary which had already been less than adequate.

Due to the financial crisis, my assignment that first year was to contact the Symphony's creditors and negotiate a compromise of the obligations due them. The most difficult task facing the board, however, was to determine how to stage concerts for the balance of the 1957-1958 season without the necessary funds. The members of the orchestra came to our immediate rescue by agreeing to donate their services for a benefit concert. Esther, who had worked at Converse College in Spartanburg, South Carolina before coming to Charlotte, suggested that we talk to Henry Janiec, a faculty member at Converse, about conducting the orchestra. He agreed and we promptly hired him for the evening. The concert was a great public relations gesture and attracted a full house, raising substantial funds for the orchestra.

At the same time, every board member was enlisted in a campaign to raise funds in the community. I went to see W. Reynolds "Rennie" Cuthbertson who was the president of City Savings Bank. After I made my spiel on behalf of the Orchestra, he immediately replied that he himself was in the process of raising funds for his favorite charity, the Methodist Home, and asked if I might be willing to make a contribution to that worthy cause. Through the years I have become accustomed to having people expect a reciprocal back rub in matters of that kind, but that was the only time it was put so directly as a *quid pro quo*. In retrospect, I think Mr. Cuthbertson was having a little fun with a youngster who was new to the community and presuming on his time as a busy bank president.

On a similar mission, John P. Kennedy and I called upon Mrs. W.S.O'B. Robinson, the widow of the Duke Power General Counsel, at her home in Myers Park. We were met at the door by the butler and ushered into the parlor where an elaborate silver tea service awaited us. Mrs. Robinson soon floated down the stairs in a blue chiffon gown and served tea. After an appropriate exchange of pleasantries, we presented our case on behalf of the Symphony, whereupon Mrs. Robinson explained that although she would love to help us, "the sheriff" was at her door. By that she meant that creditors had levied on her property – which was a light-hearted way of expressing her lack of interest in our project. Suffice it to say, neither John nor I saw the sheriff.

The following year, I was elected to succeed Bud Coira as president of the Symphony board. We were fortunate in retaining Henry Janiec as our conductor and Esther Waltenberger as our manager throughout the three years in which I held that office. Both of them were absolutely dedicated to the Orchestra and were significant factors in its recovery. One of our first challenges was to persuade the recording industry's Trust Fund for the Performing Arts to pay the orchestra members' fees for the first concert of the 1958-59 season. They agreed, but in accordance with the requirements of the Trust Fund the concert was free to the public. Hattie and I entertained Samuel Rosenbaum, the president of the Fund and his wife, Edna Phillips, who was the principal oboist with the Philadelphia Orchestra, when they came to Charlotte to attend the concert.

Later that year, the Orchestra presented Beethoven's Ninth Symphony with Metropolitan Opera tenor John Alexander performing as a soloist. We were able to engage Alexander at a bargain fee because he was related to the Alexander family that had been instrumental in founding the City of Charlotte in the eighteenth century. Due to the Symphony's limited funds, he stayed with Hattie and me on the weekend of the performance. At breakfast the morning after the concert I brought the *Charlotte Observer* to the table to read the review with every confidence that John would be favorably treated. Much to my surprise, the *Charlotte Observer* critic actually panned his performance! John took the news with good grace.

Hattie and I took John to St. Mark's Lutheran Church on Sunday morning where, because we were late in arriving, we were seated at the back of the balcony. When the congregation began singing the first hymn, nearly every head in the sanctuary turned to see who was singing in such magnificent tones from the balcony. Thus did John deliver a telling rebuttal to the music critic's assessment of his talent.

I served as president of the Charlotte Symphony until 1961 when I was succeeded by Dr. John Stuart Gaul. That spring we staged the first Symphony Ball – on the theme "A Night in Venice." The Charlottetown Mall, now Mid-Town Mall, had just opened for business so we chose that as the venue. Ball chair Chris Stoll and subcommittee chair Helen Williams engaged Jack Pentes to decorate each of the inside avenues. It was a massive undertaking and Pentes did a superb job. Stuart and I both risked our limbs by climbing frail lattice-work to mount a large CHARLOTTE SYMPHONY banner over the stairway. Governor Terry Sanford was our guest of honor.

## THE HOUSE OF THE SEVEN GABLES

Hattie and I often visited our friends Robert E. E. (Bobby) and Lorna Booker on Brandon Road in Myers Park, just around the corner from Myers Park United Methodist Church. During a visit in 1958, we could not help but note that a house across the street from the Bookers was for sale. Within a short time we made an offer which was accepted some months later. I soon dubbed it the "House of the Seven Gables" because it has the same number of gables as the subject of Nathaniel Hawthorne's classic novel. Originally constructed of dull yellow brick, the house bore some resemblance to the "gloomy and desolate" appearance of that fictional house. Upon learning that the children asked anyone who drove them home to let them off at the corner, we brightened the exterior by painting the brick a pale shade of aqua. In connection with an appraisal, a realtor recently characterized the house's architecture as "unknown." Whatever architectural style it is and whatever color it has been painted over the years, our home suits us to a "T." For the last forty-six years, the house and the neighborhood have both satisfied our every domiciliary need.

## CHARLOTTE COUNTRY CLUB

Several years after moving to Charlotte, I joined the Charlotte Country Club, which had been organized in 1910. At that time women enjoyed the advantages of membership only in their capacity as wives of members. (That anomaly has since been corrected.) Hattie and I attended various social functions at the club and at the annual Easter ball we met Rem and Gwen Rogers, who soon became our close friends. Gwen, a lovely lady by any standard, was active in the North Carolina schools' "Green Circle" program at the time, fighting to combat racial discrimination. Rem, a likeable Albemarle native who was a dead ringer for Hollywood's Lee Marvin, managed Henderson Belk's Volkswagen dealership in Charlotte until the late '60s when he opened a Porsche dealership on East Independence Boulevard under the name "Autohaus Charlotte." I represented the company until Rem died, too young, from a heart attack.

About twenty years ago, the media made an issue of the fact that there were no African Americans among the members of the club. In fact, *Charlotte Observer* publisher Rolfe Neill resigned from the club on that account. The situation was not amended until the late 1990s when I had the opportunity to work with the Robinson, Bradshaw and Hinson law firm in support of the admission of their African American partner, Frank Emory. There are still no Jewish members, although I have undertaken to interest several of my friends in filing an application.

For the past forty years, the Charlotte Club has also been the site of our family's tennis exploits. These days, my Saturday doubles group often includes Paul Bell, Dick Ferguson, Stuart Gaul, Alex Josephs, Chuck Kirby, Clarence Willard and occasionally Norris Preyer. Although we average eighty-three years of age, we defer to no one when it comes to enthusiasm for Henry VIII's favorite sport. When I observed a notice of the annual Club tournament listing "75 and older doubles" as one of the age categories, I asked Bill Francis, the tennis pro, why he had not also listed a category for 75 and older singles. Bill replied "Men 75 years old don't play singles." Nevertheless, he offered to create that category should I identify an opponent. I did and he did, and I am glad to report that my desk now boasts a pen and pencil set emblazoned with the words "Charlotte Country Club Men's 75 and Over Singles Winner 2002."

# CHAPTER 17
## PRACTICING LAW IN CHARLOTTE

What follows is an account of several matters I handled during my early years of practice in North Carolina. I believe they fairly reflect the nature of the practice of civil law in Charlotte at that time.

### THE BONNIE BRAE GOLF COURSE

Because of my experience with Mr. Davis in the school segregation cases, I had hardly arrived in Charlotte before I was contacted by John Shaw, the attorney for the City of Charlotte. John retained me to assist him in representing the Charlotte Park and Recreation Commission in a case challenging segregation on a municipal golf course. When blacks undertook to play on the Bonnie Brae Golf Course in Revolution Park, the Commission sought a declaratory judgment as to whether allowing such action would cause the title to the park to revert to the persons who had donated the land to the city subject to a "whites only" reverter clause. The question before the court was whether the Park Commission would lose the park altogether if blacks were allowed to play there. Superior Court Judge George B. Patton held that, while the reverter clause would ordinarily have caused the title to the property to revert to the original donors, the fact that the city had no other golf course on which blacks might play meant that giving effect to the reverter clause would violate the Fourteenth Amendment to the United States Constitution. For that reason the title would not revert to the donors in this case.

In an opinion by Justice Hunt Parker\*, the North Carolina Supreme Court affirmed the judgment of the trial court. From that time, blacks were admitted to play golf and swim at Revolution Park. Presumably if the case were decided today, the result would be the same, whether or not the city provided separate golf courses.

I drove to Raleigh with John Shaw for appearances in the North Carolina Supreme Court several times during the late '50s and early '60s on the *Bonnie Brae* case and several others. On each such occasion John stopped at a country church off Highway 64 where we enjoyed a small libation of Tennessee sourmash at a spring in the churchyard. It was a regular ceremony with him and I readily joined him in it. Unfortunately, I have not been able to find the churchyard since John died.

### SPEEDWAY MIDWIFERY

Two new clients arrived in our office in the fall of 1958 insisting that they had known nothing of the United States Securities Exchange Commission (SEC) requirement that issues of shares of

---

\* *Charlotte Park & Recreation Commission v. Osmond Barringer, et al.*, 242 N.C. 311 (1955).

stock must be approved by that Commission before being offered on the public radio. My partner Joe Grier and I were retained by Bruton Smith and Curtis Turner, the latter a noted stock car race driver, to represent them in trying to persuade the SEC to lift the Stop Order it had issued against them so that they could resume sale of stock in the newly organized Charlotte Motor Speedway. We immediately set to work to prepare a prospectus and the appropriate documents for filing with the Commission in Washington, DC.

Though Joe was their principal contact with the firm, most of the work on the registration of the securities fell to me because I had done such work at Davis Polk. I worked closely with both men in undertaking to extricate them from what had been a serious legal blunder. As the SEC requires that any setbacks to a project be reported, I prevailed upon them to affix a new label to their prospectus practically every time it rained. They were contrite and cooperated fully in undertaking to repair their position with the SEC. The stop order was eventually lifted and they again began to sell their stock, which soon became highly marketable.

The most interesting aspect of representing Curtis and Bruton was assisting them in the various crises that arose through the course of the construction of the speedway, right up until the running of the first race. Curtis in particular was an extraordinarily colorful character and representing him was sometimes like trying to put socks on an octopus. He was a unique individual who drew people to him like bees to a honey pot, including numbers of admiring women. Among other triumphs, he won the Southern 500 at Darlington in 1956. (That race was memorialized by a "collector's edition" scale model Chevrolet numbered "99," which a friend gave me some years ago.) A recent *Charlotte Observer* article suggesting a list of the first ten race drivers who should be elected to a proposed NASCAR Hall of Fame included Curtis Turner "because of Robert Edelstein's biography of Turner, or because for years Lowe's Motor Speedway President Humpy Wheeler has said Turner is the greatest driver he ever saw."

Some of the sub-contractors with whom we dealt were also quite interesting. For example, the Speedway engaged W. Owen Flowe to level the land on which the track was to be built, a task that was made more difficult by large deposits of rock. At one point I was asked to meet Mr. Flowe at the Speedway in order to negotiate the cost of removing the rock. He drove me around the track in his automobile to show me the problem first hand, and in the course of the drive I noticed a huge dent in the top of the dashboard. When I asked how it had happened, Mr. Flowe, who must have weighed over 400 pounds, explained that he had once put his arm on the dashboard to shift his weight. "They don't make cars like they used to," he said.

As of May 1959 construction was still considerably behind schedule and it appeared that the track might not be ready in time for the first World 600 race. Money was tight and some of the creditors were threatening to stop work. Late on the Friday prior to the Sunday opening, I received a Mayday phone call from Curtis asking me to come to the track right away because one of the subcontractors had quit work. My partner Francis Parker and I arrived to find Curtis conferring with the paving subcontractor named Propst and Propst's Concord attorney, Eugene Bost. Propst, who had been working overtime to finish on schedule, quit paving the track because he had not been paid in accordance with his contract. His equipment remained parked in the middle of the track. Francis and I spent several hours negotiating a plan for Propst to finish the work with some reasonable assurance of being paid.

As we were about to leave, Charlotte lawyer Walter Benson drove up with the Cabarrus County sheriff. Benson had filed suit against the Speedway in Mecklenburg County and obtained an order of attachment on the premises for nonpayment of an obligation due to another creditor. The order of attachment called for the Speedway to post a $20,000 bond in order to avoid being closed down. By that time it was nearly 4:45 p.m. and we were all well aware that the clerk's office closed at five. We called "Judge" Lester Wolfe, the Mecklenburg County Clerk of Court, who agreed to wait for us to get to his office in order to post the bond necessary to dismiss the order of attachment.

Curtis told us that he would meet us in the clerk's office in about an hour, whereupon Francis and I left for Charlotte. As we were driving back, Curtis passed us on Highway 29 at a speed not unlike that at which he usually traveled on the race track. Arriving at the clerk's office, however, Francis and I found that Curtis was not yet there. A few minutes later, he came puffing and blowing into the clerk's office with a shoebox under his arm. We sat in wonder while Judge Wolfe opened the box and counted out exactly $20,000.00 in cash. As we were leaving, Francis asked Curtis where he had gotten all of that money in such a hurry. With his usual good humor, Curtis replied "You don't want to know."

On Sunday, the World 600 went off on schedule, though not without a few problems. Because Propst had barely finished laying the macadam on the track that morning, it was so wet that it came up in great globs during the race. Fortunately that merely served to whet the appetites of the spectators and no serious consequences ensued.

Representing Curtis and Bruton was always an adventure. Eventually the two had a falling out and very nearly came to blows. They later lost control of the Speedway when it was forced to go through a bankruptcy reorganization. Curtis was tragically killed in a private airplane accident in 1970 while flying his Aerocommander only twelve minutes from his home in Roanoke, Virginia. Bruton eventually accumulated sufficient funds to reacquire the Speedway, which has since proved to be an extraordinary moneymaker. I should think that Curtis, whose name, so far as I can determine, does not appear anywhere on the site where his dream was realized, is probably spinning in his grave.

## THE CITY RECORDER'S COURT

Prior to the North Carolina legislature's adoption of a court reform program that drastically altered the state court system in the mid 1960s, criminal misdemeanors were tried in what was known as the City Recorder's Court. My friend and colleague, Howard Arbuckle, who became City Recorder in 1959, invited me to serve as the Vice Recorder, in which capacity I should hold court for him when he asked me to do so. It was a part-time position that would not interfere with my practice at the law firm so I accepted the invitation.

Howard liked to spend long weekends at his house in Blowing Rock and we soon fell into a routine by which I regularly held court on Fridays. Most of the cases dealt with traffic offenses, cutting scrapes or petty thievery. Cases involving driving under the influence also fell within our jurisdiction and, as this was before breathalyzers were introduced, they often represented the most difficult challenges. Until I served as Vice Recorder, I had not appreciated how many of my fellow citizens led tragic and violent lives. Many often called the police to rescue them, not infrequently from a member of their own family. The experience was an eye opener for me. The longer I served in the post the greater the sympathy I began to feel for the persons who appeared there, often the assailants as well as their victims.

At the time, the maximum jail sentence for a misdemeanor was two years but I rarely imposed any such judgment. Charles W. Tillett, who served as Recorder some time in the 1920s, was said to have once told a friend "During the time the evidence is being presented, I begin thinking about an appropriate sentence for the defendant. I know that if he didn't do that, he probably did something just as bad." It was a different culture that prevailed among the patrons of the Recorder's Court and suspended sentences were quite common.

While I was serving as Vice Recorder, the police arrested Robert Schrader, the operator of the Visulite Theatre on Elizabeth Avenue, for showing a movie called "For Members Only." The film depicted life in a nudist camp and Schrader was charged with violation of a statute that forbade the public display of obscenity. Because this was classified as a misdemeanor, the case appeared on the Recorder's Court calendar. Howard, who would have to decide the case, recruited me to see the film with him. Besides involving a rather inane plot, the film showed members of the nudist camp in various stages of undress. I'd rather not repeat what I told Howard when he asked my opinion of the film. It is enough to say that when I reported my comment to my friend Mark Bernstein, he called me a "prude." Of course, I have since developed an appropriate veneer of sophistication.

At Schrader's trial both the prosecutor and the defense called expert witnesses. Baptist minister Joe Chambers appeared for the State. Local author Harry Golden and Unitarian minister Sidney Freeman appeared for the defense. Howard ruled that the film was not obscene within the meaning of the statute and Robert Schrader was acquitted. The *Charlotte Observer* published an editorial soon thereafter which, in spite of agreeing with the judge's decision, criticized Schrader for "pandering to the prurient." Schrader was incensed at that characterization of his work and brought a civil suit against the *Charlotte Observer*, seeking damages for libel. The jury returned a verdict for the plaintiff in the amount of one dollar.

### WACHOVIA BANK'S CUSTODIAL AGREEMENT

Our partner Carol D. Taliaferro was a splendid technician in drafting wills and settling estates. A consummate gentleman, he had established an excellent reputation with the trust officers of all of the local banks. Among them was Courtney Mauzy of Wachovia Bank. After Mr. Taliaferro retired, Courtney called upon me with some frequency to assist the Wachovia trust department in handling various legal matters. In 1959, trustees of the Davis Hospital in Statesville approached Wachovia about taking on the responsibility of handling investments for a trust established under the will of a Mr. Wagner. The trustees appointed by the will were the ministers of several leading churches in Statesville. Recognizing that they were not qualified to invest substantial funds for the hospital, they wished to engage Wachovia to handle the investments as a custodial account. It was my job to prepare the custodial agreement and to go over it with the trustees at one of the churches in Statesville.

The Statesville meeting went off well except in one respect. Several of the ministers on the board had publicly expressed strong opinions on the subject of racial integration. The minister of the Presbyterian Church and the minister of the Episcopal Church were strongly opposed to integration in the schools. On the other hand, the minister of the Broad Street United Methodist Church was a staunch advocate of integration. At our meeting the Presbyterian minister actually refused to speak to the Methodist minister. Despite some uncomfortable moments, we eventually managed to execute the custodial agreement.

The Episcopal minister, the Reverend James Parker Dees, was so fervently opposed to integration that he left the Episcopal Church in

1963 and organized a separate Episcopal denomination called the Anglican Orthodox Church, which was headquartered in Statesville. It espoused a radically conservative theology and Dees became its governing bishop. The new denomination has not had much success in America but has apparently attracted thousands of members in Third World countries through the work of its missionaries. It is doubtful that the members in Africa know that their church originated out of a segregationist's racial prejudice.

## DIXIE NEWS AND THE GIRLIE MAGAZINES

In the 1960s the firm represented Dixie News Company, a wholesale magazine dealer. The sheriff of neighboring Gaston County threatened to indict the officers of the company, Dewitt Brown and his wife Othel, for promoting the sale of pornography. It was quite ironic that the Browns should be charged with such a crime, as there never was a kinder or more generous couple. In fact, they eventually bequeathed eight and a half million dollars to the Disciples of Christ Church. Having wrestled with the issue of public nudity in the Recorder's Court a year earlier, it seemed I was to return to the subject in their defense.

At our suggestion, instead of prosecuting a criminal charge the sheriff eventually chose to seek an injunction against the company to enjoin the sale of what we used to call "girlie" magazines to Gastonia newsstands. Dewitt brought copies of the magazines in question to Joe and me and we admitted (to each other) that they did disclose practically the full length of the female anatomy in the flesh. Feeling that Dewitt might be at the mercy of conservative community standards in Gastonia, we advised him that we were fully prepared to raise the First Amendment constitutional issues involved. Dewitt himself then devised what turned out to be the best conceivable defense.

When Joe and I arrived at the Gaston County Courthouse with our clients, we listened while the county attorney Charles Gray presented his case to the judge. He offered copies of a half dozen magazines of the kind to which I have referred, together with the testimony of several local citizens who were offended by the contents, after which he rested his case. We then called Dewitt Brown to the stand and he testified more or less as follows:

> "Your Honor, I understand the sheriff's concern about this matter and frankly I'm at a loss to know what to do about it. I want to protect the constitutional right of the public to purchase magazines that are generally available from my national suppliers. On the other hand, I do not want to offend the morals of the community in which they are sold. If someone is willing to appoint a representative committee of local citizens that can agree on what magazines we should not distribute to the newsstands in Gastonia I shall be glad to abide by their decision."

The sheriff and his attorney were clearly surprised by Dewitt's proposal. On the strength of it, they agreed to dismiss the case and we never heard from the Gastonia authorities again. No doubt the committee had some difficulty in deciding what materials met the definition of "pornography" under the statute. Apparently they had even more difficulty than U.S. Supreme Court Justice Potter Stewart who stated in an oft-quoted decision "While I don't know just how to define pornography I will say that I know it when I see it." Suffice it to say, it is something more salacious than a mere depiction of the naked female anatomy.

Incidentally, after the hearing I left the magazines in the Dixie News file, where they were reexamined from time to time by various members of the firm, solely for the purpose of testing them against the proper legal standard, of course.

## THE LAWYER REFERRAL PROGRAM

In 1961 the Mecklenburg County Bar Association appointed me to chair a new committee called the Lawyers Referral Committee. Similar programs had recently begun to appear in major cities across the country but ours was the first in North Carolina (the North Carolina Bar Association later instituted a similar program). The purpose of the committee was to provide members of the public thirty minutes of legal advice at a cost of thirty dollars, to be equally shared by the lawyer who was a member of the panel and the Bar Association. It has been highly successful in providing the public with an opportunity to obtain a legal opinion without running the risk of incurring a crippling fee.

Recently the leaders of the Mecklenburg County Bar Association threatened to kill the program because it was not self-supporting. Enough lawyers came to its rescue at the eleventh hour, with financial contributions and spirited advocacy, to assure its continuance. It would have been unfortunate if the program had been allowed to expire since it is one of the principal means by which the Bar discharges its responsibility to provide legal services to middle income disputants who are otherwise wary of consulting lawyers.

## CAROL D. TALIAFERRO

Shortly after his retirement, Mr. Taliaferro undertook to cement relations between the firm and the trust officers of the various local banks, whose confidence he had always enjoyed. To this end, he had a dinner party at his home on College Street to which he invited all of the firm's lawyers and the senior trust officers of each of the major banks. His intentions were excellent but the event did not turn out well. Even though all of the bankers were very fond of Mr. Taliaferro and had engaged him to represent their banks, he apparently lost sight of the fact that they were natural competitors.

Mr. Taliaferro's diplomatic instinct did prevail, however, when he failed to invite our prohibitionist colleague Judge Clarkson to the dinner, since, in the interest of social bonheur, he expected to provide his guests with alcoholic libations. In fact, however, the drinks may have flowed more freely than Mr. Taliaferro intended.

One of the trust officers told the Commercial National Bank's representative to "shut up" when he felt he had been interrupted. The firm's young associate found that expression amusing in the circumstances and began to mimic the trust officer. "Shut up, Jack," he cried whenever the Jack in question spoke, until it became quite clear that Jack was no longer amused.

In his last years Mr. Taliaferro suffered a mild form of dementia and his physician Dr. Lucius Gage admitted him to Memorial Hospital. When Dr. Gage wouldn't discharge him, Mr. Taliaferro asked Joe Grier to take out a writ of habeas corpus. After talking to Dr. Gage, Joe declined as politely as he could. Mr. Taliaferro then made the same request of Francis Parker and Bill Poe successively, each of whom declined. He never called on me to help, probably because I was so new that he had no confidence in my ability to obtain such a writ. It was apparent, however, that he needed the attention being given him there.

## GRIER PARKER POE AND THOMPSON

Following Mr. Taliaferro's retirement, the firm name became Grier Parker Poe and Thompson, which it remained for ten years. Jim Preston joined us in 1961, having graduated from the University of North Carolina Law School. We were especially pleased to recruit him because he had been editor-in-chief of the *North Carolina Law Review*. I was immediately drawn to Jim, who worked with me on several trials before developing a specialty in tax law. He very quickly justified our early confidence in him by becoming one of the best tax lawyers in North Carolina. He eventually served as president of the North Carolina State Bar. Gaston Gage joined us later that year, after having practiced on his own for a few years, and became an indefatigable litigator. He is still working on a savings and loan case which the United States government filed against our client in the 1970s. It may outlive all of us.

Not long after I became a partner in the firm, we began meeting at Joe Grier's home each Tuesday evening. After exhausting business matters, we spent the balance of the evening reviewing recent North Carolina Supreme Court cases reported in the advance sheets. From time to time, Joe played an audio tape on some professional subject for the edification of those present. Gaston Gage never tires of describing one of his first meetings at Joe's house. Francis, Bill and I were lying back in our chairs with our eyes closed, looking suspiciously as though we were asleep, while Joe sat smiling and listening intently to a lecture on tax-exempt qualified stock options.

Another story that Gaston relishes is an account of his and Jim Preston's being summoned to Joe's office one morning in 1964 to find Francis, Bill and me also present and looking quite solemn.

With serious mien, Joe soberly announced to them that they were both being fired. Before they could take another breath, however, he added, "Since you no longer have a job, we wondered if you would be interested in becoming our partners in this firm."

# CHAPTER 18
## COMMUNITY LIFE
### HORACE WILLIAMS PHILOSOPHY CLUB

Soon after we moved to Charlotte, Judge Francis Clarkson invited me to join the Horace Williams Philosophy Club. Horace Williams was a teacher of philosophy at the University of North Carolina in the early twentieth century. After some of his admiring students settled in Charlotte in the early 1900s, they founded the Club as a forum in which they could continue to discuss the subjects they had studied with Professor Williams. Among its most renowned members in the early years were Judge John J. Parker, father of my partner Francis Parker, and Ambassador Herschel V. Johnson.

Judge Parker, chief judge of the United States Court of Appeals for the Fourth Circuit for nearly thirty years, was appointed by President Herbert Hoover to the United States Supreme Court in 1930 but failed by a single vote to obtain Senate approval. Herschel Johnson was a career foreign service officer who was *charge d'affairs* of the American Embassy in England just before the United States entered World War II. In that post he facilitated highly significant negotiations between President Roosevelt's special envoy Harry Hopkins and Prime Minister Churchill. Johnson later served as acting ambassador to the United Nations at the time that President Truman first recognized Israel as a sovereign nation. I once tried to persuade Herschel to write a memoir of his experiences in the Foreign Service, but he felt that much of what he had done was too confidential to record. When he died, his sister, Mrs. Edgar Terrell, gave me his monogrammed ivory letter opener because she knew how much I admired him.

Another well known member was Harry Golden. The author of the best-seller "Only in America," Golden popularized the phrase "vertical integration" in reference to his theory that North Carolinians might more readily accept integration of the races so long as the participants were standing rather than seated.

I joined the Philosophy Club in the late 1950s, although until recently my attendance has been spotty. There are eight meetings a year and each member is responsible for taking a turn at either leading a program or getting someone else to do so. The Club has recently taken on new life thanks to the extraordinary energy of our secretary Bryan Crutcher. Based upon Bryan's assurance that he will continue in that office indefinitely, I accepted the chairmanship following Francis Parker's resignation. My principal responsibility is to give each member an opportunity to comment on the subject of the speaker's presentation and still have the meeting adjourn by 9:00 p.m. That is usually something of a challenge.

## FLORENCE CRITTENTON HOME

I became a member of the Board of Trustees of Charlotte's Florence Crittenton Home, a home for unwed mothers, in 1957 and the following year I became chairman of that board. The Board of Trustees was not responsible for the day-to-day operations of the Home, which was handled by a Board of Managers consisting entirely of women. Rather, our function was to deal primarily with real property matters. Nevertheless, over the next fifteen years I was called upon to provide legal services to the director of the Home, at first in the person of Ms. C. A. Troop and later in the person of Mrs. Helen Anderson. I was glad to do so without charge, of course, as Judge Francis Clarkson had done in the '30s and '40s.

## MORE ON MYERS PARK CHURCH

Dr. Clay Madison was appointed pastor of Myers Park Methodist in 1963. In the mid-sixties many civil rights activists from the North were making bus trips to the South in support of blacks who were seeking to register to vote and to integrate public facilities there. The media called them "freedom riders." The National Council of Churches publicly supported the freedom riders and contributed to their expenses. This did not sit well with some of our church members, who felt as though the freedom riders should mind their own business. In an effort to avoid more drastic action which might have involved withdrawing financial support from the National Council, the church finance committee prepared a letter requesting that none of the money that we contributed to the Council be spent to finance the work of the freedom riders. I spoke in opposition to the motion at a meeting of the Board of Stewards, but in the vote that followed, Nancy Akers, a septuagenarian, was the only one who voted with me.

Miss Nancy was a remarkable lady and one of my favorites, not just because we viewed the world alike, but because she remained enthusiastic about every aspect of life around her as long as she lived. Once when a police officer followed her home because he was concerned about her driving, Nancy thanked him warmly and then invited him in for a cup of coffee. Naturally he accepted. On another occasion, Judge Spencer Bell, who was Nancy's cousin, recognized her car parked on Providence Road and found her sitting behind the wheel reading a book. When he inquired if he could help her, she replied "I ran out of gas and I knew someone like you would come along sooner or later." Nancy passed away in January 1994 and I still miss her.

Bob Tuttle succeeded Clay Madison as pastor of Myers Park Church in June 1967. Soon after, Methodist churches across the country began scheduling visits of delegations from other Methodist churches in a program that was designed to effect a spiritual revival. "God loves you and I love you," was the cry. By 1970 a group of our

Myers Park members, began conducting devotional services on Sunday evenings and speaking in tongues. Some of the participants were reported to have undertaken to lengthen the leg of another member through prayer. This development troubled some church members and, perhaps more significantly, troubled the officialdom of the Western Conference, including the bishop and his administrative assistant. I learned of their concern as chairman of the Pastor-Parish Committee, which customarily confers with the bishop about clergy appointments to the local church. In that role I was also told that the bishop was considering moving Bob Tuttle to another church. When the final decision was made, I was given the responsibility of reporting this plan to Bob, who indicated that he would prefer to remain at Myers Park until his retirement which was scheduled to occur within a year or two. Bob was obviously displeased, and the experience was by no means pleasant. I especially regretted this development because I liked Bob very much.

## THE CSO UNDER JACQUES BROURMAN

In the spring of 1967 the Charlotte Symphony Orchestra undertook to engage a new conductor, and Mark Bernstein and I chaired the search committee. We arranged for the four finalists to try out for the position by conducting the orchestra through one movement of a symphony of their choosing at the Piedmont Junior High School. The finalists all auditioned on the same night so we wouldn't have to ask the members of the orchestra to give us more free time. Mark and I met with finalist Shep Coleman in the dressing room just after he had finished his turn at conducting. As he was doffing his jersey and dabbing toilet water on his chest, he mused aloud: "God, I expected them not to be very good, but they are awful!" Obviously he was not concerned about ingratiating himself with members of the committee. A well-established Broadway conductor, Coleman was apparently seeking a greater artistic challenge. No doubt he was accustomed to more proficiency in his musicians.

Jacques Brourman conducted the first movement of Schubert's Unfinished Symphony. When he finished, Mark turned to me and said, "That's our new conductor!" Of course, it was up to the committee to make the selection, but Mark's prophecy came to pass and Jacques joined the Symphony in the fall of 1967. I read a tribute in verse to Jacques at a dinner in his honor when he was leaving one summer to attend a music camp he had established in Sun Valley, Idaho:

SYMPHONY TALES –
A TOAST TO CONDUCTOR JACQUES BROURMAN

I

When that orchestra with its magic sweet
the drought of Charlotte pierc'ed to the root
and bathed each tone-deaf ear in such a shower

of which culture engendered is the flower,
our Symphony pilgrims wend their blessed way
to "metropol'tan" status, though some say,
"It's just as well the League bestows such praise
for money spent instead of money raised."
Indeed, there is no other band on earth
so gleefully spends in excess of its worth.

II

But of this task the ladies, our ombudsmen,
just say what each has often told her husband
"If more expenditure should look too rash,
the answer's clear – you simply get more cash.
And if income should still not meet outgo,
the red will be made black by Mr. Rowe."
Still some will ask who else can e'er afford
the cost of heading up the Symphony Board.
Yet others say don't worry 'bout a pres'dent
for now it seems we have a lifetime res'dent.

III

But still they manage, teetering on the brink,
to gorge their appetites with food and drink.
In truth our heroes have a date with fate
led now by him of newly hirsute pate.
No longer satisfied with "metropol'tan"
they'll  spend still more in merriment and frol'ckin'.
And with their eyes fixed prayerfully on heav'n
they've scheduled six concerts – and maybe seven.
But when it's time to make the fiscal tally
Il Duce's gone to far-away Sun Valley.

In the nine years that he served as conductor, Jacques led the Symphony to a significantly higher level of performance than had been previously attained, largely as a result of his inspiring our board to pay the members of the orchestra what then passed for a living wage, so that we at last had a contingent of "full-time" players. Jacques periodically held the board's feet to the fire until we found the money to engage another full-time player or two.  I especially liked Jacques and was sorry when he chose to resign and leave Charlotte in 1976.

Oliver Rowe, chief executive of the Bouligny Company, served as president of the Symphony board from 1965 to 1971.  We had both attended Myers Park United Methodist Church for years, and although his wife Marie was an ardent Republican, I had prevailed upon him at one time to head the Democratic Men's Club.  He accepted the challenge despite the risk to his domestic harmony.  I also represented his businesses in a number of legal matters.  In truth, Oliver had become my very good friend.  When he retired from the presidency of the Charlotte Symphony after serving in that capacity for seven years, I delivered the following verses in tribute to that redoubtable champion of good causes:

129

I

Tonight our wandering pilgrims quit their maze
to ring the rafters loud and long in praise
of one whose love for Charlotte's Symphony
near equals that he has for fair Marie,
though both have come to know that they must share him
with swooning girls who daily join his harem.
But now, if you'll excuse the muddled metaphor,
the mantle's passed to one we're none the better for.
This valiant white-maned stallion goes to graze
with other greats of old Symphonic days.

II

So now, dear friends, attend with care the story
of Captain Rowe's great rendezvous with glory.
Just fifteen years ago began this cruise.
From Bouligny's helm he sailed to meet the muse.
And, like Ulysses, heard an unknown tongue
by oboe, flute, bassoon and violin sung;
strange sounds to this a loyal Civitan-er,
whose favorite tune was the Star-Spangled Banner.
(Or perhaps our cunning friend has merely ribbed us,
and steered a course 'twixt Scylla and Charybdis.)

III

But soon our hero, warming to his task,
in all the classic symphonies did bask
til he became a music connoisseur.
To no one in the arts would he defer.
Indeed, to prove the vastness of his fame,
a Fine Arts building chose to bear his name.
But of all good works for which he's been the leaven,
there's one for which he's now a place in heav'n.
He took a modest Symphony in hand
And set its course toward honor in the land.

I served on the Symphony board until 1971, when I redirected my time and attention to the Charlotte Opera Association, largely at Oliver's prompting. Shepherd Coleman could have hardly conceived of the great strides the orchestra has made today.

## THE CHARLOTTE OPERA ASSOCIATION

Oliver Rowe invited me to join the Charlotte Opera Association's board of directors in the spring of 1967 as part of an ongoing effort to strengthen that organization. I had become accustomed to accepting his suggestions, which were usually in my best interests as well as those of the community. Within the year, Mrs. Mary Henderson stepped down as president because of differences of opinion that had arisen between her and the Charlotte Opera Guild. This temporary set-back was soon amicably resolved by the establishment of the "Friends of the Opera," a second auxiliary for young women, at a meeting attended by Emily Smith on behalf of the new auxiliary and Sally Gamble on behalf of the Opera Guild. After Mrs. Henderson's resignation, Oliver Rowe, George Daly, Caroline McMillan, John

Stedman and I were appointed as an oligarchy of sorts to govern the Association until a successor might be elected.

Oliver was president of the Charlotte Symphony at the time, so he was not in a position to assume responsibility for the Opera. John Stedman and I conspired to recruit George Daly for that office. He declined out of hand. George and I then called upon John Stedman to the same end. John told us that it was possible that he would be appointed to head a new company that was about to be organized, but that he would accept the position with the understanding that he could resign if he received that appointment. George and I readily agreed to that condition and John was elected president of the Charlotte Opera in the summer of 1969.

Less than a month later I looked up from my desk in the Law Building one day to see John and George Daly striding into my office. I should have guessed their mission! John had indeed been appointed president of the newly-organized Republic Bank. Having failed at conscripting either of them for the job, I was now the victim of a phenomenon known as the process of elimination. I accepted their challenge and assumed the presidency of the Opera in September of 1969.

At that time the Opera's annual budget was about $40,000. The productions were much better than that amount would indicate, however, because nearly everyone involved was either a volunteer or a martyr. The only exceptions were the conductor Charles Rosekrans, the soloists and a part-time secretary, Mamie Willard. Bill Mahoney, Jean Erwin and Bill Rackley designed sets and supervised their construction and painting at minimal cost. When we received a visit from the General Director of the Baltimore Opera Company in connection with our Opera America membership, he was greatly impressed with the quality of the performance, especially in view of our modest budget. We were fortunate to be able to increase the annual budget to $110,000 by 1974, due in part to a $12,500 grant that I was able to obtain from the Mecklenburg County Commissioners. That grant matched the annual contribution made by the Charlotte City Council.

In addition to acting as conductor, Charles Rosekrans gradually assumed the role of music director, in which capacity he selected the vehicles to be performed as well as the soloists who appeared in them. Over the next ten years, he was largely responsible for holding the company together and polishing its performances.

Despite such progress, the Opera was not without its share of growing pains. One evening in 1973 I returned from a professional trip to Washington, DC, just in time to make the curtain for our performance of "Tosca." Charles called me backstage to tell me that our lead, Marisa Galvany, was ill and unable to go on. He had located another Tosca, Lucine Amara of the Metropolitan Opera

Company, and she was en-route in a private plane but was still somewhere over Virginia. Charles, John Alexander (the tenor lead), Val Patacchi (the stage director) and I entertained the audience by turns until the curtain was finally raised at 9:40 p.m. Fortunately, no one left the hall while we awaited Ms. Amara's arrival. During the performance Amara sang the title role in Italian while the other members of the cast sang their parts in English. It was a bilingual night to remember! It was also quite expensive. Ms. Amara's fee was about $20,000 - at a time when our total annual budget was only $110,000! I don't recall now how we eventually raised the money but it was worth it!

### TREADING THE BOARDS

In the years following our move to Charlotte, I played a couple of minor roles at the Little Theatre of Charlotte under directors Tom Humble and John Morrow. In 1970 I asked Dorothy Masterson, the artistic director of the Golden Circle Theatre at the Mint Museum, if she might find a role for me in one of her productions. After I read for her, she offered me a role in "Dylan," a play by Sydney Michaels based on the life of Dylan Thomas, the celebrated Welsh poet. I was cast as John Malcolm Brinnin, the American poet who acted as Thomas' agent in scheduling his American tours.

I enjoyed the role greatly, especially because I had an opportunity to work with Rudy Thompson, who played Dylan. As depicted by Michaels, Thomas died in America after a fatal drinking bout. The play ended with a ship's officer reciting the poem:

> "Do not go gentle into that good night.
> Old age should burn and rage at close of day.
> Rage, rage against the dying of the light.
> Tho wise men at their end know dark is night
> because their words had forked no lightning, they
> do not go gentle into that good night.
> Good men, the last wave by,
> crying how bright their frail deeds have danced in a green bay,
> rage, rage against the dying of the light."

That poem left a catch in my throat every time I heard it. Hopefully it stirred the audience as well.

Since that date, as the reader will by now have noted, I have occasionally crafted heroic couplets in iambic pentameter as favors for my friends, attributing the verses to John Malcolm Brinnin whom I purported to have contacted on their behalf. Hattie says that about half of the persons who have heard that spiel actually believed me while the other half suspected my dissembling. I am inclined to think I am a better liar than that. I recently abandoned the practice after learning that Brinnin had died. No doubt my friends were tiring of the joke anyhow. I'm sure Brinnin never learned of the imposture. If he had, I hope he would have viewed it as the compliment it was meant to be.

I eventually assembled my John Malcolm Brinnin verses in a soft cover book entitled "A Collection of Ad Hominem Verse at One Time Attributed by Ruse to John Malcolm Brinnin," which I distributed to a few friends. It should perhaps have been more appropriately entitled "A Collection of Ad Hominem Doggerel." As there has been no demand for general publication, I have incorporated a number of them in this memoir.

I wrote such a tribute to Dorothy Masterson after she retired from the Golden Circle Theatre and moved to Baltimore. Darrell Kortheuer painted her portrait in the costume of Elizabeth I, a role she had played at the Mint Museum. Upon her retirement, the portrait was appropriately hung in the Green Room of the Blumenthal Performing Arts Hall. On that occasion I read the following verses:

### MEMORIAL TO DOROTHY MASTERSON, FOUNDER OF THE GOLDEN CIRCLE THEATRE

#### I

Today we honor one who cast her net
and wove a spell o'er all within this set
by which she challenged us to meet her goals
and steer a course 'round threat'ning thespian shoals.
When first our children studied in her class,
we learned how gently Dorothy could harass
until she drove into their doltish minds
the memory of those damned elusive lines.
Yet most of us were constantly amazed
at their performance, though their eyes seemed glazed.

#### II

But most of all we wish to pay respect
to that which made her one of God's elect.
She wheedled and cajoled us till we said
each line as it resounded in her head.
Indeed, she fashioned from our mortal clay
a worthy cast for each immortal play
and formed a Golden Circle at the Mint
that 'ere long left on Charlotte its imprint
and 'stablishéd a classic theatre clime
which introduced us all to "magic time."

#### Epilogue

So here's to our Queen Bess of noble heart
for Masterson a most appropriate part.

I originally attributed those verses to Brinnin, of course, which I suppose constituted "poetic justice" since Dorothy had cast me in that role.

My next part was as Helen Keller's father in "The Miracle Worker" at the Charlotte Little Theater. John Morrow was the director, Sue Holloway played my wife and Mary Jo Kieronski played Helen Keller. Modesty should prevent my reporting that I was named the "best supporting male actor" in Little Theater productions for 1972, but I have managed to overcome any such reservation.

Honesty requires me to confess, however, that one of the judges was my good friend the Reverend Sidney Freeman, Unitarian minister.

Several years later I tried out for a play called "Morning's at Seven" at the Golden Circle Theatre. Marilyn Carter, who had succeeded Dorothy Masterson as director, cast me as Carl, an emotionally disturbed middle-aged plumber who periodically obsessed about wanting to "go back to the fork" so that he might take another road in life. I learned even more from Marilyn than I had from Dorothy. Marilyn was quite candid: once when I was apparently overacting, she said "Let up a little, Sydnor. You're not playing King Lear."

## PLANNED PARENTHOOD

Sarah Bryant, with whom I had worked at the Florence Crittenton Home, became concerned about young unmarried girls who had become pregnant but who did not want to leave home to live in a group setting. Recognizing that the girls still needed advice and support in connection with their predicament, Sarah set up a special red telephone in her home which served as a hot line for the unwed mothers. Although the national Planned Parenthood organization had been established years earlier, there was as yet no local chapter. In 1971 Sarah assembled a group of Charlotteans who became the board of directors of a local branch known as "Planned Parenthood of Greater Charlotte," and asked me to serve on it. I was highly sympathetic to the cause and readily agreed. Sarah became the first president and I accepted the post of vice president on her assurance that I should not be called upon for any significant responsibility in that capacity – at least for a time. About a month later, Sarah informed me that she had been hired by the national Planned Parenthood organization as the executive director of the new Charlotte branch. Because she had to resign her office, I was to succeed her as president!

In time the local chapter began to help clients arrange for abortions, and, in a move that was controversial with several board members and also some members of the public, eventually developed a full-blown abortion clinic. The Supreme Court's ruling in *Roe v. Wade* gave our organization greater confidence, of course. The presence on the board of the Reverend (later Bishop) Hunt Williams, then vicar of St. Peter's Episcopal Church, lent further credibility to those early efforts. I have drawn considerable satisfaction from having helped Sarah with this work and have never wavered in my conviction that it is the best answer to a difficult problem.

## CLASSICAL MUSIC STATION WDAV

For years Hattie and I considered Charlotte something of a musical desert as it primarily featured country and pop music stations. Hoping to improve that situation, we approached some of the network-affiliates about carrying "serious" music at odd times but found that they weren't remotely interested. As Charlie Crutchfield, the head of radio station WBT, pointed out to Hooper Alexander and me, a commercial radio station cannot change the nature of its programming for a few hours a day without losing regular listeners.

In the mid 1970s, both Davidson College and the University of North Carolina at Charlotte began to show an interest in establishing a classical music station. Hattie met with interested supporters of the idea at UNC-C and I met with a similar group at Davidson College. President Sam Spencer took up the cause at Davidson, and eventually carried the day. Hooper and I served on the first Advisory Board of Davidson's WDAV in the early 1980s. Music lovers were delighted with the sea change WDAV provided in musical fare, and the station continues to prosper today. UNC-C also established a new station with the call letters WFAE, programming serious music for a time before becoming an NPR station.

# CHAPTER 19
## MEANWHILE BACK AT THE RANCH
### HATTIE RESUMES HER CAREER

Hattie virtually put her music career on hold from the time young Harriet was born in 1956 until Brenny was born in August 1958. She was determined to renew her dedication to music, however, and in 1959 she began to work with Professor Hans Heidemann. Hans was on the faculty at Salem College in Winston-Salem, North Carolina, so Hattie made that pilgrimage weekly for several years. By 1962, they were performing publicly as a duo-piano team and in 1963 they performed in a Community Concerts Series at the John Motley Morehead auditorium in Leaksville-Spray. My favorite of the numbers they played was Rachmaninoff's Suite No. 2 for Two Pianos in C minor, especially the "Romance" section.

Hans was a talented pianist who had been born in Germany and who had studied with Rudolph Serkin in Switzerland. He once told us that when he was working with Serkin, he practiced so much that his fingers became numb. He called Serkin to tell him what had happened and Serkin asked him how much he had been practicing. "Eight hours a day, just as you told me," replied Hans. "Make it ten!," Serkin said and hung up. Serkin later visited Charlotte to play in the Community Concert Series. Hattie and I entertained him after the concert and when we related Hans' story to him, Serkin laughed and said "Well, it worked didn't it?"

Hans and Hattie both matriculated in a Master of Music program at the University of North Carolina in Greensboro in 1963 under the tutelage of the pianist Daniel Ericourt who had recently joined that faculty. Ericourt had studied with Debussy in France and was noted not only for his interpretation of Debussy's music, but also for being the best exponent of French piano music in America at the time. Hans and Hattie each received their Master of Music degrees in 1966. Thus, Hattie resuscitated her music career and was once again on target to meet the demands necessary to excel as a concert pianist.

Smack in the middle of her musical renaissance, Hattie paused long enough to give birth to our fifth and last child. Mary Katherine Line, who was named for Hattie's aunt whom she loved and admired, was born on April 17, 1962. Aunt Mary and her husband Glenn Todd came from Carlisle and Hans Heidemann and his wife Patricia came from Winston-Salem for Kathy Line's baptism at Myers Park United Methodist Church.

### PREPARING FOR A YEAR IN VIENNA

Hattie and the children saw the film "Sound of Music" more times than should have been necessary for them to commit it to memory. They were not alone! It has been said that more people saw "The Sound of Music" at Charlotte's Carolina Theatre in 1965 than lived in the city at that time. No doubt the members of my family represented many of those admission fees. Before long they were talking about the possibility of going to live in Austria for a year. In time the venture came to seem more and more feasible. The children had been saving their money to buy a farm some day. Although Brenny was the principal advocate of that project, they soon agreed to devote "the farm account" to the Austrian adventure, which meant they really wanted to go.

Realizing that it would be good for the children to learn a second language, Hattie and I began to explore the possibilities. At first we considered Salzburg since that's where our neighbors, the Robert E. E. Booker family, had lived for a year and that was the home of the von Trapp family (who were the subject of the film). In time, however, we chose Vienna because that city offered so many more opportunities. The children, we decided, could become familiar with a great cultural center and Hattie would have a better opportunity for piano study, though she insists that was not a major consideration. It was not feasible for me to go with them, of course, since my income was necessary to finance the venture.

In the spring we prevailed upon Karl Gabriel, a professor of German at the University of North Carolina at Charlotte, to come to our home every Sunday afternoon to give the family German lessons. Hattie's mother sat with us for the lessons, so Karl had students ranging from age three to age eighty-five. By that time Mother Line was staying with us most of the year, although she occasionally visited her sons for several weeks at a time. When asked if she didn't miss her friends in Carlisle, she replied, "If I should go back to see them, I'd have to dig them up." She was a very practical woman.

At our first German lesson, Karl taught us to say, "Sprecken sie langsam, bitte" (speak slowly please) and "ïch verstehe nicht" (I do not understand). He was a fine teacher and helped us a great deal, but after several months of tutelage he considered it advisable to review the same two expressions. And he was right! We had given him a difficult assignment.

Gradually, plans for the great adventure became more concrete. We agreed that we should rent our house to a couple who were just moving to Charlotte. I arranged to stay with my mother. It seemed that every aspect of the plan quickly fell into place. Because the tenants wanted the house in June and Hattie and the children were not scheduled to leave for Austria until August, we were fortunate in being provided a house at Island Point on Lake Wylie by our friends Louis and Lynn Rogers. The children swam every day and I even learned to water ski.

When the time for leaving arrived, Mark and Louise Bernstein offered Hattie their station wagon for the trip to New York. Besides the five children, Hattie had to find room for about twenty suitcases, so she accepted their offer gladly. On their way to board the *S.S. France*, a state trooper stopped her on the Pennsylvania Turnpike. He was about to write a speeding ticket for which she would have been called to appear in court two weeks later. When she explained that she was on her way to New York to go to Austria for a year, the trooper exclaimed, "You mean you are taking these five children to Austria for a year by yourself! Have a good trip, ma'am!" And he sent her on her way. Louis and Lynn drove me to New York City so that I could see the family off.

Several of our friends invited me to stay with them for a time while the family was away. By September I was being hosted by a number of good-hearted souls who undertook to see that I didn't get too lonely. For much of that year I alternated a week or two with Mother and a week or two with friends. Mark and Louise Bernstein, George and Rosemary Blanchard, Judge and Cama Clarkson, Louis and Lynn Rogers, Rem and Gwen Rogers, Ace and Heathey Walker, and Bobby Booker all put me up at one time or another. I don't know how they felt about it, but I loved it. And I'm sure it served Mother well to have occasional relief from the company of her peripatetic boarder.

### VIENNA

The children enjoyed the voyage to Europe immensely, swimming in the pool every day. The ship docked at Southampton, England in late August. Hattie had made arrangements to visit the Ian Redheads en route to Austria, so they took a train to Peterborough from Southampton. The Redheads' four children made their stay most pleasant. Ian enjoyed relating the story of how Brenny was missing one day, only to be found sitting perfectly contented in a nearby pasture among a herd of cows.

After ten days with the Redheads, the family embarked from a port on the east coast and crossed the North Sea to collect a Volkswagen station-wagon that they had ordered from the factory in Wolfsburg, Germany. From there they drove to Salzburg, toured the town in a horse and buggy, and took a cable car to the top of a mountain overlooking the city. Their curiosity about Salzburg satisfied, they set out for Vienna.

Karl Gabriel had recommended a family in Perchtoldsdorf, a wine village in the 26th district of Vienna, as one that might provide our family with living quarters. When Hattie inquired of a local policeman as to the location of Perchtoldsdorf, the policeman thought she had said "Pürkersdorf" and directed her there. When they arrived in Pürkersdorf and were unable to find the address they were looking for, they took rooms at the Kuntner Pension and set up housekeeping while they searched for Perchtoldsdorf. Eventually Perchtoldsdorf was located and while their accommodations were being readied there, the children commuted to school from the Kuntner Pension.

Their Perchtoldsdorf neighbors in the adjacent duplex were landlords Henrietta and Oskar Kirchmayer, the Kirchmayer children Wolfgang and Adelheid and Henrietta's parents Herr and Frau Gilg. On the day they arrived in Perchtoldsdorf at 34 Krausgasse, the children ate a number of ripe plums from a tree in the garden, resulting in a family epidemic of upset stomachs that lasted for several days and provided an inauspicious introduction to the local schools.

D'Arcy, the oldest at 15, Sydnor and Harriet enrolled in the higher school (*hauptschule*), while Brenny attended the elementary school (*volkschule*). Hattie enrolled Kathy Line, who was just four years old, in a nursery school. All of them were suddenly engulfed in an avalanche of spoken German that left their heads spinning. D'Arcy proved best able to make the transition, perhaps because she spent much of her time with teenage friends. In fact, before the year was out she was occasionally mistaken for a native.

During a school vacation, Hattie took the children to ski at a resort called Feuerkogel near Salzburg. When Sydnor was climbing a hill he fell. One of the guides helped him up just in time for an iron bar on the ski lift to hit him on the forehead as it was passing. Sydnor was uncomplaining. "Don't worry, Mother," he said, "I'll be all right." But it was a serious cut so Hattie drove him to the local hospital. Young Harriet, who was only nine years old, volunteered to run back to their hut through knee deep snow to get the car keys from Hattie's pocketbook and was the family's heroine for the day.

Although Sydnor was only twelve years old, he was his mother's right hand during their stay in Austria. Among other chores, he got up early every morning and made several stove fires before the rest of the family awoke.

An excellent description of their first few months in Perchtoldsdorf can be derived from letters Hattie wrote to her mother.

September 11, 1966

Dear Mama – Tomorrow we move into our house in Perchtoldsdorf. The children are all in German – rather Austrian – schools learning German and only hearing German all day. Sydnor has a tutor for his math and maybe D'Arcy will need one. The kilograms – kilometers, etc. are confusing, so the director (principal) thought they should need help in that area. They are so enthusiastic about the school and the children and teachers that the fact they cannot speak the language doesn't seem to bother them. They also like the house and neighborhood. Of course, it cannot compare with our standard of living at home. We do have a bathroom, 3 bedrooms, a living room and kitchen. The house is a duplex and is the one the friends of the Gabriels wrote to us about. It is about twenty minutes from the heart of Vienna so I have to go that far for concerts but living in this suburb seems better for the children. They can walk to school and have the interesting experience of living with the Kirchmayers who have the other half of the

139

house. They are buying us a refrigerator and a bed (so we can have enough sleeping places) and they are so kind they can't seem to do enough.

We went to the Museum of Natural History today and after two hours we still hadn't seen half of it. Brenny's eyes are still popping after seeing every conceivable kind of animal, fish, bird, and bug from the Dinosaur age to present. He saw the birth of a turtle in all stages, snakes digesting mice and all sorts of lovely things. They had a whole section on deformities showing actual two-headed species of fawns, birds, and bugs. It is the building itself that makes it so unique. It is like walking through a palace – marble walls – with gilded moldings, frescoes, and paintings and wide marble staircases. In the entrance is a lovely rotunda with a view to the top. We plan to go back and see the mineral section, geology section and a couple of others. It cost 40 cents for all six of us.

This afternoon we came back after a great dinner at the Westbahnhof, put on our hiking clothes and took off for the woods. We walked over the thick carpeted ground under tall trees – so tall we couldn't see their tops. Then we climbed and climbed and eventually came out on to meadows and a lake (man-made) where folks were boating. The landscape was like in the "Sound of Music" and all the women were in Austrian outfits and stared at me in my shorts.

---

November 3, 1966

Dear Mama – We are having some Austrian weather now. All our stoves are going and the kitchen, living room and two bedrooms are very comfortable. One bedroom is not so warm and the bathroom is heated with an electric wall fixture which is great if we remember to warm it up about ten minutes before bathing.

We took a wonderful trip to the skiing resorts this week. The children had a lot of time off – three days and with the weekend that made five days, so we took Henrietta and her two children along. We lined up a nice inexpensive place for January and perhaps a place around Easter holiday. All these places are so booked up – a year ahead – we were lucky to get one for January. Now we are gradually assembling clothes – skis, boots, etc. I found a lovely snow jacket for Harriet in Salzburg. I also found a leather suit which I wanted but found the price over 300 shillings so I'll ask Santa for that maybe.

We stayed over night at the most picturesque *gasthoff* and met some people from Pennsylvania at breakfast. We toured Salzburg again and went through Mozart's house with guide and all. We saw a Kaiser's villa at Ishel and there too we saw Franz Joseph's hunting trophies. We had an English guide. This time we explored and found the Von Trapp family home. It is terribly rundown but it was interesting to see the real setting. Monks live there now and the villa is being restored.

Kathy has gradually become used to her school and is spouting a little German. She understands it very well. Brenny is enthusiastic off and on and longs for his buddies Freddie and Harry. The three older children are having a continuous ball. They are learning to make a few sacrifices too and really appreciate the USA. They don't have TV so they get to bed early.

I was able to visit the family in Vienna for Christmas and my two weeks there were truly memorable. I was impressed with the degree to which the children had learned to cope with the difference in the language and the culture. It was extraordinary how much they had developed in five months and I was delighted. The celebration of Christmas was quite different from our usual tradition in America. The *Christkind* (Christ Child) visited us on Christmas Eve and we exchanged Christmas gifts in accordance with the custom of the Austrians. The identity of the person who made the gifts was not divulged, although circumstances might have provided a hint. That evening we lit the candles on the Christmas tree and Sydnor led the other children in delivering a recitation:

"For God so loved the world that He gave His only begotten Son that whosoever believeth in Him shall not perish but shall have everlasting life." (John 3:16)

During the holiday I also visited the school and met many of the children's teachers. I was especially impressed with Frau Hedwig Danek, who was Harriet's fifth grade teacher. She was a dedicated teacher and was particularly attentive to Harriet, whom she taught a poem – "Hoffnung" by Emanuel Geibel – which Harriet can still recite with feeling, as Frau Danek insisted it should be.

Some of the teachers were less compassionate than Frau Danek. For example, Herr Lititzky, one of Sydnor's teachers, had the habit of pulling students to their feet by twisting the hair at their temples. That was actually a custom among Austrians, who are less averse to physical discipline than Americans, as a means of getting the prompt attention of the children. Brenny suffered the skin-twisting reprimand when a guard in an Austrian museum charged him with scuffing his feet on the floor. Hattie gave the guard a piece of her mind. Although she was handicapped by the language barrier, I'm sure he got her drift when she "accidentally" placed her high heel on his foot. When I visited Brenny's first year class his teacher ordered the class to stand at attention when I walked into the room. It was certainly different from conditions in American schools today.

We visited Bratislava, Czechoslovakia at Henrietta's suggestion. The country was still under Communist control, of course. Henrietta introduced us to an architect there who was quite candid in his criticism of the Communist government. We also met his mother, a dear lady, who gave Hattie a hand-crocheted doily that she still prizes.

I returned to Perchtoldsdorf again in June 1967 for two more weeks. Because I had made so many good friends in Great Britain during my studies there, I decided to stop in London on my way to Vienna. I wrote Louis Gabe, a solicitor friend, and asked him to suggest a place to which I might invite my British friends for dinner. He suggested the Wig and Pen Club on the Strand, a private club for lawyers and journalists said to have been a favorite of Charles Dickens. I invited my friends to meet me there in early June. When I reported my plans to Hattie, she wrote back immediately to ask me what she should wear to the dinner. I got the hint, of course, and invited her to join me on June 9. It was a wonderful gathering of about twenty British friends, none of whom we had seen for sixteen years. Ben Wortley came all the way from Manchester and offered a delightful and generous toast that neither Hattie nor I will ever forget. Ian Redhead was in a London hospital recovering from a knee operation so we visited him there.

Rem and Gwen Rogers, who had flown to Germany to take delivery of a new Porsche, visited Perchtoldsdorf while I was there. I presumed to show them the sights of Vienna on the basis of my two weeks' experience. Among the most interesting was Schonbrunn Palace, where we saw our likenesses reflected an infinite number of times in the Hall of Mirrors. Hattie and I also introduced them to several *heurigens*, where we partook of Perchtoldsdorf's newly-made wine. Austrians regularly serve new wines in the season in which they are bottled.

Hattie was awarded an Artist's Diploma by the Vienna Conservatory that June, based upon the work she had done there with Professor Hans Weber, and began giving a series of concerts in Perchtoldsdorf and other outlying towns and villages. Together we made plans for her Vienna debut at the Palais Palffy, to be held in July. Like her New York debut, it was highly successful and favorably reviewed by Vienna critics:

"A spirited artist . . . completely in her element, she plays with a fine musical sense and with great feeling." *The Vienna Arbiter Zeitung*

As the end of their stay in Perchtoldsdorf approached, Hattie began making plans for the family to make a European tour before they boarded the ship for home. At one time she even considered extending the tour to the Scandinavian countries. In the end, however, she decided in favor of Italy and France. In late July 1967 the family said their good-byes in Perchtoldsdorf and set out for Italy in the Volkswagen. By then the number of bags had doubled and there were twenty-five bags packed on the luggage rack in addition to the fifteen that had been forwarded to their ship. Everywhere they stopped they had to untie the bags from the rack and then tie them on again when they left. They must have looked like the Okies in Steinbeck's "Grapes of Wrath." They made their way to the Italian Riviera and enjoyed it so much that they unanimously agreed to stay there until time to board the ship for home.

I met their ship in New York on August 20th. We stayed at the Plaza Hotel for a couple of days while they got their land legs again. I flew home in time to place a huge WELCOME HOME sign in the front yard. When they arrived in Charlotte, our Brandon Road neighbors and family members turned out in force to welcome them. Within the week the children had resumed their studies in Charlotte schools and their great adventure was but a memory.

### HATTIE'S WORLD TOUR

Following their return, Hattie continued to tour extensively. She played at New York's Carnegie Recital Hall in 1968 and again in 1973. The 1968 recital was on the day that Martin Luther King, Jr. was killed. We stayed at the Plaza Hotel, and the police had set up a special emergency station in the basement. In fact, they were stationed on nearly every corner in New York City that evening and hardly anyone came into the city to attend the concert.

Hattie made a world tour in the fall of 1972 shortly after Mother Line died of colon cancer at the age of 91. Hattie had always been very close to her mother, and the tour helped her through a difficult time. She began in the Far East, flying first to the west coast and from there to New Zealand where Sydnor was attending high school. Through a mutual friend we had made a connection with Bryan and Margaret Gainsford in Christ Church on South Island and they were his hosts for a year and a half while he studied in the public high school. Getting away from home, where he apparently felt the reins were being held a bit too tightly, was clearly the best course for him. We were delighted with the manner in which he responded to the independence the change provided him. He graduated in the top 15% of his high school class and was automatically admitted to study at Canterbury College in Christ Church had he chosen to stay there. The Gainsfords were wonderful to him and we have always been most grateful to them.

The circumstances under which Sydnor departed for New Zealand bear relating at some length. Because he was serving as president of the Methodist Youth Fellowship at Myers Park Methodist Church, most of the high school students at the church saw him off at the airport. Within several hours of his arrival in Los Angeles, Hattie had a telephone call from him saying that the New Zealand consul in Los Angeles had said that he would have to have a visa in order to go to school in New Zealand. He didn't have one. Hattie then called the consul and he explained that the reason a visa was required was that a number of hippies had been migrating to his country, causing both economic and social problems.

I called the consul as soon as I got home that evening and he quickly assured me that he thought we could work the matter out. In fact, the first thing he said to me was "What a fine young man your son Sydnor is." I realized his attitude had changed during the interim between the two calls. It seemed the consul had obtained details from Sydnor as to whom he would be visiting in New Zealand. Sydnor explained that, in addition to staying with the Gainsfords while he was in school, he intended to visit the Robert Thornleys in Auckland on North Island. Dr. Thornley had served as a visiting preacher at Myers Park Church the previous spring and had invited Sydnor to visit him en-route to Christ Church. Believe it or not, Dr. Thornley had been the minister who married the consul and his wife! That coincidence provided the key to the visa Sydnor needed and he was soon on his way. It was further evidence of the truth of the old adage, "It isn't _what_ you know; it's _whom_ you know."

Sydnor was in New Zealand during the height of the Vietnam War and the widespread dissension that accompanied it in this country. When Hattie visited Christ Church High School, she thanked the principal for all the school had done for him. "Do you think we have done something for Sydnor," he asked. Somewhat taken aback by this response, Hattie replied "I've had glowing reports from his teachers." She later learned from Sydnor (not from the principal) that Sydnor had given a speech at the school criticizing the United States' involvement in Vietnam. On the heels of Sydnor's speech, the principal enjoined those attending the assembly not to be "disloyal" to their country (implying that Sydnor had been) and later threatened to have Sydnor's visa revoked. New Zealand was a member of the coalition of nations that had sent troops to Vietnam and the principal was a former Minister of Education in the New Zealand government. Fortunately Sydnor's English teacher had approved his speech in advance.

Further evidence of Sydnor's conviction that United States armed forces should withdraw from Vietnam was the fact that he bought a box of "McGovern for President" buttons to sell to New Zealanders in order to raise money for his candidate. Suffice it to say, he didn't sell many of them.

From New Zealand Hattie emplaned for Australia where she played a recital in Melbourne and then on to Singapore, where she played to a large audience at the Hilton Hotel. While she was practicing one morning, a Malaysian girl who was cleaning the room listened for a time and asked Hattie if she would please "show me how to do that." The tour continued to Athens, Barcelona and London. Returning to New York from London, Hattie played a concert on the *Elizabeth II*. In the eight years that followed, she filled similar engagements on the *Elizabeth II* as a pianist for the Cunard Lines. Hattie has some great stories to tell, including the time she nearly fell off the piano bench when the seas rose as a result of near hurricane force winds.

# CHAPTER 20
## CONTINUING TO BUILD A LAW PRACTICE

Judge Wilson Warlick of the U.S. District Court for the Western District of North Carolina retired in 1967. Several of Joe Grier's friends suggested that he should seek the appointment and Joe showed considerable enthusiasm for the idea. I offered to contact some of the members of the Bar on Joe's behalf and one of my first assignments was to speak with Jim McMillan, who was a good friend to both Joe and me. When I spoke with Jim, he said that ordinarily there was nothing he would not do for Joe but confessed that he also aspired to that appointment. Thus it developed that the two friends, Joe and Jim, were the leading candidates to succeed Judge Warlick.

The appointment was within the province of United States Senators Sam Ervin and Everett Jordan, who were expected to make recommendations to President Lyndon Johnson. When a delegation of lawyers from Charlotte visited Senators Ervin and Jordan in their Washington, DC offices, the senators let it be known that they would recommend the person who had the most support from the Mecklenburg Bar. Within a few weeks the Mecklenburg Bar Association submitted the question to a vote of its members. Jim got a majority of the votes and received the appointment just in time to be called upon to decide the celebrated *Swann* case requiring extensive busing of school children. If Joe had been appointed to the judgeship, *he* would have had to handle that "hot potato."

At my suggestion Mark Bernstein left his practice with Messers. Haynes, Graham and Baucom in January 1968 to become a member of our firm, with salutary consequences to the growth of our practice that could hardly have been imagined. At the time Mark became a partner, we wanted to change the firm's name to reflect the merger of the two practices. Since Gaston Gage and Jim Preston had already been with us for several years, we could hardly leave them out of consideration. After much soul-searching, Joe, Francis, Bill and I made the decision at lunch one day to change the firm name to Grier, Parker, Poe, Thompson, Bernstein, Gage & Preston. It was by all odds the longest name of any law firm in North Carolina and perhaps in the entire country. After a few attempts at pronouncing the entire name when she answered the telephone, the receptionist soon learned that "Grier Parker" was quite sufficient. By this means the name was salvaged – for twenty years.

Sam Woodard, a graduate of the University of North Carolina Law School, became associated with our ever expanding firm in 1969. Max Justice, a graduate of Wake Forest Law School, joined us in 1970. In time, both proved to be great strengths to the firm.

UNIVERSITY RESEARCH PARK

Established in 1966, University Research Park was intended as a site for companies that would engage in various forms of research as a complement to nearby University of North Carolina at Charlotte. The Charlotte Chamber of Commerce and Chancellor Dean Colvard of UNC-C were especially instrumental in establishing Research Park and garnering support from the city fathers. In fact, Colvard has written an interesting history of the Park. Paul Younts was also among the leaders of the project and he engaged our firm to represent the Company.

W.T. "Bill" Harris, who was then president of the Charlotte Chamber of Commerce, became the first president of the Research Park board. I worked closely with him and real estate brokers Claude Freeman and Louis Rose who undertook to recruit national companies, most notably IBM, to buy acreage and settle there. In time, David Taylor of Celanese Corporation succeeded Bill as president of the Park board.

I continued to represent the Park until my partner Grant Whitney, a former chairman of the local Republican Party, assumed that responsibility under what were for me somewhat inauspicious circumstances. When a vacancy occurred on the North Carolina Supreme Court during Republican Jim Martin's term as Governor, my partner Francis Parker, a long-time Republican, was considered a likely prospect for the appointment. The two of us called upon the president of University Research Park, who was a Republican and a strong supporter of Governor Martin, to ask him to use his influence to have Francis appointed to the Court. He did so and Francis received the appointment.

Some weeks later when the campaign in which Francis would run as a Republican was being mounted, Justice Harry Martin asked me to co-chair the Mecklenburg County campaign for the Democrats who were running. Most of them were seeking reelection. Because Harry was a good friend and because no trial lawyer likes to disappoint the members of the Court in which he regularly appears (not to speak of the fact that I am a "yellow dog" Democrat), I agreed. Somehow I considered that everyone would naturally expect me to support the Democratic ticket. That was a mistake. Although my role had little to do with whether Francis won or lost the race (he lost by about 100,000 votes statewide), it soon became clear that I should have declined Harry's invitation. After all, Francis had been my partner and my good friend for thirty years, and I had prevailed upon my client to help him get the appointment. Shortly after the election, the chief executive of Research Park began referring the Park's legal work to Grant, who had theretofore been assisting me in those matters. I can't say that I blamed him.

146

While the Park proved a temporary boon to the Charlotte business community, it did not become the center of research that it was expected to be. Most of the property has since been sold to manufacturing concerns.

## CHEMICAL BANK'S LOAN TO THE LANDMARK HOTEL

The early 1970s were good years for our law firm on a number of counts. William Rikard, a graduate of Vanderbilt Law School, and Fred Lowrance, a graduate of Virginia Law School, joined us then. William began working with Joe and Fred with me. Both have made major contributions to the firm's litigation practice. Fred has always had an abundance of energy and he accepted every assignment offered him with enthusiasm. By that time the firm had about a dozen lawyers and was netting over half a million dollars from its general practice. Within the next ten years the firm more than doubled in size and income. Specialization developed in earnest and departmentalization became firmly established.

Unfortunately that was not an equally good time for Wall Street. A great many real estate mortgage loans ended in default and the New York banks who had invested heavily in them were thrust into a situation in which they were compelled to establish "work out" teams to supervise the handling of millions of dollars worth of delinquent real estate loans. After I had moved to Charlotte in 1954, people occasionally asked me if I thought my time in New York had proved beneficial to my Charlotte practice. I often responded by saying "It has at least prevented my being intimidated by a New York lawyer." I soon had an opportunity to prove whether or not that was true in a case involving such a mortgage loan.

A Charlotte developer named Earl Crawford engaged the D.C. Turner Construction Company of Charlotte to build the Landmark Hotel in Asheville, North Carolina. Chemical Bank had organized a Real Estate Investment Trust (REIT) called Chemical Realty Corporation to engage in that market. A few months after Landmark had obtained a permanent loan commitment from Home Federal Savings and Loan Association of Hollywood, Florida, Chemical Realty made a $6,000,000 construction loan commitment to Landmark Hotel. The permanent loan agreement obligated Home Federal to pay off the construction loan after the hotel was completed and after certain other conditions were met. When the construction loan was closed in April 1973, I was named as trustee of the deed of trust of which Chemical Realty was the beneficiary. After Chemical Realty had advanced in excess of $5,000,000 on the construction loan, Crawford ran into financial difficulties and was unable to pay Landmark's bills. In October 1974 he moved all of the guests out and closed the hotel down.

Mike Berman, who was in charge of the "work out" for Chemical Bank, immediately came to Asheville and to Charlotte and retained me to represent the bank in what had clearly become a very serious situation. Fred Lowrance was also heavily involved in the case from the beginning. Berman first offered an assignment of the loan to Home Federal Savings and Loan, which refused the assignment on the ground that the conditions of the permanent loan commitment had not been met. We then brought suit against Landmark on behalf of Chemical Realty to foreclose the construction loan's deed of trust.

Before the matter could be heard in state court, Landmark's attorney Willie Green of Asheville filed a voluntary petition in bankruptcy under Chapter 10 of the Bankruptcy Act on its behalf. We filed our own petition seeking to have the hotel property surrendered to Chemical Realty on the ground that the property did not have a value in excess of the amount due Chemical on the construction loan and therefore the bankruptcy court should "abandon" the property to Chemical in accordance with established law. We prevailed in the bankruptcy court on that theory and the judgment was affirmed by the United States Court of Appeals for the Fourth Circuit on January 12, 1976.[*] Chemical then held a public foreclosure sale and was the successful bidder for the hotel at $3,000,000. It later sold the hotel to a third party.

In late 1976 we brought suit against Home Federal Savings & Loan in the Buncombe County Superior Court on behalf of Chemical Realty to recover damages for breach of its contract to take out Chemical's $6,000,000.00 construction loan. The action was tried before Superior Court Judge Walter Allen in Asheville in 1980. Fred and I went to Asheville the day before the trial and bunked at the Landmark Hotel, the subject of the suit. As we saw it, the major issues in the case revolved around two principal questions: (1) Was Chemical a third party beneficiary of the permanent loan commitment made by Home Federal so that it could compel Home Federal to honor its commitment? And (2), had all of the conditions precedent required by Home Federal in its permanent loan commitment been substantially met? It didn't help that we had earlier refused to pay Turner the contract price because the building was defective, although that case had been settled before the Home Federal case was actually tried.

The trial of the Home Federal case lasted only two weeks but the judge held the case under advisement for months. In fact, it was a full year after the trial before Judge Allen heard oral arguments in the case. So much time then elapsed without his having ruled that he set the matter for re-argument after another year. Finally, in 1983 (seven years after the action had been filed and nearly three years after the case was actually tried), Judge Allen ruled for the defendant

---

[*] *Landmark Hotel, Inc. v. Chemical Realty Corp.*, 532 F.2d 750.

Home Federal, finding in its favor on both of the issues on which the case turned: that Chemical was not a third party beneficiary of the permanent loan commitment, and that neither Landmark nor Chemical had substantially complied with conditions precedent set forth in the permanent loan commitment.

On appeal to the NC Court of Appeals, in an opinion written by Judge Hugh Wells in 1987, the appellate court finally ruled in favor of the defendant Home Federal on both grounds on which the Superior Court had relied.**

The holding that Chemical was not a third party beneficiary of the permanent loan commitment so as to enable it to recover from Home Federal was much criticized in banking journals and was clearly out of tune with modern banking practices. In ruling that Chemical had failed to comply with the conditions of the permanent loan commitment, however, the Court of Appeals may have been on sounder ground.

Before the matter was resolved, Mike Berman left Chemical to go into the real estate development business. He and I continued to cross paths, however. In the late '70s I was engaged to represent the bondholders in the Carolina Caribbean Corporation bankruptcy at the request of Stephen Case, a partner at Davis Polk. Carolina Caribbean operated an amusement park and ski resort in the mountains of North Carolina. By coincidence, Mike Berman and Stephen Case had been in a meeting together in New York City. According to Mike, my name came up and I am told they agreed to the proposition that I was "the greatest lawyer in North Carolina." Regardless of whether they were correct (and who am I to contradict them?), I once again drew some satisfaction from the fact that my colleagues thought I had met the test.

Concerning our work on the *Home Federal* case, Mike Berman wrote:

March 3, 1981

Dear Syd:

There are times when people really go the "extra mile" on behalf of their associates and I believe the Home Federal trial was one of those occasions. We here at Chemical were absolutely delighted with the diligence and professionalism that was displayed by all participants.

I thought you might enjoy reading Herbert Hyde's book and asked him to inscribe it for you as a memento of the event. Please accept this book as a small token of our appreciation for your efforts on our behalf.

Sincerely,
Mike

The book to which Mike's letter refers is a collection of Herbert Hyde's hilarious tall tales called "Genuine Hyde." I had associated

---

** *Chemical Realty Corporation v. Home Federal*, 84 N.C. App. 27 (1987).

Herbert Hyde in the case since he practiced in Asheville where the case was tried. One of the best stories in the book is called "Mr. Speaker, There Oughta Be Somewhere a Person Can Cuss Without Breaking the Law," which he delivered in the North Carolina legislature when he was a member of that body. It read in part:

> This is an iniquitous bill, Ladies and Gentlemen of the House, and ought not to pass. The present statute 14-197 reads – and I'll try to read it the best I can – I don't understand it but I'll read it anyhow – "If any person shall, on any public road or highway and in the hearing of two or more persons in a loud and boisterous manner use indecent or profane language, he shall be guilty of a misdemeanor" and put in jail.
>
> Now, it doesn't say what's profane. And it doesn't say what's indecent. And I don't know. And most folks in Swain County don't know. And if you pass this you are going to put 'em in jeopardy."

The legislators then obliged Herbert by exempting Swain County from the act!

When Mike retired from Chemical Bank, I went to New York for his retirement party where I read a limerick:

> Here's to our friend Mike Berman,
> to the South a modern-day Sherman.
> Though billed a "Black Bart",
> he's really all heart.
> If you scratch him, he's pure gold and ermine.

### FAIR TRADE LAWS IN JUDGE MCMILLAN'S COURT

In the early '70s Don Zimmerman, who had so intimidated me in my first year at Harvard and was now a member of a major New York law firm, referred a new client to me in the person of Melvin Solomon. Solomon was the president of Sam Solomon Company, a Charleston, South Carolina catalog warehouse showroom. The company had been sued in the U.S. District Court for the Western District of North Carolina for selling Panasonic products at a price less than the fair trade price that Panasonic had stipulated. (At that time several states, including North Carolina, had fair trade laws that enabled manufacturers to require retailers to maintain a certain minimum price for their products.)

Mark Bernstein had represented Bulova Watch Company for years in that company's efforts to police the fair trade prices of its products by bringing actions against those who sold the products at less than the fair trade price. Because of his familiarity with fair trade laws, I asked Mark to work with me on the Sam Solomon case. Together we took the depositions of several Panasonic representatives at Skadden, Arps, Slate, Meagher & Flom in New York City. By coincidence, the Meagher of that firm was the same William R. Meagher who had, at Davis Polk, worked with Mr. Davis and me on the South Carolina school segregation case.

Eventually the Panasonic matter came on for a hearing on the plaintiff's motion for an injunction in Judge James McMillan's court. Mark and I had a clear understanding that we should not challenge

150

the constitutionality of the North Carolina fair trade law for several reasons: (1) the federal courts had already upheld the constitutionality of such laws on a number of occasions, (2) we had sufficient defenses to win the case without raising the constitutional issue, and (3) Bulova Watch Company had a great stake in enforcing the fair trade laws, and we did not want to prejudice its position in the future. This plan was agreeable to our client. Bill Covington, of Kennedy, Covington, Lobdell and Hickman, represented the plaintiff as local counsel.

On the day of the hearing, Mark and I appeared in court on behalf of the defendant. Mark excused himself briefly and left the courtroom before the proceedings got under way. While he was out, Covington made an opening statement in favor of his client's position and Judge McMillan immediately asked him if the fair trade law under which the action had been brought did not violate the Fourteenth Amendment to the United States Constitution. Covington insisted that it did not and then Judge McMillan put the same question to me. I explained that we had not raised the constitutional question but were satisfied that our other defenses entitled us to prevail. Without further ceremony, Judge McMillan pronounced judgment that in his view the North Carolina fair trade law was unconstitutional. He then dismissed the plaintiff's case just as Mark walked back into the courtroom. While Covington, his face drained of color, stammered his protest, Mark and I collected our papers and quickly left the courtroom.

The few remaining fair trade laws were soon repealed in those states in which they remained in force. We continued to represent Sam Solomon Company in a great many matters for ten years or more, including the eventual sale of all of its stores to Service Merchandise Company of Nashville, Tennessee. Shortly after the Panasonic case was tried, Melvin Solomon, a delightful gentleman, entertained Mark and me and our wives at Charleston's first Spoleto Festival.

## MAKING THE MOVE TO CAMERON BROWN

By the early seventies the firm had become large enough to necessitate being organized into departments. Because I was still doing a considerable amount of general corporate work, representing clients like S&W Cafeterias, Delph Hardware, and Carolina Transfer and Storage Company, I became co-chairman of the corporate department with Mark Bernstein. I was also beginning to do more and more trial work, however, and by 1973 my trial practice had grown to the point that I had determined to move in that direction.

The firm moved to the tenth floor of the Cameron Brown Building on McDowell Street in 1974. George Pittman decorated our offices in his usual yellow and orange motif with plenty of bric-a-brac lying around on the furniture. Jim Preston rescued us from the ersatz finery for a time by depositing most of it in a closet, but Joe Grier soon discovered the malefaction and restored the office to its former glory.

Just after we moved into our elegant new quarters, Jim Preston and I made a pact that he would stop smoking cigarettes if I should give up my pipe, a habit which I had enjoyed off and on for at least thirty years. A few months later I walked into his office and was surprised to find him smoking a cigarette. Apparently he had started smoking again within a few days after our agreement but tried not to let me see it so that I could succeed in breaking my own habit. It's one of the nicest things anyone ever did for me. I have now been smoke-free for thirty years. Hattie smoked her last cigarette on July 23, 1957 at 3 o'clock in the afternoon, an occasion of which she will remind you at the drop of a hat. It seems she read a newspaper article to the effect that smoking had been found to be dangerous to your health. Our daughter D'Arcy, who has tried to stop smoking on many occasions without success, has not been so fortunate.

By 1975 four more associates had joined the firm, all of whom have made significant contributions to the practice. Fred Thompson, Jr. and Bill Farthing, Jr. arrived in 1974 from the University of North Carolina Law School. Both went into corporate work within a short time of their arrival. Tony Orsbon and Irvin "Hank" Hankins came to the firm in 1975, Tony from Vanderbilt Law School and Hank from the University of North Carolina Law School. Tony soon went into wills and estates work and Hank into litigation. In 1977 Heloise Merrill and Bill Porter joined us. Heloise, who came to us from Duke Law School, was our first woman lawyer and later became our first woman partner. For several years Heloise worked with me in litigation but she eventually transferred to the Tax Department at Jim Preston's invitation. Although it took me a while to forgive Jim, Heloise went on to become an outstanding specialist in pension and profit sharing plans. Bill Porter, who came to us from the University of North Carolina Law School, now heads the Commercial Contracts and Bankruptcy Division of the Litigation Department and has earned an excellent reputation as a bankruptcy lawyer. Both Hank Hankins and Bill Farthing have served as the firm's managing partners, Hank for at least fifteen years beginning in the 1980s and Bill for the last few years.

In the early 1970s I began to entertain the firm's associates at an annual sports outing and dinner at the Charlotte Country Club. We usually played tennis but because some preferred golf, we tried our hands at golf on at least one occasion. I well remember a weekend in the mid-seventies when Sam Woodard, William Rikard, Fred Lowrance and I played eighteen holes while Max Justice dispensed beer from the back of a golf cart. I had no hope of breaking a hundred, but they were willing to put up with me for the sake of playing one of the best courses in North Carolina.

After a few years, Jim Preston insisted on helping with the cost of our summer outings and I was delighted to accept his offer. We established a trophy for the winner of the tennis tournament with the understanding that it should be retired by any player who won it three years in a row. Fred Lowrance quickly retired the first trophy after the first three years. I eventually retired the second trophy after we changed the game to doubles and I claimed either Rich Schell or Mark Bernstein, two of the best players, as my partner. After all, I bought the trophy!

Eventually, the firm itself adopted the idea of a summer outing at a local country club. From time to time the associates were made responsible for the evening's entertainment which usually took the form of a skit. With the help of Regina Wheeler, Kevin Dunlap brought the house down one year with his masterful mimicry of Hank Hankins. In general, however, the results were somewhat uneven and that format was eventually abandoned in favor of a dinner and dance. One of the firm's better summer parties featured a skit written by Mike Almond in which the firm was likened to a pack of dogs. I prepared some verses for the occasion:

### PARKER POE DOG-GEREL

#### I

Tonight our firm which rarely pettifogs
has chosen to identify with dogs –
some old, some young, but each prepared to play
a role in which he's called to howl or bay
the epic tale of that immortal pack
of lupine types who pillage and ransack
the Metrolina countryside for bones
in ways that neither heav'n nor hell condones.
But now as this historic tale unweaves
we hear an age-old moral in re thieves.

#### II

For two old dogs who'd shame a Philistine
have claimed the lion's share – Poe and Bernstein.
And all the others vie for just a bite
or seek by various ruses to incite
a firm-wide revolution 'mong their peers,
recruiting them as canine buccaneers.
Among their leaders Almond and Lowrance
have sought the younger puppies to entrance
with songs of major major derring do
and dreams of major major bones to chew.

#### Epilogue

But now at dog-gerel's end,
one firm, one faith, one blend
of old dog and pup,
having plenty to sup
and higher goals yet to transcend.

Members of the firm later began spending a weekend in the fall at Joe Grier's cottage at Garden City, South Carolina. When our numbers grew too great for that venue, we moved first to Litchfield Beach, and then later to Pinehurst.

## JOHN CANSLER

At Judge Clarkson's suggestion, he and I interviewed John Cansler, who was one of the senior leaders of the Charlotte Bar. He had recently retired. We wanted to preserve his recollections of the history of the Charlotte Bar while his memory was fresh and we recorded the interview on tape. He had been practicing law since the early 1900s, when he joined his father's law firm after graduating from the University of North Carolina Law School. He was a delightful gentleman, possessed of a marvelous sense of humor. In the course of the interview, he told Judge Clarkson and me about his having taken dance lessons from a fellow student (a new step called the "fox trot") while he was a freshman at UNC-Chapel Hill in 1910. When one of the faculty members who was acting as a chaperone congratulated him on his dancing prowess, Mr. Cansler thanked him but modestly protested that it wasn't something he did well, to which the teacher responded "Listen, John, I'll give you a little piece of advice. If anyone ever again tells a damn lie in your favor, don't contradict him." I've used that story to good effect more than once.

Mr. Cansler had some great stories about Charlotte lawyers, and Judge Clarkson also made a few contributions:

Cansler: My father (Edwin T. Cansler) told me this one. Of course back in those days the place was small and lawyers practiced everything in town. They didn't have any Recorder at that time. The mayor had the mayor's court and Colonel Jones just loved to sit there all day. The mayor at that time was Dr. Brevard and it seems it was Labor Day or some holiday like that and some cotton mill hands got off so they got hold of a five gallon keg of beer and went down to Belmont springs to spend the day and drink beer. They spent the day out there, and had a very delightful time. Late in the afternoon some colored boys came by, and they got into a big fight and I don't know whose fault it was. They were all in court and they were tried for fighting.

So the case was being tried before Dr. Brevard who was the mayor. Colonel Jones was representing the colored boys and my father was representing the mill hands and they talked about that they were drinking beer and Colonel Jones said "you boys, all of you were drunk." They said "no sir, Colonel, we weren't drunk." He said "you bound to be, you been drinking beer all day. How many of there were you?" "There were five of us. We just had one case of beer." "Did you drink it up?" "Yes, sir, we drunk it up." "You mean to tell me that five of you, each had a gallon of beer and you weren't drunk?" "No, sir Colonel we weren't drunk." Colonel Jones was a hard liquor man himself. Then Judge Brevard said "now just a minute, just a minute Colonel. The court will take judicial notice of the fact that it is possible for an able-bodied young man to drink a gallon of beer all day long and not get drunk because the court has done it himself many times." (Laughter).

Clarkson: Let me tell you a story about your father and mine (Heriot Clarkson). They were great friends, but they opposed each other at times you know. One time they were before Squire Marshall in a lawsuit and Mr. Cansler said something to father that father resented. I have forgotten what it was but my father thought Mr. Cansler called him a liar. So father started to jump on him and Mr. Cansler sat back in his chair and raised up his foot. In the meantime Squire Marshall got in between them to separate them and he got Mr. Cansler's foot right in his belly. (Laughter). They said the old Squire jumped around and said "damn it, let them fight." (Laughter).

Mr. Cansler also reported on the activities of some of the Charlotte lawyers who were Civil War veterans:

Cansler: Here is a story that Mr. Guthrie told me about Captain Bason. The Captain was quite a character and he was the counsel for the Southern Railroad for years and years. And of course the headquarters was in Little Washington, so he had to go back and forth and of course he and the conductors knew each other. Well, the Captain had quite an eye for the ladies. When he took the train, he saw a very attractive young lady come up there and it wasn't very long before he was over there and making friends with her. They were chatting. Then it came night time and he had to make some arrangement in the meantime. Well, the conductor knew Captain Bason, and had his eye on him, and he was going along, and about midnight he heard low voices and he looked in the Captain's berth and the Captain wasn't there so he knew where he had gone. So he shook the side of the lady's bed and said "Captain Bason, Captain Bason, we can't have such disorder, we can't have such." Well Captain to his embarrassment could not perform when he got there, but it was a cold night and they were just there chatting. So he said "I just want to let you know that this young lady is as safe with me as if she was in her mother's arms". (Laughter.)

Captain Bason and Colonel Jones were good friends but they were constantly sniping at each other. Back in the early part of the century in the early 1900s Dallas was the county seat of Gaston County and Gastonia was just a small village. Back in those days of course they had court not more than twice a year. Well a lot of Charlotte lawyers would go over there. Well this particular rainy night Captain Bason, Colonel Jones and Judge Osborne and my father all got off in Gastonia late in the evening, and they got a hack and drove over to Dallas. They'd always stay at a big boarding house. The owner said "I'm just sorry as I can be. I've got a big bedroom here with two double beds if you four gentlemen want to get in there that would be fine." It was raining and they had no choice. So they went into the room and they questioned who was going to sleep with whom. (Laughter.) Captain Bason said "I am not going to sleep with Colonel Jones. I'd rather sleep with a dog as with him." The Colonel said "I couldn't agree with you more." (Laughter.)

Back in those days a lot of the Civil War veterans, especially those who had been in the calvary, continued to wear boots under their trousers, and Captain Bason was wearing them so he sat down to get undressed and he started to pull off his boots and then ostentatiously put them on the table right by his bed and the Colonel said, "far be it from me to inquire as to the habits of people, but my curiosity gets the better of me. Do you want to tell me just why you put your boots on the table by your bed?"

Captain Bason said "no I don't mind telling you. The first son of a bitch that starts snoring is going to find out." (Laughter.)

Finally, Mr. Cansler added a reference to General Stonewall Jackson's granddaughter who had lived in Charlotte:

Cansler: Randolph Preston's father was the beloved minister of the First Presbyterian Church.

Clarkson: And Randolph had married a granddaughter of Stonewall Jackson. Her name was Julia.

Cansler: Miss Julia's father was named Christian. Mr. Christian was furious at Randolph one time and he took to the streets saying he was going to kill him. This fella, I can't remember his name, he was a contemporary of Randolph, and he said "you know, Randolph needed some friends to rally around there to try and protect him, to keep him from getting killed, so we did; but since I've got to know him better, I think we made a great mistake." (Laughter.)

# CHAPTER 21
## VIENNA AND BEYOND
### ANOTHER YEAR IN VIENNA

As the earlier experience had proved such a success, Hattie and I decided that another year in Vienna would be beneficial to her music career and to the three younger children. D'Arcy had completed dental hygiene studies, married and launched her career in Norfolk, Virginia and Sydnor had enrolled at Duke University. In 1973 Hattie, Harriet, Brenny and Kathy Line prepared to set sail. En route to Vienna, the travelers visited the Hajmassy family in Wiesbaden, Germany. Jutta Hajmassy is the daughter of the celebrated German pianist Walter Gieseking. Jutta's husband Imré is also a noted concert pianist. During Hattie's visit to Wiesbaden, the Hajmassys generously offered her their vacation house on a mountain overlooking the Zurich Sea in Switzerland. She and the children accepted the offer for a time, but after visiting Vienna before the Swiss schools were scheduled to begin, they unanimously agreed to spend another year enjoying the exciting life they had known in Vienna.

Within a week they had set up housekeeping again in the same house they had formerly occupied in Perchtoldsdorf. This time young Harriet attended a German-speaking "gymnasium" (high school) and Brenny and Kathy Line attended the Perchtoldsdorf *hauptschule* and *volkschule,* respectively. After a time, Hattie decided that Brenny was not getting enough from his studies because of the language barrier and enrolled him in the English speaking Black Forest Academy (a boarding school) in the Black Forest near Basil. Kathy Line enjoyed the advantage of having Frau Hedwig Danek, the same dear teacher who had been so helpful to Harriet seven years earlier.

With the children settled in school, Hattie had another good year of piano study, this time with Jörg Demus, the celebrated Austrian pianist. The Hajmassys had recommended Hattie to Demus and she commuted to his master classes in Stuttgart throughout the year. He proved to be most helpful. Over the years, they have become fast friends. In fact, Demus stayed with us when he came to Charlotte in 1977 to perform with the Charlotte Symphony Orchestra. He asked Hattie what she would like him to play, and she suggested Beethoven's Emperor Concerto because she knew it was one of my favorites. He played it beautifully, of course.

Jörg visited us again in 1986 when he conducted a piano workshop at the University of North Carolina at Charlotte and played a recital at Queens College. Several years ago, we visited Jörg at his museum-like home in Salzkammergut, Austria and made a video in which he described his remarkable collection of about thirty instruments that represent the development of the piano from its origin in the early 1700s to the present day.

During Hattie's second year in Vienna, we again rented our house and this time I stayed the entire year with Mother. I suppose I had worn out my welcome with the friends who had put me up the first year. Rolfe Neill was looking for a house for a young newspaperman from Seattle, Washington to rent. The prospective tenant, the son of the publisher of *The Seattle Times,* was to be in training with Rolfe at the *Charlotte Observer* for a year. He and his wife and two young children soon moved into 1622 Brandon Road. He eventually followed in his father's footsteps, and is now the publisher of *The Seattle Times* himself.

Fortunately, it was also a good year at the office. I was just beginning to hit my stride as a litigator in several demanding cases, so that kept me busy. I was still lonely, however, and often felt the need to gather my friends around me. One evening, I invited a dozen close friends to the Charlotte Country Club and after dinner chaired a discussion of some subject that I have since forgotten. Those who attended were Nancy Akers, Mark Bernstein, George Daly, Dean Hamrick, John Kennedy, D. G. Martin, Lawrence McCleskey, Jim Preston, Ace Walker, my brothers Joe and Phil and my sister Bobbie. I gave each of the men gold cuff links engraved with their initials and each of the women a brooch, as well as an appropriate remembrance for each invitee's spouse. (In Nancy's case her daughter Mary Cathey got the second gift.) After that evening, I felt a little less lonely.

## MORE CONCERTIZING

A few years after returning from Vienna, Hattie and Ann Peschek, a soprano who had married an Austrian and was living in Vienna, collaborated on a concert tour to memorialize the two hundredth anniversary of the American Declaration of Independence. All of the music on the program was early American and they concertized both in Europe and in the United States. Hattie played compositions by Alexander Reinagle, Nathaniel Dett, Louis Gottschalk and Wallingford Riegger.

Once, when she was traveling in a semi-private train compartment between London and Peterborough, Hattie used the practice board that she customarily carries with her on tour. The keys of the practice board make no sound but are merely designed to provide a means of reviewing repertory. When the train stopped at an intermediate station, an old gentleman entered the compartment and took a seat in a corner across from Hattie. After watching her practice on the board for awhile, her fellow-traveler inquired "Would you mind playing a little louder?" He had apparently never seen any such contraption before.

Two years later, Hattie performed Rachmaninoff's Second Piano Concerto with the Charlotte Symphony Orchestra to a standing ovation in Charlotte. The orchestra then performed the same concert in Gaffney, South Carolina. By this time, she had resumed her music career in full force. Those concerts were immediately followed by solo recitals at Carnegie Recital Hall in New York, the Mint Museum in Charlotte, and Coker College in Hartsville, South Carolina. Several years later she played the Rachmaninoff Second with the Charlotte Repertory Orchestra, again to listener acclaim.

In the 1980s, Hattie had an accident which might have ended her music career. She was running along South Boulevard when she tripped over a raised place in the sidewalk, fell to the ground and drove three fingers on her right hand out of their sockets and onto the back of her hand. She managed to return two of the fingers to their sockets immediately, but the little finger was not so amenable. To this day that little finger is unable to reach its former span. Somehow Hattie has found a means of compensating for that handicap in her playing. The city was clearly negligent in not having repaired the sidewalk, so Hattie brought suit against the city and the jury found to that effect. Unfortunately, the jury also found that Hattie was negligent in not avoiding the obstacle and so she received nothing. Although Hattie made an excellent witness, we learned later from one of the jurors that they had concluded that she was much too well off and well dressed to need to be compensated for her injuries by taxpayers like themselves. And, to make matters worse, her lawyer and I had prevailed upon her to reject an offer of settlement of $40,000.00 before they jury came in!

North Carolina is one of the three states which do not recognize the principle of comparative negligence. This is no doubt a result of the political influence of the insurance companies in the North Carolina legislature.

# CHAPTER 22
## THE LAW PRACTICE GROWS

By 1980 Charlotte had a population of approximately 300,000 and the firm had grown to twenty-five lawyers, with a budget of nearly three million dollars. Not until the early nineties, however, when Charlotte acquired its NBA basketball team (the Charlotte Hornets, now the "New Orleans Hornets"), did locals begin to boost Charlotte as a "world class" city. By that time the population had grown to 400,000.

In 1982 the firm appeared to be suffering from growing pains and a professional consulting firm called Hildebrand was retained to review our internal business practices. As a result of that review, in 1983 members executed the firm's first partnership agreement in nearly one hundred years of practice! Although that fact is a tribute to the confidence that the partners had in each other over the years, it may also be a commentary on their lack of sound business judgment.

There was one provision of the proposed partnership agreement to which I objected: that which stated that a partner must begin taking steps toward retirement at age 68, at which time his compensation would be drastically reduced with each subsequent year. Complete retirement would occur at age 72, although one would continue to be provided an office and a secretary indefinitely, as well as a pension to be hereinafter described. I had planned to continue to practice law as long as I remained in good health, as had several other partners. The majority voted in favor of the retirement provision, however, so it was adopted.

By sheer good fortune I found a copy of a memo attributed to an anonymous Central Piedmont College faculty wit who found himself in a similar predicament. I adapted it to our situation, and read it at a firm outing that summer:

### MEMORANDUM

TO:    All Grier Parker Poe Thompson Bernstein Gage & Preston Personnel

SUBJECT:  New Retirement Policy Adopted by the Firm in 1983

FROM:    Management Committee

The following plan has been adopted for implementing the new firm retirement policy for certain partners:

Under the plan, older partners will go on early retirement, thus permitting the advancement of younger partners who represent our future plans.

Therefore, a program to phase out older partners will be placed into effect as soon as possible.

The program shall be known as RAPE (Retire Aged Partners Early).

Partners who are RAPED will be given the opportunity to seek alternative employment within the system, provided that while they are being RAPED they request a review of their employment records before actual retirement takes place.

This phase is called SCREW (Survey of Capabilities of Retired Early Workers).

All partners who have been RAPED or SCREWED may also apply for a trial review.

This will be called SHAFT (Study by Higher Authority Following Termination).

The new policy dictates that older partners may be RAPED once and SCREWED twice, but may get the SHAFT as many times as the firm deems appropriate.

I confess that, despite my conviction that I should never want to retire, the retirement provision has actually worked to my advantage in the long run, as will eventually become clear.

A number of equally noteworthy developments occurred in the firm in 1984. Most significantly, that was the first year since I had joined the firm that we were without the leadership of Joe Grier, Jr. Joe's son Joe 3rd had just finished law school and was about to go into practice. Joe wanted to practice with his son, who was not eligible to join our firm because of our policy against nepotism. Also, under our new partnership agreement Joe's partnership interest was about to be drastically reduced since he was approaching the new retirement age. That combination of circumstances prompted him to retire from the firm as of December 31, 1983, and form a new law firm with his son. I was disappointed, of course, since it was Joe who had brought me to Charlotte and served as my mentor in the early years of my practice there.

Following Joe's retirement, the firm moved again, this time to the 26th floor of the new Charlotte Plaza building on College Street. Bill Poe replaced Joe as chairman of the Executive Committee, and Hank Hankins became managing partner. I became chairman of the firm's Litigation Department, serving in that capacity for the next six years. My only regret in assuming that post was that I had to give up the chairmanship of the Associates Review Committee. That committee's responsibility was to conduct a review of the work of each associate every year. It was a role that I had particularly enjoyed because it kept me in touch with each associate.

At about that time, Judge Clarkson returned to the firm as "counsel" upon his retirement from the Superior Court bench. One of the most enjoyable aspects of my workday was having him stop by my office in the mornings to ask "Well, Syd, what are we working on today?" From time to time he helped me to think through some challenging legal question. But as important as his help was, I cherished even more our close association and genuine friendship. I think anyone who knew Judge Clarkson will understand my view that he was as fine a man as any I have ever known.

In December 1984 the firm celebrated its one hundredth anniversary at a gala dinner at the Charlotte Country Club. Heriot Clarkson, our founder, had first opened his law office in 1884, after having been admitted to the bar upon oral examination by the judges of the North Carolina Supreme Court. At the time of the anniversary celebration, our law firm was the third oldest in Charlotte. Only Cansler Lockhart and Craighill Rendleman (formerly Tillett Campbell) were older. Since then both of those firms have been dissolved, thus constituting ours the oldest firm in Charlotte. I enjoyed the privilege of chairing the anniversary dinner, at which Governor James B. Hunt and Fourth Circuit Chief Judge Sam Ervin 3rd spoke. Justice Jim Exum of the North Carolina Supreme Court, two former North Carolina chief justices and many other state judges were also in attendance.

We took the opportunity to unveil portraits of both Judge Clarkson and his father Judge Heriot Clarkson. The portraits were painted by Cedric Egeli, an outstanding portrait painter from Baltimore. Judge Clarkson and his wife Cama were present to participate in the ceremony, as were Eddie and Elizabeth Clarkson. The portraits now hang in our offices at Three Wachovia Center.

An editorial in the *Charlotte Observer* paid a generous tribute to the firm:

> It was obviously a special occasion. The banquet hall at the Charlotte Country Club fairly glittered with men in crisp tuxedos and women in rustling gowns. There were notables at every table.
>
> Gov. Jim Hunt was present, representing the state government, as were Associate Justice Jim Exum of the State Supreme Court and retired Chief Justices Susie Sharp and William H. Bobbitt.
>
> Representing the federal judiciary were Judge Sam J. Ervin III of the 4th Circuit Court of Appeals and Judge James B. McMillan of the Western District of North Carolina. Superior Court Judges Frank Snepp and William Grist led an impressive array of local jurists.
>
> From the academic community were the deans of three of the state's five law schools: at UNC, Wake Forest and Campbell.
>
> The event was a celebration of the 100th anniversary of the Charlotte law firm now known as Parker, Poe, Thompson, Bernstein, Gage and Preston. It has had a succession of other names since it was founded by Heriot Clarkson in 1884.

In honor of the occasion, I read a reminiscence in verse:

### ODE TO A HUNDRED YEAR OLD LAW FIRM –
#### PARKER POE THOMPSON BERNSTEIN GAGE & PRESTON

I

Tonight our pilgrims pause to celebrate
the hundredth anniversary of that date
on which young Heriot Clarkson sailed to wind
'gainst corporate giants, alcohol and sin.
Embraced the high-toned cause of common man,
whose like can scarce be found among this clan
in high styled sequined gown and black cravat,
(can any dandy here be Democrat?)
And then the plaintiff's torch he held so dear
was raised aloft by Taliaferro & Grier,

but soon the likes of William Poe and MeRB*
began this halcyon picture to disturb.

II

They sought the favor of those self-same kings
of industry and all that money brings.
Today defendants roam these halls at will
inhaling drafts of fine imported swill,
while plaintiffs wait in closets for their turn.
But let us not this macrobusiness spurn
whose P.R. counsel drafts its first brochure,
for never was a firm of lawyers truer
to all that's good and just and undefiled.
Of this, howe'er, no one could e'er be surer,
"The plaintiff's action was not timely filed."

A few months after the anniversary celebration, Judge Clarkson died of cancer after enduring the trauma of his son Frank's trial and conviction of embezzling his clients' money. I suffered through that nightmare with the Judge and appeared with several of my partners as a character witness at his son's trial. Frank was given an active prison term and, after serving his sentence, moved to Florida. In this case, the son's misdeeds were visited upon the father, rather than the Biblical converse.

For decades Hattie and I have brought modest presents to the non-lawyer employees in the Charlotte office at Christmas time. I use the term "modest" advisedly as Hattie has a penchant for finding bargains. Dressed in Christmas attire, we deliver the presents to the office early on the morning on which the firm holds its Christmas party and closes for the holiday. It is our means of expressing our personal appreciation for the staff's loyalty.

For the last twenty years I have also customarily entertained each year's class of new associates and each year's class of summer associates (who have completed their second year of law school and are prospects for full-time employment upon graduation) for lunch at the Charlotte Country Club. It is the means by which I become better acquainted with the new crop of colleagues. They appear to enjoy the tradition as much as I do. I have noted of late that there are often as many women as men in those groups. It seems that given equal opportunity, women have more than proved their ability.

### MODULAR CONTAINER'S GROCERY CARTS

In the early '80s I became involved in an action we filed on behalf of a French firm's subsidiary, Modular Container Corporation, against a warehouse-style grocery chain called Two Guys. My friend Stuart Marks, whom I had known at Davis Polk, referred the matter to me. Modular, his client, had sold Two Guys a number of grocery carts made to specifications provided by the purchaser. When the grocery carts proved to be unmanageable, Two Guys refused to pay,

---

* Lou Cunningham's nickname for Mark R. Bernstein derived from his initials, MRB.

contending that the wheels of the carts would not stay in line and so constantly blocked the carts' forward progress.

We brought an action against Two Guys in the U.S. District Court for the Western District of North Carolina for the price of the carts. The defendant, represented by Bill Diehl, counterclaimed for damages resulting from its loss of business as a consequence of the carts not working properly. William Rikard worked with me on the case. We engaged an expert engineer, Professor Ellis King from the University of North Carolina at Charlotte, to testify that the specifications designed by the defendant were the cause of the problem, rather than the workmanship. Judge James B. McMillan, who tried the case before a jury, refused to allow our expert to testify on the ground that the subject of his testimony did not qualify as a legitimate area of expertise. I was convinced that Judge McMillan was wrong in disallowing the testimony. His decision was a keen disappointment that also turned out to be a major factor in the outcome of the case.

When my colleague William Rikard was examining the defendant's president, he unexpectedly vaulted up into one of the carts that had been introduced as an exhibit and jumped up and down in it. William had not warned me that he intended any such histrionics and I held my breath for fear he would be hurt. He certainly got the jury's attention.

In the course of Bill Diehl's argument to the jury, he pointed to my client, Enrico Baretta, and exclaimed, "This man committed a fraud on my client!" The defendant had not pleaded fraud in his answer or in his counterclaim but it was characteristic of Diehl's propensity for overkill. In the end the jury found against our client on the principal action and against the defendant on the counterclaim. One of our associates interviewed the jurors afterwards and we learned that half of the jurors wanted to find for the plaintiff and the other half wanted to find for the defendant, so they ruled against both parties.

### JOSÉ MARIA ARISTRAIN

Barry Craig called our office in 1982 on behalf of José Maria Aristrain, a native of the Basque province in Spain and owner of a steel manufacturing concern of the same name. According to the associate who took the call, Barry Craig asked for a lawyer "who had attended Harvard Law School," and the call was directed to me. It became one of the most challenging cases that I handled in my legal career, rivaling the several lawsuits in the Chemical Bank's Landmark Hotel matter.

A Charlotte wholesale steel company called Intercontinental Metals Corporation (IMC) had fallen behind by seven million dollars in its obligation to Aristrain and was giving evidence of going bottom up. Harry Grim of Moore and Van Allen advised us that IMC wanted to meet with our client and a conference was scheduled in Zurich, Switzerland for the convenience of Mr. Aristrain. Mark Bernstein and I flew to Zurich just before Thanksgiving and conferred with Grim and the president of IMC, Wolfgang Jansen. I had known Jansen for several years in connection with his having contributed to the Charlotte Opera Association, which perhaps served to lubricate the discussion.

Despite that, the meeting did not prove fruitful. Within a few weeks IMC filed a voluntary petition in bankruptcy in the Western District of North Carolina. We filed a petition in the bankruptcy proceeding on behalf of Aristrain to establish our right to be treated as a preferred creditor in the distribution of IMC assets, but without success.

The bankruptcy court eventually appointed a creditor's committee and the other principal creditors were represented by Charlotte attorneys Rick Rayburn, Tom Henson, Joe Grier 3rd and Rod Dean. We met together regularly over a period of months. Eventually an arrangement was made for distribution of the remaining assets of the bankrupt with all of the principal creditors participating except the clients of Joe Grier 3rd and Rod Dean. Aristrain recovered several million dollars, including the proceeds of an insurance policy that covered their bad debts. The two creditors who did not join in the settlement continued to litigate their rights in federal court but failed in the end to establish their case for preferential treatment.

On one of the few occasions that he visited Charlotte, I took Mr. Aristrain and his associates to the Charlotte Athletic Club for lunch and the waitress spilled soup on his jacket. Both he and his associates appeared to be more deeply troubled by the incident than I should have expected, perhaps because he was accustomed to receiving the kind of deference that is usually accorded nobility! The waitress was most apologetic but even that didn't seem to help.

Whenever Mr. Aristrain was planning to attend a meeting, we were asked to keep his itinerary confidential. We soon learned why. Basque separatists who resented his doing business with the Spanish government had threatened his life on more than one occasion. Because he was not generally available to confer with us, our day-to-day contacts were with Barry Craig and Javier Imaz, one of the company's principal officers. Long after our case was resolved we learned that Mr. Aristrain was killed in an airplane accident over the Mediterranean Sea. It is possible that the Basque terrorists succeeded in their purpose. I understand they have claimed 850 victims since 1968.

## NON-COMPETE CASES

Keith Weddington came to the firm from the University of North Carolina Law School in 1986 and began to assist me in a number of trials. We worked well together and in 1988 Keith and I were presented with a series of employment cases involving the principle of unfair competition, particularly covenants not to compete. In one such case we were retained by Ellen Newcomer, a lawyer with Butler, Rubin, Newcomer, Saltareilli & Boyd of Chicago, Illinois to represent her client Wallace Computer Services, Inc. The case involved a former employee who had violated his covenant not to compete by going to work for Willamette Industries, a competitor in the business forms and computer service industry. The employee had worked in the Charlotte area so we sought a preliminary injunction in Mecklenburg County, although Illinois law would govern the case since that was where the contract was signed. Michael Stick and Stephanie Leider of Butler Rubin came to Charlotte to work with us on the matter.

Judge Frank Snepp declined to issue a preliminary injunction on the ground that the covenant was not necessary to protect any legitimate business interest of Wallace and was therefore invalid. We appealed to the North Carolina Court of Appeals where the court's judgment was reversed and the case sent back to the trial court.[*] By the time the case was remanded to the trial court, the term of the covenant had virtually expired. We persuaded Judge Claude Sitton to extend the covenant for a ten month period since that was the time during which it had been violated by the defendants. The defendants then sought discretionary review of the case by the North Carolina Supreme Court but the petition was denied.[**]

The same year, Keith and I represented Hettich America, a German corporation doing business in North Carolina, in a case in which it was charged with the wholesale raiding of Liberty Hardware Company's personnel in order to establish a hardware sales force in North Carolina. Liberty's president was Luther Mayer and the company was represented by John Sarratt, who was the husband of one of the partners in the Raleigh firm with which we were to merge a year later. Mayer was a most unpleasant adversary and at one point instructed Sarratt to bring a motion for contempt against our client for its delay in producing certain documents that had been requested by Liberty in discovery proceedings. Our client insisted it had overlooked the documents in their initial search but provided them later. The motion was heard before Superior Court Judge Preston Cornelius who denied it out of hand. It was apparent that there was no bad faith.

Our client was, however, in a vulnerable position because it had in fact hired a number of Liberty employees. With this in mind,

---

[*] *Wallace Computer Services v. Waite and Willamette Industries,* 95 N.C. App. 442 (1989).

[**] 325 N.C. 437, 713 (1989).

Keith and I worked out what we considered a reasonable settlement with John Sarratt only to learn that a newly elected Hettich America official in Germany, who had not been involved in the case at all until then, had suddenly assumed responsibility for negotiating the settlement and agreed to pay Mayer a greater sum than that which we had persuaded Sarratt and his client to accept. I was both frustrated and embarrassed.

### PARKS-CRAMER'S DISPUTE WITH THE HISTORICAL COMMISSION

Sam Powell of Parks-Cramer Company, a long-time client, called upon us in 1988 to represent his company before the Mecklenburg County Historical Commission. Parks-Cramer owned warehouse buildings on their South Boulevard property that had originally been built as textile factories in the late 1800s. The Commission's executive director Dan Morrill had proposed to have the buildings declared "historical sites" so that they could not be torn down or altered in any significant way without the approval of the Commission. The company feared that, in the event that they might decide to sell the property, any such action by the Historical Commission would depress the market price.

Keith and I appeared before the Commission and persuaded the members present to defeat the executive director's proposal. A former staff member later told us that so far as she knew that was the only time the Commission refused to accept its executive director's recommendation.

Dan Morrill wrote me the next day saying that he was not giving up. I attributed his persistence to his enthusiasm for the project rather than a lack of sportsmanship. Within a short time, Parks-Cramer sold the property and the new owners converted the entire site into an attractive shopping center while preserving the integrity of the warehouses. Thus Dan eventually had his way. I was pleased at that ultimate resolution.

### DAVID CLARK'S AUTOMOBILE COLLISION

My friend David Clark was the president of Mountain Island Freight Company. In 1989 he was driving north to his office off Highway 16 when he stopped to permit a car to turn left in front of him. His car was immediately struck from the rear by another car, and the impact knocked David's car off the highway into a ravine. The resulting injuries to his spinal column left him a quadriplegic. David, whom I had supported when he ran for Congress in 1958 and again in 1960, asked me to represent him in undertaking to recover the damages he suffered as a result of his injuries. Because he was no longer able to work and would require around-the-clock care, his damages were calculated to be quite significant. A serious legal problem arose, however, because the person who ran into David was not only an employee of David's company but he was also engaged in company business at the time of the accident. If David were limited to a recovery under the company's worker's compensation policy, he could recover only a small fraction of his actual damages, *i.e.*, the maximum established by statute (which would have been about $20,000.00 at that time). Should David be able to recover on the company's liability insurance policy, however, the recovery could be measured in millions of dollars due to the severity of his injuries.

The legal question was a close one and quite worrisome. We brought an action against the employee who caused the collision and initiated negotiations with Harold Mitchell, an attorney from Valdese, North Carolina who represented the company's liability insurance company. He was a worthy adversary. As was to be expected, he took the position that David's only recovery should be under the worker's compensation laws. Clay Davidson, who had graduated at the head of his class at the University of North Carolina Law School and joined our firm in 1988, assisted me in preparing the case for trial. A great deal of discovery was taken on both sides of the case, including depositions of the physicians who had treated David in Miami, Florida where he had a summer home. Many offers and counteroffers were made by the parties.

On the date set for trial we appeared in Catawba County Superior Court before Judge Julia Jones to try the case. While the jury was being empanelled, the defendant's attorney offered my client what amounted to $2,200,000 ($1,000,000 cash and $1,200,000 in an annuity payable $10,000 a month for ten years). I recommended the settlement and David accepted the offer. Unfortunately he lived only about six years after that and did not receive the full benefit of the annuity. Nevertheless, it was quite satisfying to have obtained such a substantial settlement when there was a real possibility that the case might never have got to the jury because of the serious legal question it presented.

## BAR ASSOCIATION ACTIVITIES

I was appointed to the North Carolina Bar Association's newly-established Alternative Dispute Resolution Committee in 1984. The responsibility of the committee was to develop a program of alternatives to litigation that would resolve disputes before they came to trial. Among the alternatives considered were mediation, arbitration, summary jury trials and mini-trials. My friend Jack Roemer, with whom I had worked at Davis Polk in New York and who had joined the Winston-Salem law firm of Petree Stockton after a stellar career as general counsel for R. J. Reynolds, was the chairman of the committee. Members who were to explore mediation as an alternative, including Andy Little who had served as Democratic chairman in Orange County when I was Democratic chairman of Mecklenburg County, made a trip to Florida to observe that state's trial court mediation program. Andy's committee developed a similar program which the North Carolina legislature then enacted into law. As a result, every Superior Court case is now referred to mediation before trial unless exempted by the court. This program has become exemplary and much admired throughout the country.

The same year, the Mecklenburg Bar Association inaugurated a new program called "Silent Partners" to provide lawyers just being admitted to the Mecklenburg County Bar with mentors from among the more experienced members. I signed up as a mentor and have participated in the program every year since then. As a consequence I have come to know a great many young lawyers over the past twenty years and make bold to say that I may have helped some of them to get started in their law practice. They have also helped me in myriad ways and many of them have become my good friends.

For many years tennis was the favorite sport among lawyers attending the North Carolina Bar Association conventions, and I participated in the men's doubles at the annual tennis tournaments. Over the years, however, golf has become the sport of choice and recent convention tennis tournaments have attracted very few participants. Mark Bernstein and I discovered the extent to which that was true when we signed up for men's doubles at a convention at the Grove Park Inn in Asheville. I went to the tennis shop at the appointed hour for our first match and when Mark arrived at courtside I gave him a report: "I have good news and bad news," I said, pointing out two young blades who were exchanging ground strokes at white heat on a nearby court. "The good news," I said, "is that we are in the finals! The bad news is that we are playing those two guys!" They disposed of us in short order.

When I was attending a North Carolina Bar Association meeting in Pinehurst about ten years ago, former North Carolina Supreme Court Justice Harry Martin challenged me to a tennis match. The match went well and was quite close until Harry fell while reaching to return a ball. As I recall, I ran to Harry's side to inquire whether he was injured, then drove him to the hospital where he learned that he had torn his Achilles tendon. The following is the story as Harry tells it:

> "The score was 5-4 and I was serving for the match. I fell down while I was trying to return the ball and Syd came running over to my side of the court. 'Would you like to forfeit the match?' he asked."

Unless Harry contacts me soon to resume the match, I shall in fact consider that he has forfeited.

In 1985 Hattie and I attended an American Bar Association meeting in London. The trip was quite pleasant and gave us another opportunity to host a dinner at Ian Redhead's Army and Navy Club for our English friends and for several couples in our firm who were also attending the Bar meeting. That gathering was the occasion for my reading the following verses about my experiences at

St. Andrew's and other British universities, the latter based upon my Fulbright experience:

### REMINISCENCES OF LIFE IN BRITAIN – AT THE 1985 ARMY AND NAVY CLUB REUNION IN LONDON

I

Near twenty years have passed since last we dined.
To us it seems that they've been more than kind
for now our comp'ny's greatly multiplied.
Our progeny have managed more to hide
the dark primeval instincts of our race
than we who carried high the Chancellor's mace
and sang the "Gaudie" lustily at school,
yet killed our fellows in a war most cruel.
But now we gather once again to sing
the praises of St. Andrew's U. and King's,
and Manchester and LSE-on-Thames
and most of all, our loyal British friends.

II

The years have flown – two score since World War II
when George and Geordie played "The Pirate" crew
and Socks taught Charlie how to dance the reel.
Now Geordie's Ian, Charlie's Syd and, we'll
be hanged, dear Socks is Sylvia Craig
whose favor all physicians now must beg.[1]
Indeed, since visiting Blun'ston Hall, it's true,
Syd may become "Sir Sydnor" e'er we're through.
We're honored by your presence here in force
and we in turn would honor you, of course.
So here's to each of you who reminisces
with us and basks in heartfelt love and kisses.

That proved to be the last occasion on which we were to see our good friend Leslie Clark, whose home we visited at Walter's Farm. He died soon thereafter in his nineties.

### MECKLENBURG BAR PRESIDENCY

I was elected president of the Mecklenburg County Bar in the spring of 1990. I worked with the Bar's Executive Director Mary Howerton, who was a superb administrator as well as a warm personality. Catherine Thompson of the Helms Mulliss firm was president-elect, and she too was most helpful.

Fortunately I was able to persuade quite a number of my friends at the Bar to chair various committees during my presidency. Both Mark Bernstein and George Daly took on significant committees and Tom Garlitz served as chairman of the Grievance Committee. I had long considered it appropriate to name laypersons to the Grievance Committee in order to give the general public a greater confidence that the process of investigating their grievances against members of the Bar was being handled fairly. To that end, I met with the lawyers on that committee who then agreed to my proposal contingent upon

---

[1] Sylvia's husband Ian served as president of the English Society of General Practitioners.

their having a veto over the names of the laymen I should recommend. My appointees were Charles McCree, my next door neighbor, and Stuart Elliott, a fellow member of Myers Park United Methodist Church. They agreed and were unanimously approved by the lawyers on the committee. They both served with distinction and paved the way to make the change permanent.

During my term and for several years thereafter I served as a representative of the Bar Association on the Criminal Justice Commission that was appointed by the Mecklenburg County Commission to recommend reforms to the criminal justice system. One of our principal tasks was trying to convince the State's Administrative Office of the Courts (AOC) to assign sufficient funds to local courts to enable us to operate effectively. Just when we were beginning to make some progress, however, the County Commission abolished the Commission. It was a frustrating outcome for dedicated volunteers like Jack Tate, Jr. and Sis Kaplan, both of whom had devoted considerable energy to devising reforms to the system. The problem of under-funding of the Mecklenburg County courts continues to be a serious one.

That year the local Bar built its first Habitat for Humanity house. We raised more than $32,000.00 in contributions from Mecklenburg lawyers, who then built a house with their own hands for a young family who could not otherwise have afforded it. James Wyatt chaired the project and his enthusiasm carried the day. I helped put in the concrete driveway, which I confess may or may not have been properly leveled. Within a short time thereafter we were contacted by other bar associations who were interested in learning more about our experience.

While I was the Bar president, Judge Jim McMillan invited me to join the Fourth Circuit's Judicial Conference. The Conference purports to be an instrument by which the federal judiciary solicits advice from the members of the federal Bar, but in truth it is primarily a social fraternity, conducting its meetings in alternate years at the Greenbrier Hotel in White Sulfur Springs, West Virginia and the Homestead Hotel at Hot Springs, Virginia. Hattie and I attended for several years. When Hattie was in Aspen at that time of year, I often attended with my partner Francis Parker. On one such occasion William H. Harbaugh, who had authored a biography of John W. Davis, was on the program. I greatly enjoyed talking with Harbaugh about the man whom we both greatly admired. This year's meeting was cancelled, which would indicate either that the federal judges do not consider that they are in need of our advice or that they are not feeling very sociable for the moment, or both.

## MERGER WITH A RALEIGH FIRM

In 1990 the firm succeeded in identifying a Raleigh law firm as a merger partner. Through the good offices of Tom Clay of the

Philadelphia consulting firm Altman and Weil, we initiated negotiations with Adams, McCullough and Beard (formerly Sanford, Cannon, Adams, McCullough & Beard). The firm had been established by Terry Sanford in the mid-1960s shortly after his term as governor expired. We soon determined that our two firms were highly compatible and the merger was consummated under the new name Parker Poe Adams and Bernstein. Without Mark's knowledge, I suggested to the executive committee that his name should be retained in view of the strength of his client base. The new name will doubtless serve us indefinitely. Having finally taken their cue from Madison Avenue marketers, law firms don't often change their names any more.

# CHAPTER 23
## MORE COMMUNITY LIFE
### PUBLIC FUNDING FOR THE ARTS

I served on the North Carolina Arts Council for two terms from 1977 until 1984. It was a most rewarding experience in that it was the means by which I became familiar with many excellent arts organizations throughout the state. I particularly enjoyed my association with Mary Regan, who was, and is still, the executive director. She is totally dedicated to the advancement of the arts and has devoted her life to that purpose. Hattie and I especially enjoyed the Council weekend retreats that were held at the University of North Carolina's Quail Roost, the former home of tobacco magnate George Washington Hill outside of Durham.

In the early 1980s Mayor Eddie Knox appointed a committee to identify a site for a new performing arts hall in Charlotte, naming Mark Bernstein as its chairman. A number of arts organizations evidenced a keen interest in the project by voluntarily banding together to support the proposal. When Harvey Gantt was elected Charlotte's mayor in 1983, he commissioned the same committee to continue its efforts on behalf of a new hall. Our fondest hopes were suddenly realized when John Belk announced that Belk Stores would contribute the site of its downtown retail store for the hall. Within a few weeks supporters met on College Street across from the Belk store for a groundbreaking ceremony. After several self-congratulatory speeches by leaders of the various organizations involved, Mayor Gantt turned a couple of spades of dirt and the project was under way! Soon funds for the construction of the hall were appropriated by the City of Charlotte and by the North Carolina legislature. Cesar Pelli was selected as the architect for the building, which incorporated both the performance hall and the Bank of America headquarters. Herman Blumenthal then agreed to contribute several million dollars to complete the funding of the hall and it was named the "North Carolina Blumenthal Performing Arts Center." The rest is history.

### THE CHARLOTTE OPERA ASSOCIATION GOES STATEWIDE

Richard Marshall was hired as General Director of the Charlotte Opera in 1977, with Charles Rosekrans continuing as conductor. Richard and Hooper Alexander, who succeeded me as board president, worked well together and the company continued to grow under their leadership. Hooper was absolutely dedicated to the company and was a model president. I've often said that the best thing I ever did for Charlotte Opera was to persuade him to join the board. Upon his retirement from the board of the association, I gave a toast:

## FAREWELL TOAST TO A RETIRING
## OPERA PRESIDENT – HOOPER ALEXANDER

### I

Tonight our Company bids farewell to one
whose leaving may portend our setting sun
for ne'er did mortal work with such effect
to bring a fledgling Opera due respect
as Hooper did for Charlotte in his term.
For twenty years he's been the pachyderm
on whom we've loaded all our cares and woes
from budget overruns to empty rows
of seats our hero bravely fought to fill.
Some say to sell a ticket he would kill.

### II

But what is more noteworthy is the fact
that Hooper Alexander's real impact
has been to stretch our minds and shape our goals
with Robert Ward premieres and Wagner'an roles,
to main-stage tours and in-house fashioned sets;
and when we aim too low he chafes and frets
and checks on Board attendance lest we shirk
our great responsibilities or work.
And lest there be some doubt of what is meant,
there'll never be his match as President.

Under Richard Marshall's leadership, an exciting new program was introduced in 1978 by which the company toured its main-stage production to other major cities in North Carolina. The tour, produced by an affiliate organized under the name North Carolina Opera Company, took the productions to Raleigh, Greensboro, Winston-Salem, Asheville, Wilmington, Durham, Salisbury, Hickory and Lincolnton. Staff member Robert Weisenfeld was assigned responsibility for managing both the tour and the performances of a local repertory group.

Until that season, the Charlotte Opera had always hired its own orchestra for each performance. Besides local musicians, quite a few players were hired from Winston-Salem, which required a considerable commute on their part. That year, for the first time we engaged the Charlotte Symphony Orchestra for the entire season, retaining the right to select the conductor of each opera.

When Mary Henderson served the company as president, she hardly ever missed a rehearsal. As a result of such dedication she came to know each opera quite well and was able to lead the applause during performances after the most popular arias were performed. As every opera aficionado knows, there are certain arias that traditionally draw applause from the audience because they feature one or more of those spine-tingling thrills for which the knowledgeable opera-goer holds his breath in anticipation. When I succeeded Mrs. Henderson as president, I sought to follow her example by attending the rehearsals and so also inherited responsibility for leading the applause. When Hooper Alexander succeeded me as president, I reminded him that he then bore that responsibility. Unfortunately, that aspect of the president's job description has since fallen by the way and it is doubtful that Charlotte audiences are yet sophisticated enough to assume that responsibility on their own.

Still the news in that regard is not all bad. Because of the example set by such veteran connoisseurs as the Reverend Loy Witherspoon and the late Leon Guttman, an occasional "Bravo!" or "Brava!" can be heard from time to time at the Blumenthal Performing Arts Center. Indeed I have occasionally been moved to such lengths myself!

Just before Richard Marshall left to establish the Contemporary Opera Theatre in New York City in 1982, he achieved a significant tour de force for Charlotte Opera. He arranged with Dr. Robert Ward (whose path Hattie had crossed earlier at the Third Street Music School Settlement) to present the premiere of Bob's new opera "Abelard and Heloise," the story of the beautiful but tragic love affair between the twelfth century monk and his young student. Because it was a premiere, we arranged for the performance to be videotaped by the South Carolina Public Television Company. Prior to the production, there was a gala dinner at the Adams Mark Hotel on the theme of a Middle Ages banquet, featuring a roasted pig with an apple in its mouth borne by four bare-chested men.

In the fall of 1982 Bruce Chalmers was hired as General Director, coming to Charlotte from the Portland, Oregon opera company. Bruce was trained as a barrister and practiced law in Canada for a number of years until his love of the arts pre-empted that career. He was a splendid gentleman whom I came to regard as highly as any general director we have ever had in Charlotte.

Bruce scheduled Carlisle Floyd's opera "Willie Stark," based upon the life and death of Louisiana's Senator Huey Long, for the 1985-86 season. He asked me if I should like to sing a small baritone role and despite a few qualms, I acquiesced. The role involved about five measures of a duet sung by a corrupt baritone senator and a corrupt tenor senator. I labored over the atonal lines for some weeks before the day of the sitz probe rehearsal (the first rehearsal of the singers with the full orchestra). When the time came for me to sing out, I was so intimidated by the sound of the orchestra that I couldn't make a sound. Afterwards I apologized to Bruce and suggested that he and Floyd consider finding someone else to sing that role. When I asked Bruce what they had decided, he told me that Floyd had said "Where could we find another face like that?" I reluctantly concluded that I must look like a corrupt Louisiana senator.

While "Willie Stark" was an artistic success, it left our budget slightly askew for 1985-86. I memorialized that dilemma in verse at Bruce's retirement dinner:

Here's to a Scotsman named Bruce
and the operas he's helped us produce.
While they've all been a lark,
we preferred "Willie Stark,"
though our budget it left a bit loose.

Cullie Tarleton, who had served as the general manager of television station WBTV, was elected president of the Opera Company in the mid-1980s. In addition to trying to meet the company's immediate financial needs by asking the directors to guarantee a bank loan, Cullie sought to remedy the Company's organizational ills by introducing structural changes designed to assure a rotation of board members after they had served six years. A meeting was called to amend the bylaws to that effect. I opposed the proposal and lobbied other board members to vote against it. We nearly defeated the amendment until two board members told me at the last minute that they had changed their minds. I distrusted what I felt would be the result of any such change, *i.e.*, leaving the operations of the Company entirely in the hands of the staff without the continuing safeguard of experienced board members. The principal authority for my position was Helen Thompson, Executive Director of the American Symphony Orchestra League, who opposed any such rule for symphony boards on the ground that it unnecessarily brought about the loss of loyal and experienced supporters. Suffice it to say, the Company's professional management has since proved quite competent and my fears in that regard have proved to be largely unwarranted.

Contemporaneously, the Company took a step backward by eliminating the main-stage tour. I was actually a party to that apostasy in that I was retained by the board to merge the Charlotte Opera and the North Carolina Opera and to constitute the product of the merger into a new corporation to be known as "Opera Carolina." The discontinuance of the main-stage tour was attributed to a need to reduce expenses. There was a rather vague declaration of intention that it might some day be resumed, which accounted for the adoption of the name "Opera Carolina." Unfortunately that has not yet happened.

The Company hired Jim Wright as General Director in 1989. Jim succeeded quite well in that post for the next ten years until he was recruited to head the Vancouver Opera Company in the State of Washington. During his tenure, Opera Carolina received a special appropriation of $40,000.00 from the State legislature, largely due to the influence of State Senator Fountain Odom. Thanks to that and other developments, the Company was soon once again in the black financially.

In 1992 I was retired from the Opera board. To make me feel better, the other members gave me a framed certificate reflecting my twenty-five years of service and appointed me to a newly-constituted

176

Advisory Board. I compounded my earlier presumption in opposing the rotation of board members by reading some verses at the annual meeting that coincided with my retirement:

### A RELUCTANT FAREWELL

#### I

Tonight a long-time Charlotte Opera fan
has forfeited the right to stand
for re-election to a board hell-bent
(with motives, that, of course, are quite well-meant)
on nominating cultural neophytes
to rediscover how one Muse unites
the arts of music, drama and design.
But can one ever possibly divine
the means of educating such a band
without this self-styled indispens'ble man?

#### II

But no more 'crimination or reproach
to mar this festive evening or encroach
upon a comp'ny's rendezvous with fate,
for each of you becomes a surrogate
through whom you'll speak his mind or work his will
to guarantee the company won't stand still.
His ghost will haunt the stage, his specter fret
'til annually you build a second set.
And now and then he may pen epigrams
that challenge you to raise 3 million clams!

I hope my listeners were amused.

We celebrated the Company's 50th anniversary at a gala dinner in 1998 just before General Director Jim Wright left for Vancouver. A memorial program, tracing the history of the Company and setting out the names of all who had ever participated in its productions or administration, was distributed to the guests.

Jim Meena succeeded Jim Wright as General Director and also assumed the responsibilities of Principal Conductor. His success in both capacities has been nonpareil. The quality of the productions, now four a year, and the support he has received from the public are unprecedented. The Company is now on the verge of meeting my challenge that they establish an annual budget of $3,000,000. Today it is doubtless one of the strongest opera companies in the Southeast.

### BUILDING DEMOCRATIC PARTY MORALE

When I became chairman of the Mecklenburg County Democratic Party in late 1970s, my term coincided with both James B. Hunt's first term as Governor of North Carolina and Jimmy Carter's presidency. Morale in the party was high and I began the practice of entertaining the most active members at a Christmas party at the Charlotte Athletic Club. Originally comprising only the Executive Committee, that group gradually grew to include a number of other activists as well. It is a custom that has continued for more than twenty-five years, though it is now held in the first week of the New Year.

About ten years ago, Parks Helms, who has served many terms on the Mecklenburg County Commission (often as its chairman), offered to host that event with me. He had long been something of an unofficial head of the Mecklenburg County Democratic Party, so it made sense that he should participate with me in the annual celebration. Almost without exception, Parks and I see government and politics alike and I cannot exaggerate the degree of admiration that I have for his courageous leadership as chairman of the County Commission. The holiday luncheon is always a celebratory occasion and recently entertained ninety Democrat enthusiasts. Calling it the "Good Democrats" luncheon, Parks and I limit the guest list to Party loyalists - no mugwumps or fence straddlers are invited. In fact, we consider the luncheon an excellent vehicle for encouraging Party loyalty.

An earlier effort to boost party morale in Mecklenburg County took the form of an organization called the Old Catawba Society. Formed some fifty years ago at the suggestion of John P Kennedy, Jr., the society unabashedly restricts its membership to Democrats. We have had the pleasure of hosting such notable speakers as Governor Terry Sanford, author Jonathan Daniels, United Nations Ambassador Harlan Cleveland, Governor Jim Hunt, President Bill Friday of the University of North Carolina, Mayor Harvey Gantt, President Leo Jenkins of East Carolina University, and many others.

One of our members asked Governor Sanford, who was our first speaker, why he had recently appointed a well-known radical black of doubtful reputation to a state office. His response struck a note that we have never forgotten, "I felt the same way about him that Prime Minister Churchill was reported to have felt when he was asked why he had appointed Lord Beaverbrook to his cabinet. I just thought I'd rather have him pissing out than pissing in," he said. Of course, that was before we had women members, a political faux pas that we have since corrected.

### SCHOOL BOARD POLITICS REVISITED

In the late 1960s Julius Chambers, representing the parents of a number of black students, brought suit against the Mecklenburg County school system to enforce the U.S. Supreme Court's desegregation orders by calling for a greater mix of blacks and whites in the schools. Judge James B. McMillan of the federal district court held that the Mecklenburg County school system was indeed unconstitutionally segregated along racial lines and ordered the wholesale busing of students in order to achieve integration.* McMillan always contended that on the evidence presented he had

---

* *Swann v. Charlotte-Mecklenburg Board of Education*, 311 F.Supp. 265 (1971).

no alternative but to rule as he did. His decision was highly controversial and resulted in a sharp division on the school board as to whether they should appeal the court's ruling. In time his decision was affirmed by the U.S. Supreme Court, resulting in the adoption of similar busing programs all over the country.*

At the height of the controversy, McMillan was ostracized by many Charlotteans, including some members of the Charlotte Country Club with whom he had formerly played golf. Hattie and I made a special point of inviting him and his wife Margie to play tennis and bridge during that time. My partner Joe Grier advised the editor of the *Charlotte Observer* that the protesters parading around the Judge's home at night with lighted firebrands were violating a federal statute prohibiting anyone from seeking to intimidate a federal judge. After an editorial to that effect appeared in the *Charlotte Observer,* the nightly protests ceased.

After Judge McMillan's death, Judge Robert Potter, a conservative Republican federal district judge, ruled, more recently, that the Charlotte-Mecklenburg School District was unitary and therefore no longer subject to court supervision. This has resulted in substantial re-segregation of the district's schools. It is ironic that the Charlotte Mecklenburg School System, which had been the first to require busing, is now among the first to reduce busing. A Harvard study by Gary Orfield and his associate Chungmei Lee indicates that such re-segregation is occurring everywhere in the country. It is equally ironic that leaders of the Charlotte Chamber of Commerce, which had led in the effort to desegregate city schools after the U.S. Supreme Court decision, have recently joined other local business leaders in an effort to reestablish neighborhood schools.

CONGRESSIONAL ELECTIONS

In 1980 North Carolina Democrats were again faced with the task of finding a good candidate to run against Congressman Jim Martin, who had held the Ninth District seat for several terms. We looked to the town of Davidson, NC and identified an outstanding candidate in Randy Kincaid, an economics professor at Davidson College. After a hard fought contest, Martin was reelected by a substantial majority. The outcome was discouraging, but not particularly surprising in view of the fact that Republicans had won that seat in every election since 1952.

When Jim Martin vacated his Congressional seat in 1984, Republicans chose Alex McMillan to run as his successor. Ben Tison, Susan Green and D. G. Martin declared their candidacy in the Democratic primary. D. G. Martin won the primary, and went on to mount an exemplary campaign in the general election. He was

---

* 91 S.Ct. 1267 (1971).

highly popular in Mecklenburg County, a fact that was reflected in the enthusiasm that his campaign attracted. I was serving as Ninth District chairman and on election night we went to bed thinking that D. G. had won by several hundred votes. To our surprise, an error was discovered the next morning in the return from a precinct in Lincoln County. McMillan was elected by a slim margin. D. G. ran again two years later, but the magic was gone and McMillan was reelected. Cam Weaver succeeded me as Ninth District chair, but her efforts to recover the Congressional seat for the Democrats were no more successful than my own had been. Indeed, the district has now been so effectively gerrymandered in favor of the Republicans that the Democratic Party has been able to mount only token opposition in the last twenty years, despite having fielded some excellent candidates.

## U.S. SENATE ELECTIONS

As his second term was drawing to a close in 1984, Governor Jim Hunt ran for the United States Senate against Republican Jesse Helms. Helms had a record as a staunch segregationist arising out of incendiary remarks he had made as the manager of Raleigh television station WRAL. In a highly dramatic development, Eddie Knox, who had been defeated by Rufus Edmisten in the Democratic gubernatorial primary, joined Helms' campaign and flew with him to Charlotte on the eve of the election. Knox's defection was generally attributed to his disappointment that Governor Jim Hunt had not helped him in his own primary campaign for Governor. Of course, Hunt was himself a candidate for the United States Senate at that time, so it was not surprising that he had not taken sides in the gubernatorial primary. In any event Knox's defection was viewed by Democrats as the ultimate betrayal. In a hard-fought campaign Jim Hunt lost his bid for a Senate seat to the man who soon came to be known throughout the country as "Senator No."

Former Governor Terry Sanford, who had served twenty years as president of Duke University after his term as Governor of North Carolina, ran for the other United States Senate seat in 1986 and won. It was the same year in which Mecklenburg County Democratic chairman Hugh Campbell and I prevailed upon Ron Harper to succeed Hugh as chairman. Although Ron initially agreed to serve, several months prior to the primary election he told us that he would have to resign because his wife Katherine had decided to run for the United States Senate. He reported that when she was vacationing at the beach she had heard a voice urging her to enter the race. She declared for the office a few weeks later.

Fountain Odom of Charlotte ran for the same seat in that primary. In deference to the candidacies of Harper and Odom, who were both Charlotteans, Sanford did not campaign in Mecklenburg County during the primary. Nevertheless, he won both the state and the county easily and Fountain and I campaigned for him in the election that followed. We put on a puppet show for him at courthouses in neighboring counties and sought to champion farmers' causes by introducing a live cow at the park on the square in downtown Charlotte. During Fountain's stump speech for Sanford, the cow relieved herself on the feet of an unsuspecting bystander.

Senator Sanford was elected and served with distinction for a full term, being especially active on the Senate Ethics Committee. When he ran for reelection six years later I had the privilege of serving as his campaign chairman in Mecklenburg County. Unfortunately he had to have heart surgery during the campaign, an event which became the principal cause of his defeat, though I am pleased to report that he carried Mecklenburg County even then.

The most noteworthy political development in North Carolina in recent years has been the meteoric rise of Raleigh lawyer John Edwards. When he first ran for public office in 1998 in the Democratic primary for the United States Senate, I supported his opponent D. G. Martin whom I had known and admired for more than twenty-five years. Although I did not know John Edwards, I labored long and hard to induce him to debate D. G. in Charlotte before the primary election. Edwards declined and then surprised us by beating D. G. in the primary. Democrats closed ranks, allowing Edwards to defeat Senator Lauch Faircloth in the election. We recently learned that D. G.'s son David 3rd won a seat in the State House from Raleigh this year, despite the fact that his Republican opponent raised a record amount of money. It seems there may yet be a second coming for the Martin family's political life.

## RUNNING FOR OFFICE

Some of my friends had suggested that I should run for the North Carolina legislature in the early 1960s. The idea intrigued me and I went to Joe Grier to ask him what he thought of the idea. "Well," Joe said, "I think that would be fine if that's what you want to do, but I thought you came here to practice law." He was right of course, and that was the end of that.

In 1992, however, the North Carolina State House seats were redistricted and my neighborhood became a part of a newly constituted district. The seat was open and I was approaching retirement age at the firm; after thirty years this seemed to be a propitious time to run. I declared for the office in February by filing in the Democratic primary. I then assembled a campaign committee chaired by Henry Doss, who had recently resigned from the First Union Bank. Having managed D. G. Martin's Congressional campaigns, Henry proved to be highly knowledgeable about campaign techniques. Ace Walker, who acted as my finance chairman, did an equally good job. Nancy Mead acted as volunteer staff and maintained the records of the campaign in impeccable fashion.

Initially both Doris Cromartie and Martha Alexander also filed to run in the same primary as mine. No doubt realizing that they would likely split the women's vote, they agreed that Doris would drop out of that race and file for a State Senate seat against Leslie Winner who had already filed for the Senate. My partner Gaston Gage had chaired Martha Alexander's campaign when she ran unsuccessfully for the legislature a couple of years earlier. She asked him to chair her campaign again and Gaston came to ask me about it. Of course, I told him that I should certainly have no objection and he accepted.

It was a rigorous campaign in which I came to be greatly indebted to the many friends who helped me. My neighbor Charlie McCree was one of my most enthusiastic supporters. Teila Hand, Joe Grier 3rd, Nancy Brame and Mary Murchison were especially helpful. I walked a great many miles across the district, knocking on doors and soliciting votes. I also managed to put up more yard signs than I had ever seen in a district election.

As primary day approached in early May, I received notice that I was to argue an appeal in the United States Court of Appeals for the Fourth Circuit on the day of the primary election in a case involving one of Mark Bernstein's clients. I undertook to get the argument postponed but to no avail. Craig Lynch and I went to Richmond together the night before and flew back to Charlotte on the afternoon of the election. (We later learned that we won the appeal.)

I immediately drove to St. Mark's United Methodist Church on Clanton Road. The Black Caucus had endorsed my candidacy and I knew St. Mark's would have a heavy turnout. When I arrived at about 4:00 p.m., I found that my opponent had been there most of the day. I also noted that a woman who was known to accept payment for her campaign efforts was meeting voters at their automobiles in the parking lot and telling them that the Black Caucus' endorsement of my candidacy was a mistake and that they should vote instead for my opponent.

I lost the primary by fifty votes. *The Charlotte Observer* staff writer Gail Smith had this to say: "It may have come down to one thing in the N.C. House District 56 race: who was in town on Election Day." Hattie insists that I lost by only twenty-six votes, since that is the number of my opponent's votes that I would have needed to win. After the election, we had a dinner for my campaign workers and I prepared a limerick for the occasion:

> Here's to our primary fray
> and to you whom we ne'er can repay.
> As you may have surmised,
> we were somewhat surprised
> to learn we have mere feet of clay.

It was a grand run but would have been grander if I had won.

Bishop Bevel Jones was appointed to the Western North Carolina Conference of the United Methodist Church in 1984, having served as senior minister of a large metropolitan church in Atlanta before being elected bishop. It proved to be a highly significant appointment for me as well as for the Conference. I came to appreciate Bev Jones as a friend while he served the Western North Carolina Conference and we often lunched together. He recently published a delightful memoir under the title "A Step Beyond Caution." Bev's ministry, both as clergyman and as bishop, has been truly outstanding.

Bev headed our delegation to the World Methodist Conference in Kenya in 1986 and Hattie and I accepted his invitation to attend as delegates. It was a fascinating experience. I saw more wild animals in the week we spent there than I had ever expected to see in a lifetime. Hattie photographed one lone zebra on our first day on the Serengetti Plain only to encounter an entire herd a few minutes later. I began reading a book from my seat in the van on the second day of the safari instead of ogling the animals. Hattie insists that I actually said, "If you've seen one zebra, you've seen them all." I hope not. In any case, she made up for my questionable manners by taking reams of photos with which she has put many of our friends to the test.

We stayed at the Intercontinental Hotel in Nairobi. One morning when I went out on the balcony of our room to view a caravan of cars that was passing in the street below, a soldier pointed his gun at me and shouted for me to return to my room. The Kenyan president, Daniel Moi, who was essentially a dictator, was in one of the automobiles and he apparently lived in constant fear of assassination. I understand he has since been replaced as president but it is still nip and tuck as to whether democracy is beginning to take a foothold there.

One of the delegates from Zimbabwe explained to us that he knew the names of all of his ancestors for the last thirty generations. It was a tradition for members of his tribe to memorize the names of their ancestors and recite them in connection with a religious observance. I have since considered teaching my grandchildren the names of thirty generations of Sydnors but unfortunately I have only come up with twenty-two generations to date.

En route to Kenya, I had a layover in Amsterdam. Between planes, I raced into the city to visit the Anne Frank Museum, the house in which Anne and her family were secreted during the War until they were betrayed in late 1944. It was an emotional experience that had quite an impact on me.

## MECKLENBURG MINISTRIES

The Charlotte Clergy Association initiated plans to organize a local ecumenical association of churches which would promote the causes in which Charlotte churches were interested. In 1986 I was invited to join the task force appointed by the Clergy Association to draw the bylaws of the new organization, which would be known as Mecklenburg Ministries. Preparations were made over the period of a year or two and the new organization was inaugurated at a service in First Presbyterian Church in April of 1988. I was installed as president and served for two terms until January 1, 1990. It was the finest ecumenical experience I have ever had. The membership included both lay and clergy members of the local synagogues as well as lay and clergy members of about one hundred Protestant and Catholic churches. Later, Muslims were also invited to join, which, in view of recent developments, may prove to have been a most prescient decision.

One of the early leaders of the organization was Father John Haughey, a Jesuit priest who was then serving St. Peter's Catholic Church in downtown Charlotte. A most engaging personality, he left his imprint on Mecklenburg Ministries and on the City of Charlotte when he left several years later to take a teaching position at Loyola College in Chicago. Because he was the subject of one of my limericks, I sent John a copy of a collection of "ad hominem" verses that I had written over a period of years. He replied that someone had slandered me by attributing such inferior verse to me and promised not to show it to anyone. I was provided an opportunity to retaliate when I introduced him as the principal speaker at a Mecklenburg Ministries Council meeting at Temple Israel some time later and read the following limerick (purportedly from Brinnin):

> With regard to your friend Father Haughey
> whose wit is so cunning and coy,
> please tell him for me
> he's confused his I.D.
> with that of BARUKH ADONAI*.
>
> *Jehovah

Nancy Mead, who served as secretary to the Clergy Association for years, was engaged as the first executive director of Mecklenburg Ministries and served the organization well. Diane English, a bright young member of Myers Park United Methodist Church, eventually succeeded Nancy. The organization continues to develop excellent ecumenical programs to this day, the most noteworthy of which have involved racial reconciliation.

## ECUMENICAL CONCERNS

Since the 1960s I have attended the annual meetings of the North Carolina Council of Churches as a delegate from the United Methodist Church. The Council is the chief means by which diverse denominations cooperate in various ecumenical endeavors. The United Methodist Church has been one of the most loyal supporters of the council, both in terms of providing financial assistance as well as in participating in a variety of programs. In recent years, North

Carolina's Catholic Dioceses have joined the Council, greatly expanding its scope and perhaps its influence. My principal ally in endorsing various civil rights causes and sponsoring resolutions calling upon the North Carolina legislature to abolish capital punishment has been Dr. W. W. Finlator, the inspirational pastor of the Pullen Memorial Baptist Church in Raleigh.

A difficult situation arose about ten years ago when a group of churches calling themselves "Metropolitan" applied to join the North Carolina Council. The Metropolitan churches customarily accepted gay and lesbian persons as clergy, which prompted some debate among the other denominations. Jimmy Creech, a Methodist clergyman who was employed in the social outreach program of the Council, spoke at length in favor of accepting the application. After a heated debate, the request was approved and the church was admitted. That approval caused such a stir that at the next Annual Conference of the Western North Carolina United Methodists, an effort was mounted to withdraw from the Council. Several of us who had attended the Council meeting spoke to the question from the floor, urging the Conference not to make such a far-reaching ecumenical decision on the basis of a single issue. After the vote of delegates was counted, the Western Conference remained in the Council by a fairly close margin.

In 1965 Presbyterian minister Eugene Carson Blake suggested a possible union of nine Protestant denominations, including the United Methodist Church. The resulting organization formed to consider the proposal was called Consultation on Church Union (COCU). Significant opposition arose to the idea of actually merging the participating denominations into one united church, however, and the emphasis has since shifted to increased cooperation among the churches in agreeing upon common ordinations, worship services and mission programs. That modified version of the movement continues today under the name Churches Uniting in Christ. As chairman of our Annual Conference's Christian Unity Commission, I am presently preparing a program on the subject for presentation to our district leadership conferences.

My interest in interfaith communication does occasionally misfire. One evening when Hattie and I were having dinner at Eddie and Elizabeth Clarkson's home, I was seated next to a guest I knew to be an Episcopalian. "I certainly do admire your Bishop James Pike," I said, in what I intended to be a complimentary tone. "Well, I don't," she responded! And that was the end of that conversation.

## DEVELOPMENTS AT MYERS PARK CHURCH

A series of outstanding ministers succeeded Bob Tuttle at Myers Park Church – Mitchell Faulkner, Tom Stockton and Bernard Fitzgerald, some of whom served the church for eight or nine years. In 1993 my friend Lawrence McCleskey was appointed pastor of

Myers Park Methodist. Years earlier Lawrence and I had worked together for a Western Conference organization of young "progressive" clergy and laypersons called the Wesley Forum, and I was delighted when he became our pastor. Within a few years, however, he was elected to the bishopric and assigned to the South Carolina conference. More recently Lawrence was appointed bishop of the Western North Carolina Conference in the quadrennial fruit basket upset that characterizes the appointment of bishops, so we have now welcomed him back to Charlotte.

Julian Aldridge succeeded Lawrence at Myers Park, which was also a source of satisfaction to me since I had long admired Julian's ministry. When Julian retired a year ago, James Howell assumed that post. The church recently spent $15,000,000 to build a new Parish Life Building featuring a spacious "Jubilee Hall" in which more casual "Church in the Round" services are conducted every Sunday. The church membership now exceeds 4,000 for the first time in history, which would indicate that the combination of James Howell's dynamic preaching and the new building augurs well for the future. There are now four services every Sunday morning and James usually manages to preach at all of them.

### REMEMBERING GENERAL ROBERT E. LEE AND HIS COMRADES

Francis Parker and I both greatly admire General Robert E. Lee, not only for his military prowess as the commander of the Army of Northern Virginia in the Civil War but also for his character and style as a Southern gentleman. In 1985 we began a tradition of going to lunch at the Charlotte Country Club on or about January 19 every year to commemorate General Lee's birthday. At my insistence Francis usually recites General Order No. 9, which was Lee's farewell to his troops.

Despite his formidable rank, Lee's troops were known to call him "Bobby Lee," behind his back of course! I once delivered the following limerick in Francis' honor on one of his own birthdays:

> Here's to a consummate gent
> Who, like Holmes, knows when to dissent.
> With a fine pedigree
> To match Bobby Lee
> And hardly a sin to repent.

From time to time we have invited others of a similar mind to join our celebration, including the late Charlottean Fitzhugh Lee, a Lee descendant, and William Pender, a collateral descendant of Union General John Gibbon. Bryan Crutcher, another Civil War aficionado, has also joined us of late.

I have always had great admiration for the soldiers of the Confederacy. They fought against great odds for a cause (the right to secede) in which, rightly or wrongly, they so firmly believed that they were willing to sacrifice their lives. While I rejoice that they did not succeed, that does not diminish my respect for them or their combat service. Because of the war's link to the abolition of slavery, many African-Americans resent modern-day efforts to honor those who died for the Confederacy. While any right-thinking person must rejoice that the war led to the end of slavery, the courage of the Confederate soldiers who fought in that war is a significant aspect of Southern history. And the desire of Southerners to honor the memory of forebears who fought there is a distinctly separate matter from that of slavery, which African-Americans should acknowledge. I recently participated with other Sydnor family members in a ceremony at the Blackstone Cemetery in Nottoway County, Virginia memorializing the life and premature death of a kinsman, Edward Garland Sydnor, Jr., who died at the age of nineteen in 1862 at the Battle of Sharpsburg (Antietam) while carrying the Confederate battle flag.

## TREADING MORE BOARDS

The Golden Circle Theatre was evicted from the Mint Museum in the mid-eighties in connection with a reorganization of the Mint's visual arts programs. The troupe found a temporary home in a community center in the nearby town of Matthews. At that time, the staff consisted of Dan Shoemaker and Janet Eisenhart, who asked me to take a part in a production called "Veronica's Room." The play was a psychological drama involving the murder of a young woman and for the first time in my dramatic career I was cast as a villain. My children did not particularly savor my playing such a role, but it was fun and proved reasonably successful. The Irish accent I was called upon to simulate was perhaps somewhat less so. I played opposite Pam Hunt, who is a talented actress.

Since the Matthews venue was not satisfactory from the standpoint of proximity to Charlotte, the Company cast about for a new home and eventually approached the Jewish Community Center on Providence Road. Barry Hantman was the Center's director and he welcomed us with open arms. My partner Mark Bernstein had recently written a play, called "The Scroll of Bar Kokhba," about a celebrated Jewish rabbi who lived in the time of the Roman Emperor Hadrian and who played a significant role in the rebellion that eventually led to the destruction of the Second Temple in Jerusalem. I suggested that the Golden Circle might present Mark's new play as a season-opener and fundraiser and the suggestion was greeted with enthusiasm by all concerned, especially the playwright! Terry Loughlin, an experienced actor and director, agreed to direct the production. Mark good-naturedly acceded to Terry's drastic editing, which reduced the work by nearly half, and the play proved both an artistic and a financial success. In fact, that production provided the income on which the theater was to operate for the next several years. Perhaps I should have asked Terry to give this memoir similar treatment!

Keith Martin was eventually hired as General Manager and the Company continued to present its plays at the JCC for several years. I served as president of the board from 1988 to 1991 and Mark took over in 1991. During Mark's tenure the Company merged with the Charlotte Repertory Theatre and some of our directors were appointed to that Company's Board of Directors. As part of the merger, the Repertory Theatre agreed to perform at least one classical play per season, since that had been the principal repertoire of the Golden Circle. Unfortunately that agreement has not been honored. Perhaps it was not a realistic goal.

In 1995 the Charlotte Repertory Theatre decided to stage "Inherit the Wind," the story of the 1924 Scopes "monkey" trial. Terry Loughlin had been chosen to direct the play and I tried out for the role of Clarence Darrow. Little did I know at the time that Leo Penn, successful film director and father of Sean Penn of Hollywood fame, had already shown an interest in that role when he and Terry were working together on a film in Wilmington, North Carolina. Of course he got the role! Sean actually came to one of the performances. At that time Janet Eisenhart and I were discussing the possibility of my playing a role in a production of the newly organized Actors' Theater. I could not be in both productions because the schedules conflicted, so I presumed to telephone Terry and ask him if he had another part for me, since I had to give Janet an answer right away. He asked me if I thought I might be able to play the part of the judge in "Inherit the Wind." My answer was in the affirmative for reasons that will become evident in the next chapter. Thus was the door opened to the greatest thespian experience of my life. And for the first time I was actually paid to play a role!

The role of Clarence Darrow fit Leo Penn like a glove, and Ed Grady, a veteran of many years on North and South Carolina stages, portrayed William Jennings Bryan to a "T." At one point when I was discouraged about my portrayal of the judge I confessed as much to Leo. He put his hands on my shoulders, looked me straight in the eye and said, "Syd, I don't know of anyone I'd rather have in that role." I never had any doubts from that moment, though I recognized that he was probably just trying to build my confidence.

Janet was without any question my most faithful promoter and several years later she tapped me for a role in "Night of the Iguana" at Actor's Theatre. It was an excellent role and I was delighted to have it. Cast as the heroine's nonagenarian grandfather, I wore a white wig and carried a cane in the interest of creating the proper illusion. The part also called for me to compose a poem during the course of the play, and I mumbled snatches of lines off-stage as they were supposed to have occurred to me. As a grand finale I recited the completed poem up-stage, and expired just before the final curtain.

When the reviews came out after opening night, the *Creative Loafing* reviewer complained that the grandfather's off-stage recitation proved an unfortunate distraction. On the other hand, Tony Brown, who is clearly a very perceptive reviewer, opined in the *Charlotte Observer* that "Sydnor Thompson proved once again that he is 'a grand old man of Charlotte theater.'" What can I say?

## THE SPORADIC BOOK CLUB

In the fall of 1992 Mark Bernstein, George Daly and I met for lunch to plan the resuscitation of a book club Mark had organized many years earlier. Mark dubbed it the "Sporadic Book Club" because he did not expect we would meet with any regularity. I was especially enthusiastic about the prospect because I had missed the literary discipline that had been involved in leading one of Mortimer Adler's "Great Books" discussion groups at Queens College in the '60s and early '70s, with Virginia Thomas as my co-leader.

We soon interested Marc Ben-Joseph, Gene Owens, Jack Perry and Dr. Bill Porter in joining us. More recently Jerry Shinn and Mel Watt have become members. I enjoy the discussions and the participants more than I could ever have imagined, though I am intimidated by the breadth of their reading and the laser-like perspicacity of their minds. We are all so voluble that it's sometimes hard to get a word in edgewise. Gene Owens recently died and we miss him greatly. His contributions to the group, often cast in some lighthearted vein not necessarily in keeping with his considerable stature as a man of the cloth, were memorable. Mel Watt does not often attend because of the demands made on him as North Carolina's Twelfth District Congressman.

# CHAPTER 24
## CLIMAX TO A LEGAL CAREER
### THE NORTH CAROLINA COURT OF APPEALS

In 1984 Joe Grier and Mark Bernstein had proposed to Governor Jim Hunt that I be appointed to fill a vacancy on the Supreme Court of North Carolina. Governor Hunt declined to make the appointment at that time, but ten years later another opportunity presented itself. In 1993, at Joe and Mark's suggestion, I submitted a resumé in connection with a Superior Court vacancy. A few weeks later I received a call from the Governor. He again declined to appoint me, saying that he had a different post in mind for me. I thanked him, of course, and went back to work.

In June of 1994 I learned that Hugh Wells, a North Carolina Court of Appeals judge, was retiring from the court. By coincidence, Wells had written the opinion in *Chemical Bank v. Home Federal Savings and Loan*, in which he declined to acknowledge that my client Chemical Bank was a third party beneficiary of Home Federal's permanent loan commitment. Mark renewed his efforts, this time to have me appointed to the North Carolina Court of Appeals post being vacated by Hugh Wells. I was especially open to the suggestion as I had recently reached my seventieth birthday and many of the clients I had served, including the Carolina Transfer & Storage Co., Delph Hardware and Specialty Co., the Downs Group, Hartford Realty Company, Parks-Cramer Company, Sam Solomon & Company and S&W Cafeterias, had been sold or gone out of business. In fact, two young members of the firm's executive committee had recently pointed out to me that my production for the fiscal year 1993 had not measured up to those of previous years. Moreover, I should soon reach the firm's retirement age. Everything considered it was an ideal time for a new direction in my legal career.

This time Mark and Al Adams, a partner in our Raleigh office, went to see Governor Hunt and pointed out that, among other factors, he should consider that I would reach the retirement age for judges in less than two years, which would enable him to appoint my successor. In other words, my appointment would provide the governor an opportunity for a "double-header."

Within a few weeks I was invited to Raleigh for an interview with the governor. The meeting was most pleasant, especially made so by reminiscences about our many mutual political experiences over the years. One subject in which he appeared to be especially interested was my view of capital punishment. I confessed to him that I had introduced resolutions at the Western North Carolina Conference of the United Methodist Church and the North Carolina Council of Churches urging the North Carolina legislature to abolish capital punishment. On the theory that this view might not recommend me to the electorate, whose favor I should soon be seeking, I blush to report that I volunteered not to introduce that subject in the course of the upcoming campaign. (If appointed, I should have to stand for election in the November following my appointment.) Of course I was able to rationalize this position in some degree on the ground that capital cases go directly to the North Carolina Supreme Court from the trial court, bypassing the North Carolina Court of Appeals.

In mid-August Governor Hunt called to tell me that he intended to appoint me to the Court of Appeals and that I should have to appear before the Democratic Party's State Executive Committee in Raleigh the following weekend if I wished to stand for election to the position in November. Needless to say, I accepted his offer with great enthusiasm and gratitude. That development was to introduce what proved to be a most satisfying, if somewhat brief, climax to my legal career.

On the Saturday following my call from the governor I attended the Democratic Party's State Executive Committee meeting in Raleigh, seeking its endorsement on the November ballot. Governor Hunt introduced me to the about 100 Democrats in attendance. So far as I could tell, he was cold sober but in the course of his remarks he compared me to Jesus. In response, I related the story that John Cansler had told Judge Clarkson and me about having been advised by his college teacher that "if someone should tell a damn lie in your favor, don't contradict him." With that kind of introduction, the Executive Committee naturally approved my candidacy.

On August 26, 1994, Chief Judge Gerald Arnold administered the oath of office to me in the federal district courtroom in Charlotte before my family and friends. Hattie assisted me in donning the black robe which is the insignia of the office. Governor Hunt introduced me again, this time omitting any reference to Jesus. Perhaps he had learned the truth in the interim. It was a highly satisfying ceremony. Determined to do justice to my new career, I began reading a biography of U.S. Second Circuit Judge Learned Hand, considered by many to have been the greatest American judge of the twentieth century. Hattie and I rented an apartment at the corner of St. Mary's Street and Wade Avenue in downtown Raleigh. We borrowed furniture from my cousin Jane Lovelace and her husband Bob, who live in Raleigh, and set up housekeeping in time for me to sit on my first case on August 29, 1994. Hattie rented an U-Drive truck to move some of the items of furniture into the apartment while I was already on duty at court. She insists that the truck's wheels did not respond to the steering wheel until it was turned 180 degrees, making the trip a nightmare!

The members of the Court, including Chief Judge Arnold, were most cordial and helpful throughout my stay, doing all that they could to make me comfortable. Somehow I sensed that, because I had been practicing law for forty years, my colleagues showed me a degree of deference not usually extended to new judges. The Court's special camaraderie was reflected in the fact that those judges who were in their offices at noon on a particular day usually went to lunch together at Belks Cafeteria. I made a number of good friends on the court, especially Jack Cozort, Jack Lewis, John Martin, Betsy McCrodden and Jim Wynn.

The judges of the North Carolina Court of Appeals hear appeals in panels of three. The responsibility for writing the opinion in a particular case is assigned to one member of the panel before oral argument. After briefs are filed and panel assignments are made, the briefs are distributed to the panel members to whom the case has been assigned. They then review the briefs and assign each case to one of their clerks, who is asked to research the matter and prepare a memorandum, including a recommendation as to how the case should be decided. I was especially fortunate in having an opportunity to hire two bright young clerks, Kurt Seeber and Ann Kirby, who had worked for my fellow judge Jack Cozort the previous year. I often agreed with their recommendations, but at times we debated the matter with such vigor that my secretary felt constrained to come to the door to be sure we were all right! It was a useful exercise and one that I thoroughly enjoyed.

Immediately after the day's oral arguments, members of the panel meet in the Court's conference room and at least tentatively decide the cases they have heard that day. According to a long-established custom, the junior member of the panel is called upon to vote first – just the opposite from the way it is done by the justices of the United States Supreme Court. That meant I had to stick my judicial neck out first in every case I heard. I eventually became fairly comfortable with the process.

About eighty-five percent of the cases that are appealed from the Superior Court are referred to the Court of Appeals rather than to the North Carolina Supreme Court. On that account, the number of cases in which opinions are published in the Court of Appeals official reports has increased almost exponentially over the years. A short time before I arrived, the Court had adopted a policy of not printing all of its opinions in the official bound volumes. The theory was that only those opinions that deal with some uncommon or important principle of law should be published. With Jim Wynn's encouragement, I usually suggested that my opinions should be published. One of them dealt with the question of whether North Carolina's coastal lands at Buxton Woods on the Outer Banks should be preserved for hunting and fishing against a threat of residential development. We ruled against the residential development.[*] An

---

[*] *Friends of Hatteras Island v. Coastal Resources Commission*, 117 N.C. App. 556 (1995).

editorial in the *Greensboro News and Record* approved the decision, much to my satisfaction:

> The community needs a new source of water, and Buxton Woods could provide it.
>
> Doesn't matter, says Judge Sydnor Thompson of the North Carolina Court of Appeals. If we open the term "public use" to a broader interpretation than the one obviously intended by the state, any number of other uses could take advantage of that opening, undermining the principle of preserving the woods.
>
> Judge Thompson has ruled correctly.
>
> Because of the explosion of development up and down the North Carolina coast, ancient maritime forests like Buxton Woods have all but disappeared from the Outer Banks. Only in the past few years has the state made any effort to protect the remaining forests, chiefly by buying them up.
>
> The state had good reasons for this belated attention to a vanishing coastal resource.
>
> *The Greensboro News and Record*
> January 19, 1995

The *Charlotte Observer* also published a favorable editorial on that same subject.

I didn't always fare so well, however. In fact, the North Carolina Supreme Court reversed two of my cases. In one case our panel had affirmed a jury verdict in favor of a homeowner who had repaired weather damage on one side of the exterior of his house with artificial siding, contrary to the policy of the residential association's Architectural Review Committee.* In the other case we had held that a woman who had been separated from her husband for two years was not responsible for his hospital bill, even though she had driven him to the hospital when he was admitted.** In that case, a women's group filed an *amicus curiae* ("friend of the court") brief on behalf of the defendant and a hospital association filed an *amicus* brief on behalf of the hospital. I suggested in my opinion that the North Carolina legislature should eliminate the previously established requirement that a woman who was at fault in leaving her husband should continue to be responsible for "necessaries," such as hospital expenses, incurred by her former spouse. One of my fellow panel members requested that I omit that paragraph from the opinion before he would sign it. So I did. A bill was subsequently introduced in the North Carolina legislature which would have excused women who are legally separated from being liable for their husband's necessaries, but it was not enacted. I do not doubt that the same hospital authorities who filed the *amicus curiae* brief in the court case also lobbied against the legislative change.

I still think we were right in both cases.

---

* *Raintree Homeowners Assn. v. Bleimann*, 116 N.C. App. 561 (1994).
** *Forsyth Memorial Hospital v. Chisholm*, 117 N.C. App. 608 (1995).

Within a week or two of the time that I began hearing cases, Gary Pearce, a veteran Democratic campaign adviser, called a meeting of all of the Democratic judgeship candidates to help us plan our campaigns. We had hardly settled into our seats before Gary told us that a recent survey had shown that we were all running substantially behind our Republican opponents. That was disheartening to say the least, but it didn't prevent Hattie and me from campaigning. Every day that I was not actually hearing cases or preparing opinions, Hattie and I traveled across the state, campaigning to retain the office. She drove while I worked. I interviewed with several daily newspapers and was endorsed by about half of them. Those who failed to endorse me usually did so on the ground that I should be ineligible to serve more than another year because of the statutory rule of retirement at age 72. I suppose that was a legitimate issue. Several good friends staged fundraisers for me, including Bill and Mary Joslin in Raleigh, and Rich and Emily Preyer in Greensboro. Having run for the state legislature just two years earlier, I was reluctant to call on my friends for help again but I really had no alternative.

That was the same year in which Newt Gingrich of Georgia campaigned for a "contract with America" to reduce taxes and to turn the country's clock back in other respects. Bill Clinton had managed to alienate the North Carolina electorate in the two years he had served as President, largely because of his proposal for a national health service program and his liberal "don't ask – don't tell" policy toward gays in the military. It was a bad year for Democrats throughout the country, and I lost the November 8 statewide election by a substantial margin. In fact, every North Carolina Democratic judge who had Republican opposition lost in that election. Ralph Walker of Greensboro won my seat.

At Jim Wynn's suggestion, I called a Raleigh photographer and arranged for him to take a group photograph of the members of the Court. Before I left I gave each member a copy. I also took that occasion to have my photograph taken with my two clerks. I need hardly say that those photographs occupy a prominent position on my office wall.

In order to finish writing my opinions, I stayed in Raleigh until December 31, 1994. Hattie moved back to Charlotte during the Christmas holidays. Before she left, we had a good-bye party for the members of the Court and their spouses. The invitations featured a photograph of me with several band-aids on my face and a gauze bandage on my head, inviting the guests to a consolation party for a victim of "Hurricane Walker." Our friends Heman and Mary Jane Clark stole the show by wearing bandages on their heads that emulated those depicted on the invitation.

Near the end of my tenure, I asked my fellow-judges how long it was considered appropriate to wait before appearing before the court as an advocate. Syd Eagles immediately volunteered, "Not before the next day!" The fact is that I have chosen not to appear before the court since leaving. Hattie and I do attend the Court's Christmas parties, however, usually with our friends Hugh and Mary Irving Campbell.

Serving on the Court of Appeals was without a doubt the most satisfying experience of my professional life. After the election, Jack Betts, a *Charlotte Observer* columnist, wrote an article about my service:

> Raleigh – Sydnor Thompson set some records during his short stay here. Last August, he became the oldest person to be appointed to the N.C. Court of Appeals, when Gov. Jim Hunt named him to the bench at age 70.
>
> And when he left Dec. 30 following the Republican landslide that swept scores of Democrats out of office, the Charlotte lawyer set a second record – for the shortest stay on the Court of Appeals.
>
> Those bits of trivia aren't what Thompson will be remembered for in Raleigh, though. Colleagues who worked with him during his four months on the bench (Aug. 29 to Dec. 30) say they were struck by his extraordinary energy and enthusiasm for the job.
>
> "He was great," said Judge Jack Cozort, who among other things serves as one of the court's unofficial historians. "He came here with so much energy and just dived into it from the very first day. And when he lost (in the Nov. 8 election when he ran for the unexpired portion of his term) it didn't diminish his enthusiasm the least little bit. He showed up the next day with a smile on his face, just ready to dig back in."

I'm convinced that being an appellate judge is the best job a lawyer could have – at least it proved so for me. I was there long enough to learn that, despite the oft-repeated axiom that a judge's personal philosophy should play no part in his decisions, *i.e.*, that a judge merely decides the case before him on the basis of the law and the facts, that axiom is a gross oversimplification. The law is not always so certain. One's philosophy of life cannot help but color his decisions, even in the case of an intermediate appellate court, and definitely so in the case of a court of final jurisdiction.

Within a couple of years of my leaving the Court of Appeals, I entertained the members of the Court and their spouses at dinner at the Charlotte Country Club on the occasion of their conducting a week of appellate arguments in Charlotte. Judge Clifton Johnson was retiring, and I chose that opportunity to show him special attention. I also invited a delegation of lawyers from Parker Poe to attend. Hattie played some Chopin and one of our local opera divas, Susan Roberts Knowlson, sang. I read some verses I had prepared for the occasion:

A TRIBUTE TO THE NORTH CAROLINA COURT OF APPEALS
BY A COLLEAGUE WHO ENJOYED A FRAGMENTARY CAREER THERE

> Tonight we're pleased to host an em'nent Court
> who've reformed the law of contract and of tort.
> They work both day and night to stay ahead.

Their opinions are first-rate and widely read.
In recent years the Court sustained a blow
which very nearly brought its em'nence low.
The Gov'nor named an old man to the post
who bore a marked resemblance to your host.
He spent such time campaigning 'cross the state
that all of his opinions were filed late;
and sadly he in recent months has learned
two cases the Magnif'cent Sev'n o'erturned.
So all in all this fifteen-minute wonder
set record marks for age, tenure and blunder.

I don't know that I have ever had so much fun!

# CHAPTER 25
## A FINISHING CANTER
### A DISPUTE RESOLUTION PRACTICE

When I accepted the appointment to the Court, I retired from the law firm as of August 1, 1994, and thus qualified for the firm's pension program. The firm's partnership agreement allows a retired partner to serve as counsel to the firm after retirement and provides him an office and a secretary for as long as he cares to have them. Thus, I returned to my office at Parker Poe within a week of leaving Raleigh and Betty Helton, who had been with the firm for many years, agreed to be my secretary.

The pension is computed as a percentage of the average partner's annual earnings and, under the partnership agreement, I was given the option of choosing that pension for life or for ten years certain. Fortunately, I chose the former, with the added benefit of giving Hattie a stake in taking good care of me! In addition to my pension, I am also entitled to a percentage of the fees I earn from clients other than those I represented prior to my retirement. I soon decided not to undertake any trial work but to devote my time to mediations and arbitrations. Fortunately I had taken an American Arbitration Association course in March 1994 to learn how to mediate civil actions in the North Carolina Superior Court. As I have stated, the North Carolina legislature, acting on the recommendation of the North Carolina Bar Association, had recently adopted a statute that called for all Superior Court actions to be mediated prior to trial, unless exempted from that requirement by the Court. By January 1995, the program was under way and I was certified as a mediator on the strength of my AAA training.

Within a few weeks of my return I was in touch with Andy Little, with whom I had worked on the North Carolina Bar Association's Dispute Resolution Committee in the '80s. Andy had established an organization called Mediation, Inc., which was engaged in training mediators, as well as conducting mediation conferences. Andy and Thorns Craven, another principal of Mediation, Inc., met with my friend Lou Bledsoe and me and invited us to join Mediation, Inc. We accepted the invitation enthusiastically and are conducting mediations under the auspices of that organization to this day. It has been a splendid connection and I have come to regard all of my fellow mediators, including Andy, Thorns and Lou, Lynn Gullick of Greensboro, and Jim Billings of Raleigh, very highly. Andy and Thorns conduct an excellent 40-hour training course for persons seeking to qualify as mediators and I have acted as a coach in that course from time to time.

Well over half of the cases that I mediate are settled at the mediation conference and a great many more are settled by the parties before trial. It is a highly successful program, alleviating both mental anguish and financial expense when cases are settled out of court. For that reason, it has been a most satisfying experience. I have published articles on the subject of mediation for legal periodicals in order to encourage its use.[*]

In addition to Superior Court mediations, I conduct mediations for the North Carolina Industrial Commission (worker's compensation) and the federal Equal Employment Opportunity Commission. I have also conducted arbitrations for the American Arbitration Association since the '60s, having served on their regional advisory committee for about twenty years. More recently I qualified to conduct arbitration proceedings for the National Association of Securities Dealers, work that has increased considerably since the stock market depression of 2000.

In 1996 I was appointed to the North Carolina Bar Association's Dispute Resolution Council and for about five years served as chairman of its Ethics and Professionalism Committee. One of our major projects was preparing Rules of Ethics for North Carolina arbitrations, in which endeavor Professor George Walker of Wake Forest Law School carried the laboring oar. In fact, he drafted the Rules. His work has subsequently been adopted by other professional organizations throughout the country.

Our Committee, with the approval of the Dispute Resolution Council, also sought to persuade the North Carolina Bar to adopt a rule of professional responsibility requiring every lawyer to acquaint his or her client with the various alternative dispute resolution procedures that are available in North Carolina before filing an action on behalf of that client. The North Carolina Bar Council declined to adopt our proposal. According to my best information, the Bar Council based its decision on the ground that it would expose lawyers to actions for malpractice if they failed to advise their clients of the availability of such a procedure. The Superior Court for the 26th Judicial District has, however, adopted such a rule for members of the Mecklenburg County Bar, as have a number of other states. It is not the first time that the Mecklenburg Bar has led the way! Since then the Supreme Court rules governing state court mediations have been amended to incorporate a similar requirement.

## RETIREMENT

In March 1995 the firm staged a retirement dinner for Francis Parker and me. The dinner was the occasion for the presentation of our portraits, painted by Greenville, South Carolina artist Michael del Priore. Francis' portrait was an excellent likeness of him. While mine was perhaps not so faithful a likeness, I appreciated the painter's version nonetheless because I had always wanted a square

---

[*]  "Mediation Myths," South Carolina Lawyer (March/April 1998 issue).

jaw.    Mark Bernstein delivered a highly commendatory and somewhat exaggerated appraisal of my career, while Bill Poe praised Francis' considerable contributions to the firm.   We each received a splendid mahogany humidor appropriately engraved.   Jim Preston read a clever poem for the occasion, establishing his credentials as the true poet laureate of the firm, though I confess that the subject matter may have prejudiced me in its favor.   He wrote:

### CHARLES WILLIAM SYDNOR

#### I

Out of Virginia he came,
A true son of E. C. Glass;
Charles William Sydnor his name,
they say he was first in his class.
> And he went up to Syracuse,
> Cold windy Syracuse
> To learn, box and find his own lass.

#### II

Over the ocean he sailed,
Joining the forces of good,
Risking, that right might prevail,
His virile young body and blood.
> So he marched across Europe,
> And he fought across Europe,
> Until justice rolled down like a flood.

#### III

Back to the Orange our hero
Repaired and commenced to define
His future.  It soon became clear.  Oh,
A life in the law he designed.
> He had found his career,
> And he captured a dear
> Companion in sweet Hattie Line.

#### IV

At Harvard young Sydnor excelled
At learning the law.  And he wrote
Learned articles wherein he spelled
Out the mysteries of Blackstone and Coke.
> Then he went back to Britain –
> Jolly old Britain.
> For what?  Economics, you Bloke.

#### V

Our bar'ster was called to Wall Street
To work on his skills and renown,
At John W. Davis's feet
He learned how to lose – trying *"Brown."*
> He rolled into Washington
> Got rolled up in Washington,
> It proved an inhospit'ble town.

#### VI

Meantime his family had grown
By D'Arcy and Sydnor and so
He decided to give them a home
Far away from the ice and the snow.
> The Lord said, "It's Charlotte –

Take them to Charlotte;
Join Bill and Francis and Joe."

## VII

There Sydnor repaired to the bar,
Established himself in the courts,
Arguing near and afar
On contracts and easements and torts.
    He became a Recorder
    To restore law and order
    And jailed all unsavory sorts.

## VIII

Hattie meantime was so cheery.
At piano she was a delight.
And what's more 'bout every two years she
Produced a new child while in flight.
    Little Harriet, Bren, Kathy Line –
    We wondered how they had the time.
    But back then we didn't work nights.

## IX

To every human endeavor
The Thompsons have given their verve.
"The Party," the church, and le culture
Were blessed by their calling to serve.
    And they gave like plutocrats
    To aspiring Democrats
    Without thought of their fiscal reserves.

## X

Eventually Sydnor was called
To the High Court in Capitol City.
He went and then promptly was mauled
By a runaway elephant – a pity!
    For he loved all his cases.
    The opinions in his cases
    Were thorough, learned and witty.

## XI

Sooner he is back than expected,
Scarred but extremely alive.
Judicious and fair and respected,
As a mediator he will thrive.
    Yes, he's opening files
    And using his wiles,
    But strictly from nine until five.

## XII

How do we sum it all up –
A life lived so "splendidly"?
As long as there's wine in the cup,
I'll say what it means to me:
    "Through joy and strife, Sydnor,
    You taught us life, Sydnor,
    And we give it back – lovingly."

My own contribution to the event paled in comparison:

**A FINISHING CANTER ON THE RETIREMENT OF
TWO BELOVED PARKER POE PARTNERS --
FRANCIS PARKER AND SYDNOR THOMPSON**
(With Apologies to Oliver Wendell Holmes, Jr.)

I

Tonight our faithful laureate lifts his pen
to sound in verse a sonorous amen
to two careers that spanned o'er forty years
and now bring one and all to brink of tears
for feats undone as well as feats performed,
for heights unscaled as well as bastions stormed.

II

Ten short years ago this comp'ny laughed
to hear the laureate's memo In Re Shaft.
But now the scythe has harvested their crop.
No longer will they toil in that sweat shop,
no longer deadly sausages be fed
while self-respecting gentry lie abed.

III

No more with business stratagems assailed,
no more with others' coups d'etat regaled.
No more condemned to redact model forms.
No more constrained to meet new timesheet norms.
While you their patrons furnish their support,
they will in luxury's lap dance and cavort.

IV

Old lawyers do not die; they fade away
and so will they you honor here today.
They'll spend their days in halcyon resorts,
recounting tales of glory on their courts.
To help them savor their short brush with fame,
remember, "Judge" and "Justice" is their name.

The following year, Susan Twiddy, now Mrs. Reed Fountain of Raleigh, who was working in our Charlotte office as a summer associate, interviewed me in connection with an Oral History Project that was being conducted by Professor Walter Bennett at the University of North Carolina Law School. I spoke at such great length about my life and work experiences that Susan must eventually have had second thoughts about the interview. She saw it through nonetheless and the product now resides in the Southern Historical Collection at the Louis Round Wilson Library in Chapel Hill, by coincidence the same repository as that selected by my Uncle Joe for the letters that my great-grandfather Dr. Charles William Sydnor wrote to his fiancée during the Civil War.

Mark Bernstein retired in 2002 and I had an opportunity to return the compliments he had paid me on my retirement. I read the following verses:

**ON MARK BERNSTEIN'S RETIREMENT**

I

From York, PA he came to meet his fate.
On Providence Road he soon became first mate
to brothers Ed and Larry whom he raised,

though we are told the neighbors were amazed
that those three strapping boys did survive
the pommeling they gave each other's hide.
Yet Mark, the first born, always kept afloat.
It's why in later life he built a moat
around his house as a protective fringe
should Ed or Larry seek to wreak revenge.

## II

In time Mark made first mate at Parker Poe
and we all learned how much that he did owe
to those two brothers who had made him strong
enough to pin his partners when they're wrong.
Indeed, as head of Management Committee
he drove us hard and showed us little pity.
And just to be quite sure he could us drub
he toned his muscles at the Tower Club.
Now finally the firm may have some peace
when daily tests of phys'cal prowess cease.

## III

It's true that Mark has served our law firm well
and caused our income annually to swell.
So let's be clear: We hope you'll hang around
and keep your num'rous clients on the ground.
Don't let your new abode atop Beech Mountain
reduce the flow of that financial fountain
from which we've drunk our fill for many years.
Don't cause your co-retirees any fears
that you might those good-paying clients shirk
and put us men of leisure back to work.

Gaston Gage retired at the same time and Jim Preston paid him tribute at the same dinner by purporting to show photographs of high points in Gaston's career on the wall of the dining room. Jim pointed to and then described the imaginary photographs at length while we craned our necks to see. Eventually, we all caught on. It was a triumph of subtlety. Al Adams and Bill McCullough retired in 2003. A number of Charlotte partners attended a similar gala dinner at the Cardinal Club in Raleigh to do them honor. Jim Preston retired this year. He now joins Francis, Mark, Gaston and me in the lunches we have at La Bibliotheque Restaurant to celebrate each other's birthdays.

In 2003 Mark Bernstein nominated me for the North Carolina Bar Association's General Practice Hall of Fame. Surprisingly enough, I was inducted into that organization at the June meeting of the Bar Association in Asheville. Hattie saw to it that all of our children and a number of our grandchildren attended the ceremony to demonstrate their loyalty. George Daly, who had received the same honor a year earlier on my recommendation and who deserved it far more than I, also attended my induction. George has properly earned a reputation for championing unpopular causes at the bar by defending hippies, conscientious objectors and the like. I have often said that the closest I ever came to supporting an unpopular cause in my law practice was saying a good word for George Daly. I even wrote a tribute to him for the Atticus Finch series in the North Carolina State Bar Journal several years ago.[*] That may not be enough to win me a seat in heaven, but it's a good start.

I marked significant birthdays of both Mark and George by seeking to capture their distinctive personalities in limerick form:

> Here's to our honoree Mark
> Now nearly as old as the Ark.
> His soft endoplast
> is aging quite fast.
> But his bite is still worse than his bark.

---

> If the phone catches George in a mood
> he may seem telephonic'lly rude
> but he waxes quite svelte
> indeed butter won't melt,
> when he's asked to bring suit or be sued.

I recently nominated my friend Bill Joslin of the Raleigh bar to receive the Liberty Bell Award. Presented by the Young Lawyers Division of the North Carolina Bar Association, the award honors members whose exemplary careers have demonstrated lifelong service to the law. Among those who have received the award in the past are such outstanding North Carolina lawyers as McNeill Smith, Congressman Richardson Preyer, Katherine R. Everett, Senator Terry Sanford and Governor James B. Hunt, Jr., all of whom I have known personally and admired greatly. I thought Bill belonged in that company. Apparently the members of the committee agreed with me: he will receive the award in a Law Day ceremony in May 2005. I shall have the privilege of introducing him and have already prepared some lines for the occasion:

### A Toast to a Compleat Lawyer - William Joslin

I

> Bill's pilgrimage began at Broughton High
> where from the start he caused the girls to sigh.
> At Chapel Hill he showed scholastic worth
> and high among his classmates won a berth.
> Soon Bill responded to his country's pleas
> and sailed in uniform the seven seas.
> Then luckily in time he heard the call
> to practice law and once again stood tall
> by claiming honors at Columbia U
> and editing that law school's Law Review.

II

> Then Bill's renown was broadcast near and far;
> he stayed his plan to join the Raleigh bar,
> for Justice Hugo Black had heard report,
> a fellow Southerner could help his court.
> He sent for Bill and hired him as his clerk,
> an opening that Bill could hardly shirk.
> It's clear that Black's opinions for that year

---

[*] "George Daly, North Carolina's Lone Protector of the Bill of Rights," 6 N.C. State Bar Journal, p. 28 (2001).

are those of all he published without peer.
Then finally, with natural misgiving,
Bill came back home to try to make a living.

III

Well, you all know the story from that point.
Bill built a Raleigh practice, ball and joint.
In time selected there to head the Bar,
he recently was named a "Joe Branch" star.
In public service few have been his match –
conservancy or gardening a patch.
For the Democratic Party he would die,
perhaps the only man more so than I.
But in matrimony William's done the best
by enticing Mary Coker to his nest.

Epilogue

So here's to Bill and here's to Mary too
We're glad to follow in your retinue.

Our law firm has grown by leaps and bounds in the last decade. About ten years ago Parker Poe opened an office in Spartanburg. A few years later we recruited several Columbia lawyers and set up an office there. Most recently, lawyers from a major law firm in Charleston, South Carolina resigned from their own firm and established a Parker Poe office there. With approximately 175 lawyers practicing in five offices, Parker Poe is now the third largest law firm headquartered in North Carolina and, according to the National Law Journal, is among the 250 largest law firms in the country (we are 247th). Several new divisions of the firm's transactional department have recently been established and have grown significantly in a relatively short time, especially those involved with public finance and capital markets. Litigation continues to be the strongest department in the firm, however, though that may be a personal bias.

I continue to come to the office every day that I am in town. I confess, however, to having become something of a "10 o'clock scholar." I enjoy spending an hour or two in the morning running, having a leisurely breakfast, reading the newspaper, struggling with the crossword puzzle, and puttering about in the garden.

## RIGHT HANDS

Most lawyers will acknowledge that a good administrative assistant is indispensable to their practice. My assistants at Parker Poe have been no exception. The first secretary assigned to me after I was admitted to the Bar was Jane Street. Jane is the daughter of the late C. P. "Gabby" Street, who was the president of McDevitt and Street Construction Company. I believe it was her first job and she did well in the short time we worked together before she married. When Jane left I hired Almeda "Meda" Whitescarver, who proved to be an excellent secretary. She eventually moved to Atlanta, however, where she was hired by the Kilpatrick law firm. She retired young, reportedly because her grandmother died and left her a substantial legacy.

When Meda left the firm in the sixties I hired Deans Cree who had worked for a lawyer in Laurinburg before moving to Charlotte. Deans stayed with me until 1973 when she left for a position at the Underwood Kinsey law firm. She was very bright and especially helpful but found our practice somewhat stressful. I dedicated some verses to her at a firm send-off held in her honor:

### TO MY HELPMATE DEANS REID CREE

Today Grier Parker gathers here to cheer
for one whose grace and charm are no veneer,
for one whose very nature is genteel,
whose tiny feet bear no Achilles heel.
A lady first and last from head to toe
who now 'ere midnite flees the Ball to go
to other climes wherein the grass grows green
where neither stress nor tension e'er is seen.
So let us all exclaim from bended knee
"Godspeed to thee, our princess Deans Reid Cree!"

Several years ago, Deans went to Cleveland, Ohio for a back operation and by some tragic quirk of fate died on the operating table. She was an absolute dear and I was quite fond of her.

Judy Carden and Diane Daniels both worked with me when our offices were in the Cameron Brown Building. Diane was exceptional. Before leaving to take a position with Cato Stores, she prepared a job description for her successor, including tips on how best to handle the ogre that I sometimes became. After we moved to the Charlotte Plaza in 1984 I had a new secretary every two or three years. They included Joan Bartley, Diane Martin, Mary Shoupe, Pat Black, Dayna Lowe, Melinda Bell, Sebra Bennett and Tami Vaughn. They were all fine individuals who performed their duties well. Most of them left to take positions in other firms that paid better because at that time Parker Poe's secretarial salaries were not competitive with those of other large firms. Mary Shoupe was the sole exception. She left to have a baby, which was, of course, the best reason of all.

Betty Helton worked with me for ten years after I returned from the Court, longer than any of my other administrative assistants. She has an excellent sense of humor and it served both of us well. In 2004 Betty told me that she intended to retire at the end of the year. At first I did not believe her. In fact, I told her that she would miss me too much. It appears that I was wrong, however, as she did indeed leave on December 31, 2004.

I cannot conclude this section without relating a rather extraordinary event that occurred with one of my secretaries. Francis Parker is once again the source of much of this story. It seems that he was sitting in Joe Grier's office one morning when he and Joe heard a commotion in the hall. In the next moment Joe's secretary and my secretary bolted through the door entangled in what appeared to Francis to be a half nelson wrestling hold which one had on the other. Joe managed to separate them and then called an emergency firm meeting within the hour, indicating his view that one of the secretaries would have to be dismissed. In response to the question voiced by one of the other attorneys, "Which one should we let go?" Joe replied, "Syd's secretary, of course." To which I am reported to have expostulated, "What kind of a partnership is this anyhow!" Apparently it was not that kind of partnership after all because the two ladies both continued in the office and soon seemed to get along just fine again.

## PROFESSIONAL CONCLUSIONS

According to Professor Roscoe Pound, the Harvard legal savant, a profession is "a group of persons engaged in the pursuit of a learned art in the public interest, no less so because it is a means of livelihood." The question is when does the "means of livelihood" overshadow "the public interest." In the late 1960s, Grier Parker Poe and Thompson instituted a billing procedure that was becoming common among law firms of that day - keeping time records as a basis for billing clients. Under this system, clients were expected to pay fees based upon the amount of time devoted to their matter rather than the result achieved. Eventually, slavish adherence to billing from time sheets became a practice that raised almost as many questions as it resolved. It continues today only because no satisfactory alternative basis for billing has been devised. The most welcome aspect of my retiring from active practice was being relieved of that irksome and ethically ambiguous exercise.

Because larger law firms appear to find it necessary to operate under strict budgetary constraints, including establishing production goals for their lawyers based upon a more or less assigned number of hours billed at designated hourly rates, their law practice reflects certain characteristics of a commercial enterprise. Lawyer advertising has also become commonplace. I was recently solicited to contribute to an arts organization by a lawyer who actually signed the letter in the name of his law firm.

When I assumed the office of president of the Mecklenburg County Bar, it was clear to me that one of the greatest challenges confronting our profession was the degree to which the practice of law has become money-driven. Therefore, I appointed a task force on professionalism. After several meetings, the task force delivered a report recommending the establishment of a standing committee on professionalism, which was soon done. That commission has addressed its attention to means of assuring that lawyers' fees are fair and appropriate to the work performed, the implementation of bar programs designed to provide legal services to those persons who cannot afford to engage a private attorney and the development of programs designed to prepare new lawyers for the ethical challenges that the practice of law entails. While the effort has been a noble one, I am the first to admit that it has fallen short of stemming the swelling tide toward commercialism.

This year a subcommittee of the Professionalism Committee of the North Carolina Bar Association of which subcommittee I served as chair revised and submitted a Lawyer's Creed and Principles of Professional Courtesy to the North Carolina Bar Association. It was approved by the Chief Justice of the North Carolina Supreme Court, and adopted by the Bar Association for circulation among North Carolina lawyers. I am pleased to have played a part in the revision of the Creed and Principles, both of which appropriately reflect the challenges that we face as a profession.

I must acknowledge that the degree to which lawyers or law firms lose sight of the high ethical principles that advance the public interest depends upon the individual lawyer and the individual law firm. Parker Poe Adams & Bernstein, now the oldest law firm in Charlotte, has a rich professional and cultural heritage that goes back a hundred and twenty years. There was considerable public testimony to that effect on the occasion of the firm's one hundredth anniversary celebration in 1984. I have every reason to believe that its reputation in that regard will continue.

# CHAPTER 26
## IN PURSUIT OF THE SYDNOR GENE

After hearing the accounts my grandmother Bessie Sydnor Thompson's father had told her of our Sydnor progenitors, I determined to investigate the family history for myself. My great-grandfather Dr. Charles William Sydnor had been raised in Frederick County, so in 1965 I went to Winchester, Virginia, the county seat of Frederick County, to visit the clerk of court's office. I had already identified the home of Dr. Sydnor's father, Richard Mitchell Sydnor ("Spring Hill") in Marlboro, a crossroads store and post office in Frederick County. Within a few hours, I established that Richard Mitchell was a veteran of the War of 1812 and served in the Virginia legislature from 1858 to 1862. His father William Fauntleroy Sydnor had received a grant of Frederick County land in 1784 from his own father, William Sydnor of Lancaster County, Virginia. Thus, in one afternoon's research I traversed seven generations back to the Northern Neck of Virginia. I had caught the genealogical bug for which there is no known cure. The search soon became a consuming hobby which I continued to pursue intermittently for the next thirty-five years.

I soon began a correspondence with the Reverend Charles E. Sydnor, a Baptist minister from Pasadena, California whose work I discovered in an article in the *William and Mary Quarterly*. He was the first to acquaint me with the identity of the original immigrant Fortunatus Sydnor, who had emigrated from England to a plantation on Indian Creek in Northumberland County, Virginia in about 1660. Fortunatus is apparently the ancestor of every American Sydnor I have since been able to identify.

### SYDNOR OF VIRGINIA

Over the next five years I devoted many hours to the study of the Sydnor family history and accumulated a great deal of information. Much of it was gleaned from a study of the records of various Virginia counties in the Virginia State Library. I spent several weeks in Richmond and later in Lawrenceville, visiting my sister Bobbie and working in the genealogy section of that library.

Equally important, however, was the information I garnered from other Sydnors who had been undertaking to solve the same genealogical puzzle. Principal among them were the aforementioned Reverend Charles E. Sydnor; Garland S. Sydnor of Richmond, Virginia; Vera Morel of New Orleans, Louisiana; and William Burton Sydnor of St. Louis, Missouri. I also met Floyd W. Sydnor of Richmond, Virginia, who, as a professional genealogist, had devoted many years of study to the subject, though he showed no interest in our sharing research.

Based upon my early research, I wrote an article entitled "Sydnor of Virginia" which was published in Volume XX of the Northern Neck Historical Society Magazine in December of 1970. In it, I traced the descendants of the immigrant Fortunatus Sydnor for the first five generations in this country.

While attending an American Bar Association meeting in London in 1985, Hattie and I visited two sixteenth century Sydnor homes, one in Suffolk County and the other in Norfolk County. By that time I had gone a good deal further in my research and had been able to identify Blundeston Hall in Suffolk County and Carrow Abbey in the City of Norwich, Norfolk County, as homes of my forebear William Sydnor, who lived there from 1570, when he acquired Blundeston Hall, to 1612, when he died in Norwich. We were cordially welcomed by the current owners of both homes and by the senior warden at Blundeston's Church of the Virgin Mary, for which William Sydnor served as patron during his lifetime.

### THE SYDNOR REUNION OF 1987 IN RICHMOND, VIRGINIA

By 1987 I felt I had enough information to schedule a family reunion in Richmond and in the Northern Neck of Virginia. About two hundred and fifty persons attended the gathering, and we chartered three buses to transport the group from the Marriott Hotel in Richmond to the Northern Neck on the east side of the Rappahannock River. The sites we visited also included the homes of the ancestors of those Sydnors who had settled in Hanover County from counties east of the Rappahannock. Many of their descendants now live in or near the City of Richmond. We spent most of our time in Lancaster and Richmond Counties, the former being where Fortunatus originally acquired land and established a tobacco plantation. The reunion was a great success, although for the most part it drew only those Sydnors who lived in Virginia and the neighboring states. Nevertheless, I had already come to view myself as the self-anointed "patriarch" of the Sydnor family.

In the years that followed I pursued the Sydnor gene relentlessly, both in the United States and in England, determined to develop what had started as a "paper" into a full-blown "book." Besides carrying the search back to fifteenth century England, I determined to undertake to identify every American descendant of Fortunatus Sydnor the immigrant. In the process, I have met hundreds of interesting Sydnor kin over the last forty years, which represents the most satisfying aspect of the project.

Perhaps the most notable discovery that resulted from my research was that my great-great-great-great-great-great grandmother was Esther Ball, the elder half-sister of George Washington's mother Mary Ball. Their father, Joseph Ball, had married again after his first wife died. Esther married Rawleigh Chinn in Lancaster County, Virginia, and their great-granddaughter

Sally Chinn married William Fauntleroy Sydnor, my great-great-great grandfather. It sounds complicated, but it establishes the link to Cousin George. He was my half first cousin seven times removed. On the strength of that kinship both of my sons have acquired early nineteenth century oil portraits of their cousin in the Gilbert Stuart style.

## THE SYDNOR REUNION IN ENGLAND

Ten years after the 1987 reunion, I suggested to Hattie that we might undertake to assemble a body of Sydnors who would be interested in visiting England to see the houses in which the Sydnors had lived as well as the churches and colleges they had attended. I had identified those places to my own satisfaction with sufficient certainty to justify the trip. Hattie was willing to go along with the idea so I began to correspond with the present owners of the Sydnor homes, the vicars of the churches and the appropriate officials at Oxford and Cambridge. They all appeared to be sympathetic with my purpose and Hattie and I went to England in the spring of 1997 to prepare the way. It was on that trip that we had dinner with our long-time friend Lucia Halpern, daughter of Melvin and Cristina Halpern of Charlotte, and met her future husband John Davies, a London solicitor. Lucia was working there for Goldman Sachs.

We were given a cordial welcome everywhere we went. On our return, I extended an invitation to the American Sydnors, from Massachusetts to California and from Florida to Wisconsin, to make a similar pilgrimage. The Mann Travel Agency of Charlotte was instrumental in helping me plan the trip, especially Elaine Crutchfield of that company. She and one of her colleagues even flew to New York to help us assemble our passengers there.

When we initially mailed the invitations, Hattie considered it possible that we might have as many as thirty acceptances. In the end, eighty-six pilgrims crossed the Atlantic together on a commercial airliner in July 1998. That number included our sons Sydnor and Brenny, Sydnor's two girls and our daughter Harriet. Kathy Line, who was momentarily expecting her first child, was on that account unable to go. D'Arcy and her two children joined us later for a visit to Vienna. Brenny was our official photographer and filmed the entire trip on a camcorder. He did a splendid job and made it possible for us to make a pictorial history available to all who wanted it.

The first night in London we had a gala reception and dinner at the Barclay Hotel. Each branch of Sydnors was introduced in turn, according to their county of origin – Dinwiddie County, Halifax County, Hanover County, Frederick County, Richmond County, all in Virginia, and Lincoln County, Missouri. Dr. Brantley Sydnor of Roanoke, Virginia, who is descended by three different lines from Fortunatus Sydnor, was introduced as the person who might boast the most Sydnor genes. He was roundly applauded, though he insisted that it was not of his doing. Actually I am descended from Fortunatus by two of the same lines as is Brantley. There were a considerable number of marriages to cousins in the Northern Neck of Virginia of the eighteenth century.

The tour began with a bus trip to the Village of Blundeston in Suffolk County and the City of Norwich in Norfolk County on the first day, and ended with a visit to Gray's Inn of Court in London five days later. In between we visited the Villages of Denton, Egerton and Brenchley, and the Town of Canterbury in Kent County, St. George's Chapel in Windsor Castle, Oxford University's Magdalene College, Cambridge University's Gonville and Caius and Christ Church Colleges, and Lincoln's Inn of Court in London. All-told we spent six days on chartered buses from early morning to sundown, carrying boxed lunches for convenience. We were accompanied by two guides for whom Mann Travel had made arrangements.

All of the sites we visited were intimately connected with Sydnor family history during the fifteenth and sixteenth centuries. Richard Sydnor, born in 1465, was raised as a member of the congregation at St. James the Great Church in the Village of Egerton in Kent County, where he was later memorialized in a stained glass window depicting his coat of arms. He served as treasurer to King Henry VIII's daughter Princess Mary during her childhood. He subsequently became chaplain to King Henry VIII and chancellor of the Order of the Garter which convened in St. George's Chapel at Windsor Castle. Because of Richard's prominence in the early 1500s and his undoubted acquaintance with such eminent lieutenants of Henry VIII as "the four Thomases" – Cardinal Thomas Wolsey, Sir Thomas More, Lord Chancellor Thomas Cromwell and Archbishop Thomas Cranmer – I consider him a fit subject for a biography, which may become my next project. A detailed summary of the posts he held during his lifetime appears in W. D. McCray's Register of Magdalen College, Oxford, so hopefully there is plenty of material available for that purpose.

Richard's nephew Sir Paul Sydnor purchased Brenchley Manor in the Village of Brenchley in Kent County from King Henry VIII after it was forfeited to the King by Cardinal Wolsey. Wolsey had fallen from grace when he could not arrange an annulment of the King's marriage to Catherine of Aragon. Paul Sydnor's son William married his step-sister Ursula Berney after his widowed mother had married Sir John Berney and the family had moved to Suffolk County. It was William who acquired Blundeston Hall.

William Sydnor of Blundeston Hall was the great-great-great-great-grandfather of the noted eighteenth century British poet George Crabbe whose poetry was much admired by William

Wordsworth and whose epic poem "The Borough" was the inspiration for Benjamin Britten's opera "Peter Grimes."

On our last night in London we once again staged a dinner through the courtesy of our friends Ian and Ann Redhead at the Army and Navy Club in London. We invited all of the Sydnor kin who had made the trip as well as a number of long-time English friends. Ian Redhead led us in singing the grace we had sung before evening meals at St. Andrew's: "Sit nomen Domini benedictum per Jesum Christum salvatorem nostrum. Amen!" Young Harriet played the harp for our guests. At the close of the festivities we all stood and sang the "Gaudie" ("Gaudeamus igitur, juvenes dum sumus, gaudeamus igitur, juvenes dum sumus, post jucundem, juventudem, post molestam, senectutem. Nos habebit humus, nos habebit humus," meaning "Let us rejoice, etc."), which is the international student song featured in Johannes Brahms' "Academic Overture," and which I had learned at St. Andrew's. That was an especially poignant moment for me. During the evening I read some verses that I had penned to mark the occasion:

### CANTERBURY TALES REVISITED

#### I

We're here again to pay sincere respect
to you who taught us how to speak correct.
We Sydnor pilgrims now have made our way
to Blundeston and Brenchley for a day,
to Egerton and Denton where we saw
the sites where ancient Romans brought the law
and where our forebears crawled forth from the mold
to gird their loins and 'complish deeds untold.
To St. George Chapel where Sir Richard prayed
and for King Harry did whate'er he bade.

#### II

To All Saints Church where Paul of Brenchley kneeled,
and Thomas Wolsey's woods became Paul's weald.
To Oxford's Magdelene College where our John
contributed two books we found weren't gone,
and finally to Cambridge and to Caius
where William Sydnor learned his a, b, c's.
No wonder that some then gave up the ghost
and chose to disappoint our Gray's Inn host.
So now we thank you folks who've welcomed us
with smiles and tea where'er we stopped the bus.

I received word last December that Ian's heart was giving out and that he wasn't expected to survive. I had just learned that our mutual friend George Poston had died in November. Wanting to reach out to Ian somehow, I immediately made a video tape on which I reminisced about our times together and mailed it to him, but I fear that he did not live to see it. I admired Ian's many excellent qualities of character. In physical appearance, mien and charm he reminded me of the actor Hugh Grant.

After our English rendezvous, our immediate family went on to Vienna to visit the Austrian friends with whom Hattie and the children had lived in the '60s and '70s. Between Henrietta Kirchmayer and her sister Gerhilt Radakovics, they were able to put all of us up during our stay there. On our last night we entertained about twenty-five of our Austrian friends at a Perchtoldsdorf heurigen.

When we returned to America my seventh cousin Walker Sydnor of Lynchburg took on the responsibility of soliciting our fellow pilgrims to make gifts to three churches for which our Sydnor forebears had served as patrons in the 1500s – The Church of the Virgin Mary in Blundeston, All Saints Church in Brenchley and St. James the Great Church in Egerton. In each case the money was used to purchase a suitable memorial identified and inscribed as a gift from "the Sydnor family of America."

The Blundeston memorials are a glass-covered wooden case to house the church's guest book and a number of wrought iron candlesticks attached to the ends of the pews, all dedicated to the memory of William Sydnor of Blundeston. The Brenchley memorial is a high-backed bishop's chair made of oak and yew, dedicated to the memory of Paul Sydnor of Brenchley, the father of William of Blundeston. The Egerton memorial is a supply of the recent edition of the Church of England's hymnal entitled "Book of Common Praise," dedicated to the memory of William Sydnor of Egerton, the grandfather of Paul Sydnor of Brenchley, and to William's son Richard Sydnor, Chaplain to Henry VIII. The Blundeston warden Mrs. Iris Mayes and the St. James Church secretary Mrs. Janine Burgess have proved to be charming correspondents and we could not have been more pleased with their choice of memorials. Another delightful English couple whose acquaintance we made on that trip and with whom we have enjoyed a continuing correspondence is Clive and Margaret Charrington of Old Cryals Farm, which was once the property of Paul Sydnor of Brenchley Manor.

A curious thing occurred shortly after we returned from England. My seventh cousin Eugene B. Sydnor of Richmond, Virginia, who served in the Virginia State Senate, asked me if I might speak to John Belk to see if he had any interest in acquiring the Williamsburg, Virginia mother store in the Southern Department Store chain established years earlier by his grandfather Lincoln Sydnor. I arranged for the two to meet in Charlotte and upon John's insistence that he name a price, Gene suggested $5,000,000. After making a cursory investigation, John declined the offer and within a few months, the store was placed in bankruptcy. Whenever I see John Belk he inevitably reminds me that I tried to sell him my cousin's bankrupt store for $5,000,000!

I completed the "Sydnor Family Saga" in 2000. An 1,175-page genealogy, the book traces the Sydnors from fifteenth century England through Fortunatus Sydnor the immigrant to every identifiable branch of American Sydnors today. It was published by my friend Roy Matthews of Monarch Printers in Charlotte. I have recovered most of the cost of 500 copies by selling the books to my Sydnor kin at cost. I have also contributed copies to about twenty public and private libraries throughout the United States. Several of my contemporary Sydnor cousins were especially helpful in providing genealogical materials that were incorporated into the "Saga," especially William E. Sydnor of San Luis Obispo, California, Bradley K. Sydnor of Phoenix, Arizona, and G. Granville Sydnor 3rd of Seattle, Washington. After Floyd Sydnor died, his daughter Elizabeth Weakley made his papers available to me and I found that most of our research had been parallel.

From time to time someone who learns of my enthusiasm for the Sydnor genealogy asks why I have not demonstrated an equal interest in the Thompson family history. The answer is simple: the Sydnors were sufficiently prominent in sixteenth century England that it is possible to trace their line through various legal documents such as deeds and wills. The name Thompson, however, is much more difficult to trace and is one of the ten most common names in the United States. At any rate, my cousin David Thompson of Newark, Delaware has prepared an excellent genealogy of our Thompson family history since 1800 ("The Thompson Family," privately published in 1999).

Nancy Layne Albin, a cousin on my mother's side, has prepared an equally fine genealogy on the Layne family of Virginia. I do have something of a "rogue's gallery" of my Layne ancestors, which I have had restored and framed at considerable personal expense. Hattie does not, however, show them the same deference that she does my Sydnor ancestors, whom she allows to grace the wall of our guest room. Until she finds a wall on which they may be featured, the Laynes are biding their time in a dresser drawer and my mother's spirit is awaiting their liberation.

# CHAPTER 27
## BACK AT THE RANCH AGAIN

Hattie taught piano at the Community School of the Arts through most of the 1980s but altogether retired from teaching in about 1988. She has maintained her loyalty to the school, however, and was elected a lifetime member of its Board of Directors. In April 1985 she chaired a Community School fundraiser called "Promenade on the Mall," involving presentations by arts groups spread over five blocks in downtown Charlotte. After Hattie had begun making plans for the event with the Arts Council, she learned that Freda Nicholson, the director of Discovery Place, was planning a similar function. It was a remarkable coincidence. Hattie called Freda and they agreed to work together and share the proceeds. The event featured gala dinners at the Marriot and Radisson hotels and proved to be such a smashing success that the Arts and Science Council later adopted the idea as a New Year's Eve celebration.

Hattie's connection with the Community School was the occasion for our meeting Dzidra Reimanis, an émigré from Latvia who is one of the finest piano teachers in North Carolina. Her students usually place among the winners in local music competitions. Dzidra has become one of our closest friends and is virtually a family member. We rarely celebrate a birthday or holiday that Dzidra is not present. I learned in time that Dzidra was living in a refugee camp in Halle, Germany at about the same time that I was billeted ten miles away in the Village of Benkendorf during the war. She is a splendid emissary for her native Latvia.

In the mid-1980s Hattie was diagnosed as having a cancerous growth in her nasal cavity. Her dentist, Dr. Richard Yeager, discovered it. Dr. Bill Kirk, a Charlotte dental surgeon, removed the tumor by separating the upper jaw from its base on the <u>inside</u> of her mouth (a procedure that had only recently been developed). The operation lasted eight hours but left no visible scar. Dr. Kirk undertook to graft skin from her leg onto the roof of her mouth where the tumor had been excised but the graft did not take. As a consequence, she wears an obdurator that covers the opening in the roof of her mouth. It has not affected her speaking or singing voice in any way. In fact, she is now at the point of having become a fifty-year veteran in our church choir.

For some years, Hattie and I entertained partners, clients, neighbors and other friends at a party at our home for an evening during the Christmas holidays. In the early 1980s, Hattie decided to convert that occasion into a brunch which is held on the second Saturday in December. That party has become a highlight of our Christmas season and, if we are to believe our guests, of theirs as well. About three hundred guests attend each year. The hours are staggered and the upstairs is opened so that our house can accommodate such a large number. Omelets are the favorites. Hattie's invitations are always unique. They usually take the form of a puzzle of some sort. It is not unusual for an invitee to fail to decipher the puzzle until it is too late to attend the party. We also entertain the Ownbey Sunday School Class for breakfast on the Sunday following our Christmas party.

Beginning in about 1986, Hattie and I began to take the family to the Doe Run Lodge on the Blue Ridge Parkway in southwest Virginia for a long weekend over the New Year holiday. The grandchildren especially enjoyed sleeping in the lofts there. For the last twelve years, however, the family has instead spent the week between Christmas and New Year at the home of our friend Bruce Clayton in Hilton Head, South Carolina. We take tennis lessons every morning and play bridge every night. At the New Year's Eve dinner everyone writes down his or her goals for the New Year (if he or she wants to eat) and the evening is capped off with games of charades until midnight. Brenny has hosted that New Year's Eve dinner for the last several years. The grandchildren participate in all of those activities from the age of seven or eight.

## ASPEN

For several years in the 1970s, Hattie worked with a twelve year old piano student from Korea named Chung-A Song. In the summer of 1977 Chung-A was offered the opportunity to study at the Aspen Music School during what had come to be known as the Aspen Music Festival. Because no one else was available to take her there, Hattie agreed to accompany her. The Festival runs from mid-June to mid-August every year and attracts the finest professional musicians in the country to teach in the music school and perform in the Aspen Festival Orchestra. Music lovers like Hattie are in their element with two or three concerts to choose from daily. I heard Mendelssohn's Scottish Symphony there recently, reliving the experience of hearing it in Edinburgh when I was on my way to St. Andrew's University in 1945.

Hattie immediately fell in love with Aspen and she has returned every summer for the last twenty-eight years. In fact, she has made another life for herself there, and for other members of the family who visit her as well. Within a year or two of her first visit, she found a position as pianist at the Aspen Chapel, a nondenominational community church which was presided over by the Reverend (now Dr.) Gregg Anderson, a Methodist-trained clergyman. She has performed special music regularly for Sunday morning services. Early on she stayed for the summer with Dr. Fay Whitsell and his wife Betty at their home near the Chapel on Heather Lane and continued to stay with them every summer for about twenty years. The Whitsells and their children Cynthia Dutkin and Debbie Mohn were most hospitable to Hattie through the years and to me as well when I visited there for a week or so each summer. More recently Hattie has alternated her summers between staying with Heinz and Karen Coordes and with Hailey Dart, who are strong supporters of the Chapel. Heinz is a gourmet chef and Vietnam War hero; Karen is a master gardener and seeker after truth; and Hailey, English-born, is the most sophisticated and cosmopolitan lady I have ever met.

For the last several years, Hattie has also been responsible for organizing and conducting an annual benefit brunch that raises $60,000 or more for the Chapel. She has made many close friends in the Aspen community during her annual three-month sojourn there (despite having to solicit contributions for the benefit!). A number of those friends have also befriended me on my visits there. They have made me feel a part of the Aspen family.

Thanks to the hospitality of my friends George Madsen and George Wombwell, I have attended a marvelous community-wide bible-study group on Tuesday mornings when I am in Aspen. The entire gamut of theological views is represented in the group – from quite fundamentalist to quite liberal. It even includes a member of the Jewish faith. In order to keep the peace, no participant is allowed to address the comments of any other person directly. Sometimes the comments are like ships that pass in the night, but it works. My friend Dr. Jay Baxter attends as often as his physical health permits, especially when I am in town.

Occasionally someone pays me a compliment for "letting" Hattie spend her summers in Aspen, as though I had any choice in the matter. It's just the price I pay for the privilege of having her with me for the other nine months.

Not everyone sees it in that way. Several years ago when I was having my gas tank filled at the Providence Road Amoco station of my friend James Stancill, he asked me why he hadn't seen Hattie lately. I told him that she was in Aspen for the summer. "The whole summer," he replied. "What does she do there?" I told him that she was playing the piano, and without hesitation he asked, "Do you suppose she could teach my wife to play the piano?"

## EXERCISE

Hattie and I woke up one beautiful spring morning in 1977 and decided to run to the Park Road Shopping Center for breakfast. We got as far as Queens College when Hattie heard something snap in her leg and suddenly went lame. She was taken down a peg or two by my having to return to the house and bring the car to collect her. She had torn a ligament and remained hobbled for a week or so. That was only a temporary setback, however. Determined to improve, she has now advanced her running prowess to the point that she recently received honorable mention in a national ranking of marathon runners in her age group. She usually wins her age group in 5K and 10K races as well. In fact, she has won her age group in the San

Diego marathon the past six years in a row, raising more than $30,000.00 for the Leukemia-Lymphoma Foundation in the process. I am satisfied to settle for a 5K once or twice a year.

Since that fateful morning in 1977, it has become my custom to run a mile every morning, most recently with my dog, Taffy. About a year ago, however, Taffy, a sixteen year old cocker spaniel, became stone deaf and totally blind. I became quite solicitous of her welfare after that and even began to view myself as her "seeing eye man." No doubt that empathy derives in some measure from the fact that, like Taffy, I have become a senior citizen.

Several months ago, Hattie suggested that Taffy had become so miserable that we should perhaps have her put to sleep. When I first broached the subject to our veterinarian, she insisted that there was no need to consider such drastic action until Taffy stopped following me around. I regret to report that Taffy did recently stop being able to follow me. When I took her back to the vet, she was injected with a liquid that took her within a few minutes. I held her head and she died without moving a muscle. I have decided that I shall follow Hattie around as long as I can still move, for fear of the consequences if I do not!

When I run in my neighborhood in the early mornings I try to speak to anyone whom I encounter, including cyclists and those behind windshields. I can run on the street at that early hour to save my knees from the impact of the cement sidewalk. People usually respond, of course, but when they don't I take it as a challenge for the next time I see them. I'm simply trying to do my part in maintaining Charlotte's reputation as a friendly city. I make a special point of acknowledging children. I learned that lesson from my friend Carlyle Marney who once wrote that he always tried to "catch the eye" of any child he encountered. It's wonderful what our friends can teach us if we listen.

I run in the Midwood Park Festival 5K in May of each year and watch as most of the runners, including Hattie, soon disappear from view around a corner. Several years ago I was running alone near the finish line when I suddenly heard two women conversing behind me. I immediately took heart from not being the last runner, when suddenly the women passed me – walking! It is true that they were "speed-walking," but that was little consolation at the time.

I'm still running despite such embarrassments, though it now takes me about ten minutes longer to complete a 5K than it did when we first began twenty-five years ago. I take shorter steps out of a concern for my knees, which I am told are usually the first to go. It is a far cry from the seven-minute mile in Army boots that was required of us in the Army's basic training.

Years ago I also joined the Charlotte Athletic Club, which later merged with the Tower Club in the late 1970s. The club provides physical training classes at lunchtime each weekday, which I usually attend at least three or four days a week. For some years the club featured stationary spinning, aerobics and strength training classes. More recently yoga and pilates have become popular and I find those newer exercises quite challenging. I have told the trainers that they have saved my life and I'm sure it's true. Until I began to exercise regularly I occasionally had a troublesome backache. From time to time I attended the Priester Chiropractic Clinic operated by my neighbor Bud Priester and his son John. My back is now so much stronger as a result of daily exercising that it has been six years since I visited the Priester Clinic. Although the Tower Club has given notice that it will close at the end of this year, I am determined to find another facility to provide me the same outlet. I intend to join the Downtown YMCA in the Wachovia Center, which offers the kind of classes I like.

In addition to setting a fast pace on the footpath, Hattie runs a tight ship when it comes to diet. For breakfast I am required to drink a concoction consisting of granular lecithin, powdered wheat bran, oat bran, wheat germ, yeast and flax seed dissolved in a glass of fruit juice before partaking of a bowl of cereal and a cup of green tea. I am allowed only two eggs a week, virtually no red meat or butter, and red wine (our usual alcoholic indulgence) only on weekends and special occasions. Of course, I try to create as many special occasions as possible. Finally, I have to choke down a handful of vitamin pills every morning as I leave for the office. But it's worth it to be permitted to live there.

### THE CHILDREN

**D'Arcy.** D'Arcy, our oldest and she who bears the name of the noted St. Andrew's professor, attended South Carolina University for a time and then trained as a dental hygienist at Central Piedmont Community College. When she was in her late twenties, she began to exhibit signs of a malady which was eventually diagnosed as a schizo-affective disorder. As a consequence, she has been hospitalized from time to time. The problem has been brought under control with medication but it has certainly been a trial for D'Arcy and a matter of great concern for those who love her. By sheer determination D'Arcy has continued as a dental hygienist for the past twenty-five years. Hattie and I are both proud of the strength she has shown in overcoming her difficulties and of the marvelous compassion that virtually exudes from her being. I have concluded that her own vulnerability may account in part for her extraordinary sensitivity to the feelings of others. At a time when D'Arcy was not well, she married Gary Wall and gave birth to a daughter, whom she named Wesley. The marriage did not last. Her husband managed to spirit Wesley away at a time when D'Arcy could not prevent it. We later located Wesley when she was nine years old, but the prolonged

219

separation has left the relationship somewhat less than satisfactory. D'Arcy's children by Allan Lewis Kluttz, whom she married in 1985, were born in the late 1980s – Allan Lewis, Jr. January 24, 1986 and Ruth Sydnor March 11, 1988.

**Sydnor.** On Sydnor's twenty-first birthday he was riding in the front seat of an automobile being driven by his friend Blair Peery on Marsh Road in Charlotte. Another car, speeding in the opposite direction to escape from the police, lost control on a curve and ran headlong into Blair's car. Sydnor was thrown into the windshield and was badly cut about the face and head. Hattie arrived at the hospital first and, as she recounts the experience, was looking at his head and trying not to let him see her concern when Sydnor undertook to console *her*. "Don't worry, Mother, I'll be all right," he said. It was exactly the same reassurance he had given her when he had been hit in the forehead by the ski lift in Austria nine years earlier – and in the same words. Eventually Sydnor recovered damages from the malefactor's insurance company with the help of my partner Max Justice. Because his sister Harriet was just embarking upon a serious study of the harp, Sydnor generously devoted most of his recovery to buying his sister a beautiful Salvi harp. We should have known then that he was destined for the career he soon chose to pursue.

After having obtained an A.B. degree from Duke University, Sydnor enrolled with my encouragement in the Duke Law School. In November of his first year, he came home and told his mother and me that he had been meeting with the Reverend Bob Young, chaplain to the University, about the possibility of transferring to the Duke Seminary. I won't say that either Hattie or I was surprised. He had talked about a possible career in the church since high school, and we had both recognized a special quality in him since childhood – a marked sympathy for the feelings of others. Our pastor Bob Tuttle had encouraged his interest in the ministry. Having learned that he was not interested in practicing law as a career, the combination of circumstances seemed to dictate its own solution. After talking it out with us one night until early morning (during which conversation I reminded him that he would never make any money and would often have to put up with difficult church members like me), he finished the semester in law school, and then transferred to the Seminary. It was clearly the right choice for him and both Hattie and I have often had occasion to thank the Lord that Sydnor made that decision. So have many other persons whom he has helped. He graduated from Duke Divinity School in December 1980 and immediately accepted his first assignment as minister to the Wingate United Methodist Church in Wingate, North Carolina.

Sydnor had married Janet Hansen, a classmate at the Seminary, in July 1980. Their daughter Laurel Adaire was born on June 11,

1982. Angela Clare Sydnor came along on December 6, 1984. When Janet obtained a pastorate in Texas, the family moved there and Sydnor served in several different Methodist conferences there until he and Janet decided to go their separate ways. Sydnor then returned to North Carolina and applied to Bishop Bevel Jones for an appointment. The assignment, immediately forthcoming, was to a small church in Whittier, a community in the mountains of western North Carolina. While he was serving there, Sydnor met Kelly Stone, a nurse practitioner who has since also qualified as a mid-wife, and they were married in 1992 in Kelly's hometown, Decatur, Alabama. I read a tribute to them at their rehearsal dinner:

### A WEDDING TOAST TO KELLY AND SYDNOR

I

Tonight our families gather to extol
the virtues of two hearts become one soul
For who has known a pair less prone to feign
than Kelly and her doting preacher swain?
While she incarnates Florence Nightingale,
he searches still for Gal'hads Holy Grail.
While he chants masses and intones "Amens,"
she conjures diagnostic strategems;
While she invents new med'cal paradigms,
he praises God and sings soft requiems,
Yet Jung most often seems to be the gem
that crowns our Sydnor's heav'nly diadem.

II

But who are we to question by what right
disease is cured, the blind regain their sight.
If Karl can help then, Lord, so let it be.
Let flesh be healed and let the blind man see.
But pardon us if we prefer to bet
on Kelly and her scientific set.
For this we know – there certainly is no prettier
than she on earth – at least in greater Whittier.
So let us toast them well and their increase.
May babies come in numbers e'er they cease.
Though just in case a churlish stork delays,
they'll start with two angelic girls to raise.

Sydnor has been serving the First United Methodist Church in North Wilkesboro since 1997, which is the longest any clergyperson has served there. Both Hattie and I have come to know and appreciate many of his parishioners. We have particularly enjoyed getting to know his parishioners Bill and Frances Casey and Vicki Church and her mother-in-law Peggy Church.

Sydnor joined the Naval Reserve as a chaplain about fifteen years ago and has risen through the ranks to Lieutenant Commander. He recently received word that he will be called to active duty with the Marines in January 2005. He will train for six months in this country at Cherry Point, North Carolina and be posted to Iraq for seven months after that. Hattie and I are preparing ourselves for that day. Sydnor is taking it in stride, of course. No doubt he will again prove that he chose the right profession.

**Harriet.** Harriet began her study of harp with Elizabeth Roth in Charlotte and continued those studies privately with Jackie Myers after she enrolled at the University of North Carolina in Chapel Hill. It soon became evident that she was serious about a career in music. After she graduated from the University of North Carolina she matriculated at Indiana University as a freshman with a major in harp. In order to qualify to study with the teacher she wanted at Indiana, she was required to study for a year in Paris with Odette LeDantu, the renowned French harpist. Miss LeDantu died during that year so Harriet finished her studies in Paris with one of Ms. LeDantu's students. She then studied harp at Indiana for five years under Suzanne McDonald, one of the finest harpists in the United States. Harriet has since carved out a notable career for herself as a concert harpist. She teaches harp at DePauw University in Greencastle, Indiana, and is the principal harpist with the Terre Haute Symphony Orchestra. Hattie and I recently flew there to hear Harriet perform a harp concerto by the American composer David Ott with the orchestra. It was splendid!

Soon after Harriet had graduated from Indiana University, she married Dr. Kevin Moore, a psychologist on the faculty of DePauw University, whom she had met in college. The wedding ceremony was performed by Sydnor 3rd at Myers Park United Methodist Church and the reception was held in our garden with appropriate embellishments, including large canvas tents as safeguards against bad weather.

I delivered a tribute at their rehearsal dinner:

### A WEDDING TOAST TO HARRIET AND KEVIN

I

Tonight we honor Harriet and Kevin
whose marriage vow is surely made in heav'n.
For these two stalwarts soon will cast their lot
to live as one when Sydnor ties the knot,
though let us not forget that God is He
who actually sanctifies this sapling tree
from which great Moores and Thompsons soon will spring,
perhaps indeed a noble queen or king
For from this union only style and class
can characterize descendants, nothing crass.

II

While Harriet plays the late King David's lute
Young Kevin's best at Trivia Pursuit.
In fact, the Thompson clan will surely rue
the day it met the Kevin Moore IQ.
And yet the Moores will also never hear
of one so charming, innocent and dear
as she who all agree combines the traits
of Pollyanna and St. Joan – those greats.
No doubt his fate will be the same as mine

Harriet and Kevin have two beautiful girls, Alice Caitlin Sydnor Line, born August 11, 1993, and Rebecca Elizabeth Sydnor Wolfe, born September 25, 1996. Both girls brighten our lives and the lives of all who know them in their home town of Greencastle, Indiana. As the middle child, Harriet made peace early on in life with her older and younger siblings and soon became the family's mediator. She's a good listener.

**Brenny.** When our son Brenny was two or three years old, he attended nursery school at our church, as did all of our children. One day Brown Chism, the church secretary, remarked to him that his shoes were on the wrong feet. Brenny gained immortality in the church annals by responding, "But these are the only feet I have."

Brenny enrolled as a sophomore at St. Andrew's School in Middletown, Delaware in 1975. He did well academically and made the wrestling and cross-country teams. When Hattie and I attended his wrestling matches, we often found ourselves in contortions similar to those in which he was engaged on the mat. After graduating in 1978, he enrolled at the University of North Carolina at Chapel Hill and promptly pledged Pi Kappa Alpha fraternity. Within a couple of years, he bought a house in Chapel Hill with the help of a friend. It was the first evidence of a strong entrepreneurial bent. Brenny graduated from the University of North Carolina in 1985. After spending several months touring Europe, he entered upon a career in residential real estate brokerage. With some help from Hattie and me, he soon began to acquire houses and apartment buildings until he now owns and manages about thirty units. Several years ago he purchased our interest in the properties that we helped him acquire, very much to our financial advantage. For the last few years, Hattie has joined Brenny in his real estate firm, Brenneman Thompson Properties, having qualified as a broker.

This last decade ended quite happily when Brenny found a soul-mate in Karen Parker, whose parents live in Monroe, North Carolina. Karen is the director of Domestic Violence Services for the local United Family Services. They became engaged while visiting the Great Wall of China this year, and were married in Brenny's garden on October 9, 2004. He had acquired the home next door to the Clarksons' Wing Haven several years earlier. They were his godparents. A *Charlotte Observer* columnist recently commented on our good fortune in acquiring Karen as a member of the Thompson family. Both Hattie and I heartily agree with him.

I undertook to memorialize the occasion in verse:

### A WEDDING TOAST TO KAREN AND BRENNY

I

A toast to two who've earned domestic bliss
Who now will wed, no longer be remiss.
for both have found a mate who meets their need,

so let them wed "with all deliberate speed."
No juv'nile fancy fashioned this courtship
At last our Brenny's won her ladyship.
He set out on this mission years ago
to find the one who'd make the right duo.
Who'd have thought that she would find his call
to wed concealed in a niche in a Chinese Wall.

II

While Karen heads a group that fights abuse,
Bren's ownership of acreage is profuse.
No doubt they're better off than we who've borne them,
One thing is sure – we certainly shan't ignore them,
for Bren has promised to attend our dotage
in case we lose our shirts in agiotage.
But no more talk of money or of age!
Today romance has moved to center stage
and on their Ridgewood portal now is graven
"The world is welcome to this new Wing Haven."

Brenny is actually the poet in the family. His work is excellent and he frequently shares it with friends by e-mail. He has an extraordinary penchant for making friends. And no friend, once made, can escape his attention. E-mail is his bread and butter.

Thanks to the good work of our mutual friend Henry James, Jr., the real Wing Haven is still safeguarded in perpetuity as a charitable trust, with Dia Steiger currently acting as its outstanding director.

**Kathy Line.** After graduating from St. Andrew's School in 1981, Kathy Line matriculated at Davidson College and spent her junior year, as I had done, at St. Andrew's University in Scotland, although under somewhat different auspices, of course. In 1987 she enrolled at Wake Forest Law School. She did quite well there, being elected to the Law Review, and, on graduating, was hired as a clerk to North Carolina Court of Appeals Judge Jack Lewis. The next year she interviewed with the law firm of James, McElroy and Diehl in Charlotte. Bill Diehl, who, as I have said, has a reputation for being a bit of an ogre in court, was among those who interviewed her. The first question he asked her was "Young lady, does your Daddy know you have come here?" "Yes, sir," she replied, "He sent me." And she got the job. She was assigned to the litigation department. A chip off the old block!

The most notable occurrence in our family in 1994 was Kathy Line's marriage to Patrick E. Kelly, who is also a lawyer. It was a grand wedding with all the trimmings – rehearsal dinner at the Myers Park Country Club, wedding at Myers Park United Methodist performed by both Sydnor 3rd and a Catholic priest (Pat is Catholic) and a reception at the Charlotte Country Club. Pat's is a military family so his father, Major-General James L. Kelly, and several of his brothers participated in the ceremony in uniform. We were absolutely delighted with Kathy Line's choice of a soul-mate. At the wedding rehearsal dinner, I read a poem:

### A Toast to My Daughter Kathy-Line and
### Pat Kelly at Their Wedding Rehearsal Dinner
#### I

Tonight we honor Kathy-Line and Pat
as well as those by whom they were begat
for each descends from an illustrious clan
that's greatly dignified the race of man.
And now that these young stars are due to wed
new heights for homo sapiens lie ahead.
For whom more surely doth the Lord anoint
than one who cut his teeth at old West Point!
And where breathes so commendable a bride
as St. Andrew's and Davidson provide!

#### II

In fact, our honorees have earned their spurs
by winning law degrees – both "his" and "hers".
Though surely it invites argumentation
that two attorneys share one habitation.
Still we divine some traits distinctly regal
that characterize this combination legal
sufficient to avoid domestic frays
at least as bad as characterized O.J.'s.
Indeed, we prophesy the perfect match –
pure harmony with offspring by the batch.

Kathy Line and Pat have three remarkable children – Julia Davenport, born June 7, 1998; Audrey Rowland, born August 30, 2000; and John Sydnor, born July 2, 2002. After giving birth to her third child, Kathy Line gave up practicing law, which has worked very much to the children's advantage.

### LIKE MOTHER, LIKE DAUGHTER

As Mother entered her 80s she became somewhat forgetful. By 1984 her forgetfulness had progressed to dementia. Mother's last year was especially difficult. During that time, I made a special effort to continue to visit her nearly every day and we often went for a drive, during which time she enjoyed a cigarette.

Mercifully Mother died in her sleep in 1985 in her 83rd year. I miss her every day of my life, no doubt in part because of her utter devotion to me, as described in the dedication of this memoir, but also because of the indefatigable spirit she demonstrated, at times against considerable odds. That extraordinary spirit never faltered, even when her mind began to fail.

Hattie, Chick and I went to Richmond in October 1997 to celebrate our sister Bobbie's seventieth birthday (she moved to Richmond after she married Clayton Inge) at a restaurant operated by her daughter Jan's husband, Lee Nichols. The Nichols' precocious five year old son Danny stole the show. I read the following verses that evening:

#### A TOAST TO MY SISTER BOBBIE –
#### A BELOVED SEPTUAGENARIAN
#### I

Tonight we meet to honor Barbara Jane

whose life has been exempl'ry (in the main).
Lynchburg, Virginia was her natal place.
A Tuesday's child, she was "full of grace."
"Memorial" was the birth hospital's name
and "Memorial" the street to which she came.
Though Garland-Rhodes did give her some slight pause,
she soon won friends' and teachers' loud applause.
She claims the greatest cross she had to bear
was being Sydnor's sister and his heir,
though equally demanding was the role
of guiding younger brother Chicker's soul.

II

At Lynchburg College she soon won her spurs
and met Clay Inge who whispered "his and hers".
And though embarked upon a new career,
she chucked it all for him she holds most dear,
and you who've gathered here to celebrate
can thank your lucky stars she took the bait.
Then she became West End's belov'd librarian
and rivaled in that role the fabled "Marian"
until she chose to rest upon her oar
and pass on to her grandkids bookish lore.
But this we know and have known from the start
Our Bobbie's always had a loving heart.

It was a grand occasion and I am especially pleased that we did it then because Bobbie now suffers from an increasingly severe case of Alzheimer's.

I recently made a contribution to Bobbie's alma mater, Lynchburg College's Centennial Hall, in her honor. Her name will soon be emblazoned on one of the bricks at the entrance to the Hall. Before her illness, Bobbie ran the children's library at the Reveille United Methodist Church in Richmond. She also served for some time as a staff member for the Richmond Public Library. Like our mother, she has been an omnivorous reader.

### BROTHERLY LOVE

Soon after my stepfather died in the late '80s, my brothers Chick and Phil and I realized that we should not see each other as often in the future, since Phil lives in Columbia, South Carolina and would have less occasion to visit Charlotte. We agreed to meet for lunch in Fort Lawn, South Carolina, an approximate half-way point, about once a month. The arrangement has served us well. We also go to Atlanta together once a year to see a Braves baseball game. Phil makes the arrangements. I relish those trips too. Though I have no particular love for the City of Atlanta (jealousy, of course), I am incurably addicted to Braves baseball, having followed their itinerant course since Spahn and Sain led them to glory in Boston during my law school days. Ours has been a most rewarding brotherhood, even though Phil prefers the St. Louis Cardinals.

Chick, who graduated from the Philadelphia Museum School of Art, worked for several advertising firms before establishing "The Thompson Agency" with his son Stuart. He continues to paint for pleasure, and has also published two books of photography entitled "The Doors and Gates of Charleston" and "Atlanta, A City of Neighborhoods."

A former newspaperman, Phil has served as director of the Executive Institute of South Carolina, which trains state employees in their responsibilities in much the same fashion as that service has been performed in North Carolina by the Institute of Government in Chapel Hill. Hattie and I attended a retirement dinner in Phil's honor in Columbia in June of this year. A number of South Carolina government officials, including former Governor Robert McNair and Congressman James Clyburn, also attended. Phil recently finished writing a biography of Governor McNair which is being published by the University of South Carolina Press. It deals as much with significant events which occurred in South Carolina during the McNair Administration as with the life of the governor himself. Phil was the principal speech writer for both McNair and his successor, the late Governor John West, whose biography Phil has also been commissioned to write. Phil's wife Virginia ("Ginny") presided at his retirement dinner with her usual aplomb, underscoring again the strength she has provided him in the role of consort. Ginny recently retired from a successful public relations career in banking.

## ANNIVERSARIES AND BIRTHDAYS

In June 1997 our children surprised Hattie and me by hosting a fiftieth wedding anniversary party for us in a picturesque hotel in the mountains. Everyone in both of our immediate families was invited to attend and the party was a great success. I long ago became accustomed to being told what an extraordinary person Hattie is. Of course, I agree. She is the most highly disciplined human being I have ever known, not only in practicing piano and running but also in nearly every walk of life. For example, she makes our bed so promptly in the morning that I sometimes barely escape being rolled up in the bedclothes. In more than 50 years, I have never been able to capture her remarkable persona in verse. The closest I have come is in this limerick:

> Here's to my heroine Hattie
> who saves me from foods that are fatty.
> The light of my life,
> she's the finest wife
> since Mother married Daddy.

Both Hattie and I recently reached our eightieth birthdays. In May 2003 we celebrated Hattie's natal day by inviting a number of our former colleagues from Davis Polk and Wardwell to join us in New York for a celebration. Many of them had left New York about fifty years earlier, as we had done, but they were sufficiently intrigued by the idea of a reunion that they turned out about thirty-five strong, including spouses. The idea originated with Jack Roemer, who had left Davis Polk to become general counsel to R. J.

Reynolds in Winston-Salem. Unfortunately Edgar Appleby was unable to attend because he was in Paris putting the finishing touches on a book of poetry he had written – in French! The von Falkenhausens came all the way from Germany. Bill Kaynor was our photographer. Other former Davis Polk colleagues who attended included Gil Dwyer, Warren Eginton, Bill Ketcham, Felix Liebmann, Stuart Marks, Merlin Nelson, Jack Roemer, Louis Stanton and Ross Traphagen.

Henry King, who was one of our contemporaries, had stayed on at Davis Polk and had served as its managing partner until quite recently. Through his good offices, Davis Polk entertained all of us at a dinner at the firm, and Philip Potter, who had become a litigation partner there, gave everyone who attended an appropriate favor. Two nonagenarians Hazard Gillespie and Nelson Adams, both of whom were leaders of the firm when we were there and had retired many years earlier, were the biggest hits at the dinner. In the course of the evening, I read verses I had penned in honor of the occasion:

### DAVIS POLK ALUMNI'S 50-YEAR REUNION

I

Tonight our pilgrims meet to celebrate
the golden anniversary of that halcyon state
in which they practiced million dollar law
with men who ate their adversaries raw,
who brought Cravath's best clients to their knees
and won them as their own at higher fees,
who fought like tigers for their clients' right
to earn great gobs of money day and night
and spend it as they chose from year to year
or will it to a playmate they held dear.

II

Then those of us who ventured far afield
in time determined that our fates were sealed.
By moving from New York to fields beyond
we soon became big fish in a little pond.
'Til then one day we saw four great banks merge
and form two banks that made our practice surge.
Now we in Charlotte watch the mountains come
to see Mahomet, looking for a plum.
Whereas in days of old we came to you.
Now New York comes to us; is it our due?

EPILOGUE

Yet be assured of this, all you good folk.
We'd welcome any day old Davis Polk.

The next day we sailed up the Hudson River on a boat that belonged to federal district judge Warren Eginton. It was skippered by his son John. We had a steak dinner aboard as Warren's guests, capped off with a delicious candle-lit birthday cake which tested Hattie's lungs.

Finally, after we attended the Bartholomew Episcopal Church service on Park Avenue at the invitation of Merlin and Janet

Nelson, Bill Ketcham hosted hors d'oeuvres and cocktails on Sunday noon at his club at 11 East 54th Street. The Brook Club, which derives its name from a poem by Alfred Lord Tennyson, is one of the oldest men's clubs in New York City.

It was a birthday that Hattie will not soon forget. And it was a surprise!

Not to be outdone, Hattie set about to celebrate my eightieth birthday in February of this year. Unlike the party I planned for her, mine came as no surprise to me because I insisted on helping her make up the guest list. It was held at the Charlotte Country Club and I was surrounded by family and close friends, who delivered toasts of greatly exaggerated encomia. Two of my former colleagues at Davis Polk and their wives received special recognition for "coming the farthest" – Gil and Carol Dwyer and Phil and Trisha Potter. Unfortunately several of my closest long-time friends were unable to attend – Bill and Mary Joslin, John and Barbara Kennedy and Bill and Lil Stapleton, to name a few.

Hattie performed her "Victoria Borge" routine on the piano, in which she simulates Mozart and Chopin composition styles in renditions of "Happy Birthday." Several guests undertook to compete for the role of poet laureate. The degree to which they succeeded may be determined from reading the contributions of Mark and Louise Bernstein, Ace Walker, George Daly and my brothers Chick and Phil set out in the Appendix. My friend Jack Perry, former U.S. ambassador to Bulgaria, whose retiring to Charlotte I consider one of the best things that has ever happened to the city, couldn't make it to the party but he sent me a poem that represents the apogee of clever verse. It is also included in the Appendix.

### FINALE

In recent years Edwin and Lou Jones have been most generous in entertaining Hattie and me at the Cypress retirement community where they live. Hattie is quite impressed with the Cypress, and would move us there tomorrow if I should give her any encouragement. Some of my former partners are already living there. It is a splendid facility and I have promised to move there before I die, which may, of course, require a sense of timing beyond my ability to arrange.

Brenny occasionally asks me if I have any pearls of wisdom to impart to his generation. While I am tempted to deliver a sermonette, so far I have avoided it on the theory that I should not likely contribute any unique insights. If I were to make any such philosophical observation, however, it would be this. On the basis of eighty years of candle-burning, occasionally at both ends, I have become aware that everything I do, everywhere I go and everyone I meet soon bring to mind other things I have done, other places I have

229

been and other persons I have known, living or dead. To that degree, I live in the past, as well as the present.

Brenny also recently asked me what plans I have for the future. I do not recall how I answered him at the time, but on reflection I should say "More or less what I have been doing." And the same goes for each year thereafter – for as long as the Lord will allow. So far it has been only "the best of times." Indeed, each year seems to be more satisfying and more rewarding than the last. If I were asked why that is so, I should have to say that it is because of the richness of the relationships I have enjoyed, especially those with family, colleagues and friends, as well as the causes I have been privileged to serve.

> 'Tis here they say the journey ends
> And little doubt it must be so;
> But as I tell my bestest friends,
> I hate to go.
>
> from *Man's Days*
> by Eden Phillpotts

# POSTSCRIPT

Since the curtain dropped on this peregrination as of December 31, 2004, my dear sister Bobbie has died. Although we did not see each other very often in recent years, I feel her absence keenly, especially because she reminded me so much of my mother.

Life at 1622 Brandon Road and 401 South Tryon Street has continued apace. Sydnor 3rd served his stint as a chaplain in Iraq (now promoted to Naval Commander) and returned safely in the summer of 2006 to accept an assignment as senior minister at First United Methodist Church in Morganton, North Carolina.

Hattie has continued in her career as a concert artist and is scheduled to perform a recital at Queens University in Charlotte on May 24, 2007 to benefit the Friends of Music there. She will run her ninth consecutive marathon in San Diego on June 3, 2007, and will leave for Aspen soon thereafter. I still run an occasional 5K and manage to finish it.

Parker Poe Adams & Bernstein, under the leadership of Managing Partner Bill Farthing, now numbers more than 200 lawyers in six cities in North and South Carolina. I'm just thankful that my key still fits the door. Ashley Hogewood recently retired as the head of the Real Estate and Commercial Development Practice Group (RECD) and has joined the "of counsel" veterans at their celebratory birthday lunches. The burgeoning RECD practice that he has led now comprises 48 lawyers organized by geographical regions and is one of the firm's fastest growing areas of practice. I'm still enjoying my work as a mediator and was recently accorded the privilege of being called as an expert witness in a case involving proper mediation practice.

My interest in politics has not abated one whit. If anything, it is stronger than ever – stimulated by a recent tragic revelation of corruption in the North Carolina legislature. It constitutes a fresh challenge for all who are dedicated to good government. Both Hattie and I continue to be enthusiastic supporters of John Edwards in this campaign for the presidency.

I recently had a note from Nick Urbano, a gunner in the old 879th Field Artillery battalion, who ordered a copy of the memoir, despite having such poor eyesight that he doubted he would be able to read it. How's that for 69th Division spirit!

In October Hattie and I shall attend our 60th reunion at Syracuse University and the Chancellor has kindly undertaken to arrange a book-signing for me. I hope someone there recognizes me.

April 9, 2007

# APPENDIX

# VERSES FROM AN 80TH BIRTHDAY CELEBRATION

### *Syd's Favorite Things*
(Sung to the tune of "My Favorite Things"
from "Sound of Music")

Here we are gathered to celebrate Sydnor,
to toast his achievements within the past four score.
And soon you'll discover what pleasure it brings
to sing about all of his favorite things.

When the Judge bites
and the fee stings,
when he is feeling sad,
he'll simply remember
his favorite things
and then he won't feel so bad.

Winning at tennis
and turkey in Carlisle,
backing a cause that he knows to be worthwhile,
teaching the Ownbey class in the spring.
These are a few of his favorite things.

Researching Sydnors on Virginia vacations,
winning elections and long mediations,
flying to Aspen on USAir wings.
These are a few of his favorite things.

Poetry written by John Malcolm Brinnin,
roles in a drama that he can excel in,
opera productions where he pulls the strings.
These are a few of his favorite things.

ABA meetings and great Christmas brunches,
Lake Junaluska where he throws the punches,
political lunches where everyone brings
tidings of victories, his favorite things.

When the knees creak
and the sight fails.
When he is feeling cold,
he'll simply remember
the things that we sing
and then he won't feel so old.

Mark and Louise Bernstein

# El Syd at Eighty

I'm certain I shall never find
a man who's taken more
engagements of the soul and mind –
worthwhile pursuits of every kind –
some physical, some more refined,
both in and out-of-door.

My first encounter with him came
at church, and right away
I knew that life would not be tame,
if one should choose to play his game;
I did, so quickly I became
a Thompson protégé.

Enlistments then began to flow;
first Ownbey, then John P.,
then ESU, then Oliver Rowe,
then Democratic Party, so
before I could say "Syd go slow!"
my time was never free.

But yet it's been a heady ride;
one I would not have missed.
I'm grateful that I qualified
to tilt at windmills by his side,
to try to keep up as he cried,
"Engage!  Don't just exist!"

My zest to engage is running short;
but not so for El Syd,
from service on the Upper Court
to striving on the tennis court,
he brooks no curbs of any sort
more than he ever did!

So Happy Birthday to you, Syd.
I think you'll live forever!
With all you're doing at your age,
and your desire to be on stage,
if one suggests you disengage
I know you'll answer "Never!"

Ace Walker

## Headline: "Governor Announces New Judicial Appointment"

Governor Mike Easley announced today that he is submitting legislation to the General Assembly calling for the creation of a new seat on the North Carolina Court of Appeals. This legislation is a part of the Governor's initiative to involve senior citizens in government. The Governor indicated that he would appoint Sydnor Thompson of Charlotte, formerly a Judge on the Court of Appeals, to the new seat, which will carry an eight year term. In making the announcement the Governor said, "Judge Thompson served with distinction on the Court of Appeals, and his undeserved failure to win re-election in 1994 has long been an embarrassment to those of us who value independent and wise judges."

Knowledgeable court house observers hailed the announcement. Judge Thompson was widely acclaimed and respected during his previous altogether too brief tenure on this Court. But, there was also some speculation that the appointment of Judge Thompson was not just a well-deserved recognition of his talent and character, but was also aided by the behind-the-scenes work of several current members of the Court who had previously served with Judge Thompson and who were especially eager that Mrs. Thompson return to Raleigh with him. Though this speculation could not be confirmed, it is known that the Thompsons created a brilliant social and intellectual life for the Court in Raleigh, which some compared to the salons of Eighteenth Century Paris. Judge Thompson declined to comment for this article, but Mrs. Thompson stated that she intended to open a branch of her new real estate practice in Raleigh when she returned there.

Members of the Charlotte Bar uniformly praised Judge Thompson. One source said, "Sydnor Thompson has more friends than most of us have acquaintances. Syd is generous with his friends, and even better is generous with his adversaries."

Another source said, "Sydnor has been patriot, paterfamilias, philosopher and poet. He has received many laurels, but never one he cared to rest upon."

Well, Sydnor, of course these things are not to be, much as you deserve them. But you have been an example to us, an exemplar of energy and judgment, all your long life, and we thank you for it, one and all.

George Daly

## Ode to Bro'

He's a Legend in His Own Time;
some say "a Legend in His Own Mind."
A man who in 80 odd years
has accomplished e'en more than appears.

He's been a scholar, soldier, a member of the Bar,
whether <u>in</u> the court, or <u>on it</u>, he's gone quite far.
As a community leader, he can't be denied.
To the arts his talents he's gladly applied.

His views on politics you may contend
are left of center, which he will defend.
In fact, for his candidates many hours he'll log.
He'll even admit he's a "yellow dog."

But this event is special for all
as years of great memories we recall.
And to this octogenarian we <u>must</u> implore,
how about giving us 80 more!

Joe Thompson

# *A Birthday Toast*

Here's to my much older sibling.
'bout his years there can be no real quibbling.
But he makes a great showing
to keep us from knowing
'til the food down his chin begins dribbling.

We all know that Syd loves the courts.
As a judge he got glowing reports.
But on courts made for tennis
he's really no menace.
Seems he's better at torts than at sports.

Syd likes to discuss all things weighty
from the Bible to the sad fate of Haiti.
He likes to laugh hearty.
He's the life of the party,
so let's toast him as he now turns eighty.

Syd thinks he's a great politician
improving our ailing condition.
But try as might
he can't win a fight
from a constantly left-wing position.

Among Syd's great passions are three.
The law, his church and fam'ly.
There's no point concealing
just how I am feeling.
You've been like a brother to me.

                                        Phil Grose

# The Thompson Dilemma

St. Peter said to the Boss, "Well, Boss
Old Thompson's turned twice-forty;
One of these days he'll be coming Up."
And the Lord did say, "Oh. Lordy!
We'd better make some careful plans,
Old Sydnor's a disrupter."
St. Peter said, "Hard to instruct.
He thinks *he's* the Instructor."
The Lord said, "He's a good Methodist,
full of enthusiasm.
But if he doesn't like our ways
he might provoke a spasm.
I don't know if he'll feel at home
with our sinners and our publicans.
What if he wants to cleanse our ranks
of all our stout Republicans?"
St. Peter said, "Well, Boss, if Thompson's
awful, let's be frank:
Surely You can handle him
by simply pulling rank."
"I'm not sure, Peter," said the Lord,
"I've watched him eighty years,
and when it comes to taking orders
he's got stopped-up ears."
St. Peter said, "Well, maybe we can
head off many a spat
if from now on we say that Heaven's
officially Democrat."
"I don't know, Pete.  You know some say
I've got a Liberal bias.
And those Conservatives make a show
of being mighty pious.
If I leaned Left, our Right-wing friends
might start to acting funny,
like stopping all their gifts to us —
and they've got all the money!"
"Yea, Lord," said Peter, "I admit
your arguments are weighty.
But still I must remind you, Sir:
Syd Thompson's turning eighty!"

The Lord, He thought, and thought, and thought,
and finally He said,
"Since turning Democrat is risky,
let's do this instead:
We know if Sydnor comes Up Here
he'll make an endless fuss –
insist on making Heaven
Democratic, even Us!
Let's keep him down on earth
and let him missionary there –
until the planet's Democratic-Methodist,
I declare!
Why, he'll outdo Methuselah,
and as his deeds increase,
those of us in Heaven
can enjoy a little peace!"

Jack Perry

# INDEX OF CHARACTERS

242